qo choti

$8^{56}$

# AN AMERICAN VISITOR

# BOOKS BY JOYCE CARY

## *Fiction*

AN AMERICAN VISITOR

SPRING SONG AND OTHER STORIES

CHARLEY IS MY DARLING

THE CAPTIVE AND THE FREE

A HOUSE OF CHILDREN

NOT HONOUR MORE

EXCEPT THE LORD

PRISONER OF GRACE

MISTER JOHNSON

A FEARFUL JOY

THE HORSE'S MOUTH

TO BE A PILGRIM

HERSELF SURPRISED

THE MOONLIGHT

THE AFRICAN WITCH

## *Nonfiction*

ART AND REALITY

# AN AMERICAN VISITOR

## BY JOYCE CARY

*Harper & Brothers, Publishers, New York*

*Printed in the United States of America*
*Library of Congress catalog card number: 61-10241*

# AN AMERICAN VISITOR

# I

'BUT WHAT IS HASLUCK doing with the miners? What does she want if she isn't a miner or a trader or a teacher or a missionary?'

'Just walking.'

'All the whites are like that—a homeless lot wandering about and never satisfied with anything.' This was from a gloomy-looking horse-boy at the end of the line. He had been discharged for eating his horse's rations.

'And that is because they are damned,' said an old brown gentleman in a turban. He was darning a green silk stocking with brown wool. 'They do not know the peace of God because they are idolators and heathen. They have set their hearts on the vanities of this world —on wealth and power and indulgence,' and he was about to give the assembly pious edification for the third time in half an hour when he was interrupted by a headman of carriers called Henry with a remark that everybody knew where Hasluck had placed her heart; and he added a suggestion so obscene and droll that even the old Mallam laughed.

Eight of the worst blackguards in Gwanki were sitting in a row waiting for the white woman to come out of her tent. Since two o'clock through the hottest hours of the day they had been calling every minute or two.

'Mam, you wanta cook.'

'You wanta boy, mam.'

'Missy Mahrie, this is Henry who ask you—you my fader and mudder—tree pound a month.'

Hasluck had no servants of her own. It was said among other scandals that she was too poor. She had travelled the five days' journey from Kunama to the Niger bank with a party of three prospectors or rather with the youngest of them, Cottee, called Redhead because his hair was yellow. She was his friend. She fed with him, and his boy, Mallam Musa, waited upon her. Every day Redhead and she marched together and at night they passed among

*13*

the boys' huts arm in arm, strolling towards the forest. Sometimes they laughed so much that they appeared to be drunk. Sometimes they quarrelled and then the man behaved like a bridegroom, apologizing and paying compliments until the woman was once more laughing.

It was agreed by everybody that Cottee loved and desired Hasluck, and as he was generous to his people all wished him well. It was considered that the woman would be lucky to get such a man, tall, handsome and young, powerful as a horse. But whether he had succeeded in the affair before the big quarrel of the night before was a question that had been debated all over Gwanki by dozens of carriers and servants. Gossip is the major pastime of Africa.

'Of course he did,' said Henry. 'Missie Mah-rie is a good-for-nothing like all these white women. Why, she slept in the same hut with Red-head every night. And that's why he quarrelled with her. She didn't suit him.'

This raised another laugh.

Henry was just out of gaol for robbing carriers' women. He was a miserable-looking object, not much more than the dirty framework of a negro hung with the rags of an old khaki shirt whose flaps in front and behind dangled in ribbons over the greasy legs of a pair of dress trousers. His hat was bright green felt shaped like a pudding basin; a lady's hat begged from Hasluck.

Henry had travelled with the party as a headman, and that was why he claimed authority to give the woman the worst of characters.

But he was contradicted by the Mallam whose authority was better because he was Cottee's servant, and because he was the only man of substance, the only honest man in the gathering. 'It was because Cottee desired her and she would not admit him.'

Nobody wished to believe this. But nobody could deny the superior probity of the witness; and truth was desired, it was interesting as truth, even though it would be useless to retail. They turned to the Mallam.

'I was there on my mat among the loads not three paces away and they knew I was there. But they did not mind.'

'They have no shame, these whites.'

'Because they think of us as dogs,' said the gloomy horse-boy.

'Pardon, my scissors have fallen. Thank you with God's blessing.'

'Did she scratch him?'

'No, they talked most shamelessly. She said, Another day perhaps and he answered Why not now, and she said, Because she must think.'

Henry laughed and spat. 'Ah! these girls are all the same—they all talk like that.'

'And then he said that she was making play with him. She'd been with other men before. But she answered that those were secrets she had told him as a friend, but she was sorry for that foolishness more than all the rest. Then they quarrelled.'

'So that's what she is,' said a huge Yoruba, a fellow ponce with Henry, and he called out in a laughing voice, 'Mam, you wanta good boy. I big strong boy fit to do you good.'

'Mam, you wanta cook.'

The judge, Gore, called the Stork because of his long thin legs, his long neck and long face and long beak, came up and said, 'Clear out.' They scattered before him laughing, to gather again five minutes later, a yard or two closer to the tent, as soon as he had hurried away to stop another fight at the water's edge.

Gore had been sent up river to Gwanki to meet a pagan deputation of Birri chiefs and take them home by steamer. His district officer, Bewsher, had described the trip as a nice little holiday for a good boy, and he had in fact expected three or four days such as he loved, stretched in a long chair on the decks of steamers or under a tree in the bush, smoking cigarettes and reading the last batch of *The Times* and knowing that he was miles from a telegraph office, messengers, typewriters, clerks and fellow officials.

Gwanki was the loneliest port on the Niger. It consisted of a broken piece of gaspipe rail and two old palm planks rotting at the edge of a mud bank. Its liveliest inhabitants for three hundred and sixty days in a year were a couple of baboons scratching themselves in a human manner and barking at a distant fisherman; or two crocodiles half awash in steaming ooze.

But the opening of a new section of the Birri reserve which brought the prospectors and the Yankee journalist had coincided with an unexpected fall in the river, threatening an early end of the steamer transport; every trader for fifty miles round had hurried to the shore. There were two hundred blacks and six whites on the bank: fifty

15

families each with its babies, loads, yams, pots and invalids festering in the sun, and already there was no food to be had for money.

So that the young man, far from enjoying a holiday, had spent one of the most exhausting and miserable days in his life trying to prevent a riot which was obviously inevitable, a task so depressing to him that even some of the natives, in the midst of their own troubles. were amused by his lugubrious perspiring features, as he pushed here and there among them.

And Gore, on his part, as he climbed the bank for the fiftieth time after holding court of pie powder between three screaming women armed with each other's faggots, thought he had never seen so many miserable, worried people together, not even in the largest and richest capitals.

Even the whites were miserable. Here at the top of the slope old Jukes was still scuttling about like a scalded rat hunting for a lost load, and Cottee, lounging with his hands in his pockets, wore a condescending expression which was in him a mark of extreme disgust.

Jukes was the senior partner of the firm; a little yellow old man with gold spectacles and a thin beard. He resembled a last century don even in his voice and polite nervous manners.

Jukes was in a panic about his whole expedition. It was known that he had children at school and it was said that he was on the edge of bankruptcy, so that he could not well avoid being worried. He had committed himself.

But God knows what was wrong with Cottee who had no responsibilities and everything he could want.

The moment they set eyes on Gore they came towards him; but he, who had been avoiding them and their worries all day (on the last meeting Cottee had told him that the Yankee woman had no money and what was he going to do about it) at once changed direction. He made a vague gesture as if to say, 'I'm busy.'

He was in fact busy, for though this work was futile, it had to be done. He had sat down already twenty times and each time some new outbreak had made him jump up again. Even now a shriek from the unseen slope behind him was pulling him that way, and over beyond Jukes he could see a new family party just emerging from the bush path; two men with enormous loads of cloth, two women with nets of hardware, one carrying a baby, three weary

16

children of various ages and an old crone shuffling and wheezing fifteen yards behind in terror of being abandoned. Not one of them had the least chance of a place on the boat.

The prospectors had caught him. They burst into speech together. It appeared that they were still arguing about what Cottee called the American crisis—whether or not the American woman, invited by Cottee as a guest, but now at loggerheads with him, had any right to expect them to pay her fare to Birri and perhaps keep her there; whether indeed it was possible to make her such an offer.

'I say, Gore, about Mah-rie, if I gave her anything she'd throw it at me——'

'Mr. Gore,' panted Jukes, 'I hope you understand that it was not on my responsibility——'

Gore stared at them with wide eyes affecting complete preoccupation. He didn't want to have anything to do with this ticklish problem.

'Excuse me, just a moment,' he said, politely inclining his head like a shopwalker called away, and he stretched his long legs towards the hardware dealers.

'This is a bad place you've come to, friends. The boat cannot have room for you and there are many bad people about. You will be robbed here. Go back to a village before it is dark.'

The men stared at him from under the dark roof of their overhanging loads. Their eyes expressed both the stupidity usual to carriers with loads on their heads, as if their brains were actually made dense by compression, and the profound suspicion of stupid people confronted by an official. The women looked if possible more stupid, but also more hostile and obstinate. The three children aged perhaps between eight and twelve, exhausted, covered with sweat and dirt, stood in a row, the two elder holding the young one by the hands. His naked protruding stomach showed a large umbilical hernia. With open eyes and mouths they gazed in terror at this white man. Go back! What a cruel thing!

'If you're too tired, you'd much better camp in the bush. You'll only get robbed here in the crowd.'

No one spoke. Then the old woman arrived and began to scream. Here they were and here they'd stay. What had they done to be turned out? They were going to Alo, and no one should stop them. They were honest good people who had never done any wrong.

17

She would not listen to the suggestion that the steamer could not hold any more passengers. She didn't want to listen. She was showing her sons and daughters-in-law that she was still useful to them—she wasn't yet quite worthless. She was fighting for her place in the scheme of things, no doubt the more valuable to her that it was nearly lost. Though she couldn't carry a load or keep up even with the youngest grandchild, she had a voice still and she wasn't afraid of anybody or anything. What could frighten her now? She lived every hour with terrors worse than death and suffering beyond physical pain. 'Go back?' she shrieked. 'What have we done? Tell me that. Who are you? These men are good men, traders of repute.' The small child, to the horror of his two brothers, began to cry. Luckily he did so in silence. Great tears poured down his cheeks and splashed on his swollen stomach.

One of the men began to utter words. 'Yes, baturé (white man) we've come—you see—sell cloth and potash—catch fire-boat here.'

A chorus of yells from somewhere down the bank made Gore turn half round. Nothing could be done for these people. It wasn't that they were too stupid to understand the position but that they didn't want to. They weren't even thinking about it. They were feeling.

Still, that was true of everybody. It was what you had to reckon with.

'Of course it's not your fault,' he said, trying another approach; and for a moment the parties stared at each other, the traders with wilder blanker stupidity, Gore with his head turned to one side, with the most insinuating polite air, and a large drop of sweat on the extreme end of his nose. The children gazed up at the sparkling drop with the faces of rapt cherubim.

'I'm not blaming you for anything,' he murmured. The drop fell and the children's eyes suddenly became downcast as if in demure modesty.

'What have we done?' shrieked the old woman. 'Tell me,' and down the slope the yells sounded like murder.

He turned hastily away. It was no good. One would have to begin further back. A long way further back. And as, carefully avoiding the agitated Jukes who appeared to be abusing Cottee, he made for the new scene of disturbance, he remembered with sardonic amusement the Yankee woman's remark, almost the only one he had heard from her lips, that Gwanki reminded her of home, 'everybody just worried to death.' He liked that piece of cynicism from the worried little woman because it gave him a glimpse of feelings very like his own.

The only contented people in Gwanki except Cottee's Mallam were old White of Berua, a senior resident going on leave, who was reading his novel, probably Trollope, half-way down the slope, and the Birri chiefs sitting in the middle of the beach. The expressions of these naked warriors as they gazed upon the antics and miseries all about them, were like those of aristocratic travellers in barbarian parts or visitors to the Zoo monkey house. They watched with calm, interested faces as if from another and more distinguished state of being. Beside each man, his spear, standing point downwards and ready for instant use, guaranteed that distinction.

But the Birri, besides enjoying a Victorian self-confidence and dignity founded on a complete idea of things, were sure of getting to their destination. If this steamer did not come for them another would be found. They had their servant Gore to take charge of them. Everyone else in Gwanki except the whites had a ten to one chance of being marooned on a mud flat twelve hours' march from the nearest village. That was why women with babies on their backs were fighting like polecats for two feet of cracked mud on the water's edge, and why two convicts, three carriers, a runaway police servant and a horse-boy as well as the headman Henry, had applied for a cook's post. It would give them a free passage to Birri. And if the Birri pagans made war against the government there would be rich pickings. In wartime everyone threw money about.

As the evening wore on they pushed their faces almost through the tent fly. 'Mam, you wanta clean boy do all ting you like.'

They were insolent, and used double meanings because the humour of the thing appealed to them. There was no wilful cruelty in their pestering of the wretched woman who had last been seen flying for shelter with red eyes and her nose in the air; they did not insult and worry her because they disliked her, but because she was weak; because the restraint of fear had been removed from them. They were wandering men.

The sun was going down. It was like a huge bonfire on the far side of the river where the bank grew thin in the distance; a hair line between the sky and the water. A tapering patch of crimson joined the red blaze with the flock of dugouts rocking against the shore just below, and against the red path could be seen the three prospectors, now as black as everyone else, playing cards at their crooked table, which was sinking in the mud.

Mallam Musa finished his stocking and approached the fly. 'Missy Mahrie,' he said in English, 'I finish you work.'

'Come right in, father Musa.'

Musa went in and they heard her say, 'But this is beautiful work, Musa. Where did you learn to do woman's work?'

'Women could not do work like that, mam. It is too difficult for them.'

'Women are no good at all, are they, baba? (father). What shall I do without you?'

The Mallam did not trouble to agree with so obvious a truth. His thank-you was intoned as if to Allah rather than any human benefactor, as he salaamed himself out of the tent.

'What did she give you?' they asked him.

But with an austere face he gathered up his work-bag and descended the hill towards his master.

'It was paper money,' said Henry, and the whole group flung themselves towards the tent. But at the same moment the fly was thrown back and Hasluck came out so suddenly that they jumped away from her in alarm.

But she stood looking at the sunset and did not pay any attention to them.

She was a little woman with dark brown eyes and pale brown hair which was coiled in a tight plait at the back of her round head. Her cheeks were also pale, but in this light they had a becoming tinge of pink. Her face was broad, her nose small, her chin short and round, her mouth rather big. The blacks thought her extremely handsome and especially admired the mouth, a feature they understood. It was her best feature, well cut, sensitive, but they did not admire her smallness or her thin figure. She was dressed in bush kit, a pocketed yellow shirt and jodhpores.

They crowded round her holding out their characters. All had chits, some of them ten years old. These can be bought at great discount. They implored her. The horse-boy went down on his nose and cried out as if for mercy. Henry bowed and cringed, drawing in his head like a tortoise who expects a knock on the nose.

'I beg of you, mam, I headman for Mr. Cottee and Mr. Jukes. I Birri man—I wan go back to Birri. I be very good cook before. You take me Birri—I do all ting for you.'

He was carrying his pudding bowl hat in his two hands, and at every bow he pushed it forward in a gesture of original and profound humbleness. It was like a monkey's first sketch of prayer.

Hasluck looked round at them as if surprised. She would not take the papers, but said, 'I don't want a boy, I can't pay any boys.'

Nobody believed this. It was understood as bargaining. Henry screamed. 'Two pound a month—two pound, mam. Very cheap.'

'But I've seen you before, haven't I?' she said dreamily.

'Yaas, Missy Mah-rie. I Henry, Helleman Henry.'

'Yes, you were in gaol, weren't you?'

'Oh, mam, I no do nutting—dem bad people in Kunama catch me for nutting—because I poor Birri stranger.' Henry was in consternation. His eyes were opened to their widest to show his innocence. But the rest pushed him aside. They waved their papers. 'Mam, mam, look my book. I cook to guvnor.'

She looked at another. 'And you, Ali, you were in the stocks at Kunama for selling little girls.'

'Oh no, mam—oh no.'

She raised her voice. 'I think you are all very nice people and if I wanted a cook and a boy I think I should take Henry and Ali because I know something about them. But as I do not want anybody just now I must say good night to you.'

Then she walked away. The boys pursued her for a few minutes, but at last, when they saw that she was laughing at them, they suddenly grew abusive and shouting to each other that she was a worthless bitch, a low kind of white and so on, they left her.

The sun had set. All over the bank-side lanterns were flickering, fires sent up a tawny glow against a sky of lapis. The noise of the crowd sank into a regular loud hum as the people gathered round their cooking pots and became more good-tempered.

The card players had sent for a candle-lamp. They were now four. Old White had joined them. The lamp falling askance on his face threw the shadow of his parrot's beak across one downcast eyelid as he surveyed judicially the weak and strong points of his hand.

21

Cottee was lounging back with a peevish expression, his eyebrows raised. Allday, the expert, a pug-nosed fellow with enormous shoulders, more like a deep sea bo'sun than a scientific man, sat as usual with one thick arm locked over the back of his chair. His forehead was wrinkled not in thought but patience. It was like a fossil from some palæozoic beach.

Little Jukes was still worried. His little grey beard wagged as he talked to White and his spectacles as usual were falling down his nose.

Marie, staring at them out of a dark corner, hoped that Mr. Jukes was not telling the old judge some scandal about her. She had enough enemies already among these Britishers.

And the sad thing was that she had never wanted to quarrel with them. She liked them so much. Mr. Jukes had done his best to spoil her, and Frank had been a perfect darling. You had only to look at Mr. Gore to know what was meant by the aristocratic tradition. But he had run away from her as if she bit. No doubt somebody had told him that she had been abusing the British Empire.

Why couldn't she remember to keep quiet about the Empire. Yes, but it was because she liked these people so much that she hated to see them fixed in positions of domination and cruelty, in an artificial structure where even kind little Jukes and good-natured Frank were obliged to play the part of exploiters; and Mr. Gore, who looked like a St. Francis, to be a tyrant over the conquered.

# II

THE STEAMER DID NOT arrive till three o'clock in the morning. It would not have arrived then if the bold Captain Osho, anxious to save time and money for the government, had not pushed on by moonlight down the Gwanki reach. As everyone had foreseen there was then a riot. The hordes at the top of the bank rose up like an army and charged down the slope. Those in the front places who had waited longest were at once flung into the water and their goods scattered.

Gore was seen for half a minute by the light of a burning load of corn waving his long arms and opening his mouth to an extraordinary extent; before he, too, was pushed over the edge.

What saved the ship was the depth and softness of the mud which prevented any of the storming party of waders from reaching her.

Henry made good use of this excellent opportunity for which he had been waiting. That was Henry's superiority as a man of business. He never let go. Uttering piercing yells, striking out with his fists, trampling with his large hammer-shaped feet upon the soft bodies of the women gathered for security near the boats, he forced his way to the tent where Hasluck was sleeping. It was already demolished. Half a dozen heavy bodies had tumbled through it from above. But the woman herself, dressed in pyjamas of some red sunproof material (she used these sometimes as a kind of morning dress), was standing at the water's edge gazing at the ship.

'Mam, mam, de boat,' Henry bawled at her, grinning.

'Yes, it's the boat. What do you want, Henry?'

'I put you loads on de boat.'

'Can I go on board without a ticket?'

Henry laughed. 'You no want ticket. Dey no ask you for ticket. Mam, I be you boy—I come to Birri.'

She was absentminded, dejected. This was encouraging to Henry because a woman who is not only alone but dejected is easy to

23

manage and easy to rob. She looked at him with a mournful expression and said, 'You're a Birri, aren't you?'

'Yes, Mam, I wan go home to Birri again.'

'And you were turned out of Birri?'

Henry poured out voluble explanations of this incident. It was the wicked judge, Bewsher, who had listened to the wicked chiefs and turned him out. But he had only wanted to help the poor Birri people. In fact, he said all those things which might be expected to appeal to a woman of Marie's prejudices. For they were very well understood already.

'Well, Henry,' she said at last, 'you do have a kind of right to be helped back to Birri and I guess if you can get me there, I'll risk your cooking. But you'll have to wait for your pay.'

'Yes, Mam—we get der—you stay here, mam.' He turned and hurled himself towards the ruins of the tent.

Henry was full of zeal and even affectionate zeal. He meant to be a good servant. In fact, his furious energy, his reckless blows right and left soon cleared space on the bank and brought the labourers to their work. In ten minutes Mam and the first batch of her loads were gathered in one of the outermost dugouts with half a dozen Birri on guard.

The ship had touched the mud fifteen yards out and could not come nearer. She seemed to be nothing but two decks joined by pillars and surmounted by an awning. Engine-room, funnels, and the single paddle wheel which drove this elegant cage over the water were in the stern.

Marie, wrapped in a blanket with her hair in a pigtail, sat in the middle of a row of pagans. Their seven faces were turned outwards. But the Birri were watching the embarkation of Cottee's loads, a business which they understood, and when one of them nearly tumbled into the water they exploded in a roar of laughter which nearly upset the dugout.

It was Marie who had seen a thousand steamers and knew very well how they were made and where, who gazed with an entranced face at the white ship as it floated against the pitch darkness as if in mid-air, with its narrow bulwarks of pearl, its railings and cordage of spider's web, its pillars like ivory needles in the cold unflickering constellation of its own moons; like a piece of another magic world where even machines had grace and dignity. The greasers on a boat like that ought to be seraphim.

'Mam—Mam,' Henry bawled from the shore, 'you catch dem red box dar.'

But she did not hear him. He scrambled over the dugouts, leaping from one to the other with the desperate agility of the landsman, and pulled at her blanket.

'Mam, Mam, dem red box—you money box.'

She looked over her shoulder with the same absentminded expression and said, 'What about it? Isn't it here?'

'I no see um here.'

'I don't see half the loads—there's only four here.'

'You wait—I go look dem red box.'

'But there's no room for anything else in this boat.'

Henry looked at her. He was studying his mistress. He knew already that she was easy-going, that she hated trouble, that she did not stand on dignity. Now he could see that she was one of those whites who, like chiefs, are careless about their own property, who trust things in the hands of their servants, who say, as it were, 'I really haven't time to bother about these trifles.' She was not at all perturbed about the absence of the red box.

'I tink, Mam, if you go to ship now, I come after.'

'I think so too, Henry,' giving him a glance in which was betrayed a little surprise at his usefulness. 'I can see you're a real treasure.'

'Yes, Mam, you trust me.' He sprang away with large baboon-like leaps which expressed the exultation of his spirits. Ambition gave impulse to his muscles. He began to see a new career opening before him; that is to say, easy money and plenty of it, easy drinks, easy women. In what other direction could he make a career, for he had learnt to despise his tribe, he belonged to no community ready to admire or record his feats of courage or art. His only hope of glory and honour was in having cash which confers distinction everywhere; and of happiness in drink and women which taste the same everywhere. He dived into the crowd, yelling, kicking.

There was the box called the red box, actually a black uniform case with a red cabin label still pasted on its lid. It was half buried under the ruin of the tent.

The box was important because it contained all Marie's cash and

25

most of her reference books. The moment Henry set eyes on it, he perceived that here was his first opportunity in the new career. He pulled back the catches and threw back the lid. There was the cash box among a pile of papers. Unluckily at this moment, just as he had dived head and shoulders into the case to cover his operations, he felt a sharp prod behind, and furiously twisting himself round saw the judge Gore, looking down at him with an interested expression.

Henry banged the lid and jumped up. 'Mam tell me bring dem box—he no shut proper——'

'Are you with Miss Hasluck now?'

'Yaas, sir—I cook to Mam Hasluck.'

'Where is she?'

'She go for boat, sah, I show you, sah. You come dis way.'

'Bring that box along.'

And Stork made him carry the box down to the waterside and put it in a dugout. He did not leave him until the box was actually on the upper deck of the steamer.

Henry was now growing alarmed. But to his relief, as soon as his mistress appeared, Stork quickly dived back to the lower deck where the Birri were making themselves comfortable by pushing the Yerubas over the side.

Gore did not avoid responsibility for Miss Hasluck. The prospectors were in ambush behind their bed-nets. Gore's bed was just beyond them. His admirable boy had left his bath ready; with joy he inserted his long goose-rump into four inches of muddy Niger. His long feet on the deck wrapped over each other in congratulation of this happy hour, this successful escape. Things had turned out remarkably well.

The dimmed lights, the scattered beds, the discreet figures moving here and there in pink and green pyjamas with tooth mugs in their hands, the murmur of European voices, the ripple of the water against the side gave pleasing recollections of the leave boat. This upper deck was a piece of civilization.

Dreamily he sponged himself under the arms, turning up his eyes towards the canvas like an El Greco saint in ecstasy; at this moment Jukes, quivering with agitation, appeared before him and exclaimed that he was extremely sorry but would Mr. Gore give him a moment before he turned in; the thing was urgent. If he would come over for a night cap.

Gore said that he would be delighted. But he did not look delighted.

He was received with most impressive warmth of feeling. How good of him to come. He would excuse the invitation at such a time. A chair, a cigarette, a glass. 'You know Doctor Dollar.'

Doctor Dollar, whose heavy pale face thrust under a patched net of white muslin hung in the air like a conjuror's illusion, turned up his green eyes and gave a slight nod. 'I'm hearing you have the Hasluck on board.'

'You know the lady?'

'I know of her. All the poleetical old women in the country are talking about her.'

The prospectors' beds formed a kind of corral on the port rail. Jukes in pyjamas sat in the hollow of his green net like a gnome in a mossy cave; Allday, fully dressed, rode backwards upon a chair with his thick arms folded on the top bar. He looked as grave as Jukes was agitated.

'Mr. Gore,' Jukes pounced, 'do you realize that Miss Hasluck is a very dangerous agitator?'

'Teaching self-determination to bare-arsed apes,' rumbled Allday like a bassoon.

'Really—I'd no idea.'

The scene was comic, like all those between the solemn excited deputation of laymen and the languid bureaucrat. Gore's expression was exactly that of the young dude in the play who says, 'Well, really—what violent people.' The two miners stared at him with appeal, with exasperation, with hope supported by the excellence and irrefutable soundness of their case.

'You understand, Mr. Gore, it's a vital question for us—we can't *afford* to have trouble.'

'Really, I'd no idea—self-determination.'

Gore shook his head at the very notion, and then took a drink of whisky as if to restore his nerves. 'She might be a nuisance,' he agreed.

The miners looked at each other as if to say, 'My God, this is the kind of people responsible for our safety, for the government of the Empire. This nincompoop, this imbecile.'

27

'Self-determination.' Gore gazed pensively at the shore where a few red embers still marked the fires. He was disturbed. Self-determination was a dangerous kind of intoxicant·for conceited, truculent savages like the Birri. Here was a new factor in a situation already bad enough.

'The most dangerous kind of stuff possible for these raw savages,' Jukes pounced again.

'Oh! you'll find the Birri are pretty thick-headed.'

'In fact, you don't intend to do anything.'

'Well, you know—really to do anything effective, you'd have to——' he paused. He was obviously afraid that if he embarked on explanations he would have to·talk too much, begin with habeas corpus and go on through political expediency to the powers of assistant district officers.

'Begin further back,' muttered Cottee, who, stripped to the waist, was hanging over the rail with a cigarette drooping from his mouth. It was one of Gore's favourite remarks.

'That sort of thing.'

Cottee spat his cigarette-end at a bubble on the stream. 'Do you mean,' he asked with mild scorn, 'stopping Mah-rie's passport, or civilizing the Birri or federating the bloody world?'

'That would do.'

'Something like your old friend the Holy Roman Empire.'

'H'm.' Gore swallowed a yawn and wondered how far Cottee was being funny at his expense and how far he was trying to give him ideas. Cottee was fond of educating people.

The two miners were staring at the young men as at a couple of performing monkeys. Nothing could exceed the disgust of Dollar's puffy face turned up towards them. 'Vera illuminating,' he said.

'And meanwhile,' said Allday, 'these Bolshies do what they like.'

Cottee, still looking at the shore with an effect of indifference to these old fogeys and their absurd notions, was understood to say that if Allday was an Amurcan girl brought up on Freud and the fourteen points mixed in with Valentino and turned loose in a wilderness of notion salesmen and ward politicians, he'd be Bolshy. But the fact was that the poor bitch didn't know what she was or what she wanted. That was the trouble.

'Why all this pairsonal feeling?' said Dollar with a sly look. He'd heard about the Cottee's affair.

Gore said sleepily that the lady didn't sound very dangerous.

But Jukes at once retorted with indignation that she was extremely so. Anti-British propaganda of the worst kind. And she didn't understand the first thing about these people.

Gore made a desperate effort to look sympathetic and interested. 'Anti-British?' he murmured.

From below, where the mass of black bodies seethed in a temperature as hot as blood, voices boiled up into sharp loud cries. A heavy thump made the ship tremble from end to end as if in pain.

Gore, suddenly alert, bent his head sideways at the deck. His expression seemed to say, 'What's all this fuss about? After all, you're the lucky ones.'

Cottee threw himself back and flopped into a chair.

'Has she touched you yet?'

'Good Heavens no,' repudiating the very idea.

'You might do worse than take her on,' he continued with the same bored and discontented air. 'She'll give you some thrills—but of course thrills are hardly in your line, are they?'

'She's got a temper, has she?' said Dollar, raising his head and opening his eyes.

'Not at all. The best natured of bits——'

'Oh! I see—you were referring to an amorous technique.'

'Nothing you'd understand,' murmured Cottee towards the rail with a face even more disgusted than that which had marked his contempt of the old fool Jukes. For though the young man himself talked familiarly enough of the woman, nothing could express his loathing scorn of an old brute who should allow himself the same indulgence.

'No, old fellas like Jukes and me don't understand anything? Neither about tin nor government nor even women. That so, Jukes?'

Cottee, taken by surprise, looked quickly over his shoulder and meeting the gooseberry eyes fixed coldly upon him, turned red; and after sitting as it were pinned for a moment or two, decided to pass the thing off. He laughed and answered something to the effect that he would guarantee that Doc knew a good deal at least about the last subject.

And when Dollar continued to stare at him with that green, spiteful little ball, he became quite genial and made several jokes in

29

very much the same taste as the doctor's. One would have said that he had become a different man. But in fact he was only showing a different side of that good-natured sensitive character which had made him friends everywhere. Cottee hated to waste any of the good things in life, and among these good things he valued very highly the regard of his friends and neighbours.

Suddenly a violent clatter was heard and a tall figure in scarlet singlet and drawers, with an extremely red face, was seen charging down upon the beds. As he came he was heard to say loudly that something was intolerable and that he would appeal to the captain. The violence and directness of his charge seemed for a moment likely to overturn at least one of the beds on top of the party. Gore and Cottee jumped up.

But when the infuriated stranger, going full speed, was within a foot of Allday's bed, his eyes swivelled aside and then he himself, by a peculiar gliding movement which did not acknowledge a change of objective, passed completely by and was gone. Possibly the sudden apparition of the very tall Gore and Cottee, especially Gore, who in his blue pyjamas was a somewhat striking object, rather like a blonde vulture in a hospital coat, or a glance from Dollar's eye which was capable by some quality of its own of taking all the fire out of the most generous emotions and leaving them flat and disgusting, had diverted his rage.

'What you call a delicate hint,' said Cottee.

'Yes, I must really tear myself away—good night, Mr. Jukes. You'll let me know if there's anything I can do.'

A glimpse of Dollar's upturned face full of sour contempt for these graceful attitudes gave Gore his only moment of amusement since he had been pushed into the mud by the crowd.

That was the kind of accident which moved his sense of humour, especially when it happened to himself. The best joke of his year had been a tornado which blew off his roof in the middle of a dinner party, smashed most of his crockery and soaked the guests to the skin in one minute. Dollar also belonged to that order of the comic, the disastrous, the squalid, the ruinous; together with Harry Tate's motor and Rosinante.

The prospectors were on their feet full of politeness and apologies. Allday crushed his hand and growled that Mr. Gore would understand their position; Jukes hoped that they had not been troublesome. Dollar's head was suddenly withdrawn into his net and his bed creaked violently as he rolled himself up in his sheet.

'Good night, good night.' Gore smiled his way backwards out of the corral, and at once turning round with a quite different kind of expression, a most exhausted and bored expression, dived towards his bed.

A short figure in a brown coat started up with a pale anxious face. 'Mr. Gore!' Gore, inexpressibly startled, gazed at the woman. What on earth was she doing out of the lady's cabin?

But for some reason her nervousness made him obliging, even too much so.

She wanted an advance against her next remittance. She hadn't been able to go to bed, she confessed, because without her fare she felt like a bank robber.

But the next remittance was not due for a long time.

'Not at all. Delighted.' Gore was already unlocking his office box, a large square trunk of black tin chained to the leg of his bed.

'It's very kind of you, Mr. Gore.'

'Good Heavens!'

'Are they going to let me into Birri?'

'Birri? Why not? It's as open as Piccadilly or—or Broadway. At least the part that isn't still in the reserve. You can't go there, of course, without special leave.'

'So I needn't be worried any more?'

'No need at all.'

'Is that a promise? You really will get me in?'

'Yes, of course you'll get there.' He was counting out the five pounds, chiefly in florins. 'I'd better give you a bag for this. Here's a Treasury bag—you'll find it stronger than the cotton ones.'

'I just don't know how to thank you, I can't say how I feel.'

'Don't mention it. Delighted. Anything you want.'

He noticed that the lady had the foreign habit of a rapid accelera-tion. Whereas at a first meeting she was formal, even excessively so, after the old-fashioned American style, in another minute her eyes began to sparkle and her cheeks to flush, her whole expression said plainly, 'Isn't this delightful—to meet a new friend.'

And this suddenly alarmed him like an attempt upon his privacy, to break into the time and peace which legitimately belonged to himself. He explained with an abruptness as unexpected to himself as his first excess of good-nature that he was only doing his job.

But Miss Hasluck, in the act of turning the corner with her bag, answered that all the real angels said that. No doubt an Americanism. He locked his box and clambered joyfully into bed.

'Good night, judge'; like the note of a distant banjo.

This came from the next bed, and surprised him so much that he failed to answer it.

'And thank you.'

'Don't mention it.'

But she certainly had the power, as Cottee had suggested, of conveying a great deal of emotion in a few words.

He was glad she hadn't been squashed. In this damn country one forgot—what did one forget—he was too sleepy—one read too many newspapers—too many facts—got out of touch——

The tumult below deck had fallen to a bubbling gasping noise like a sleepy child's last convulsive sobs.

# III

THE JERK OF THE STEAMER from the fourth shoal below Gwanki waked Henry from his afternoon sleep. He was with the rest of the Birri in a forward corner of the lower deck.

It was three o'clock and extremely hot. He awoke with unusual quickness for a native, that is to say, in less than a minute, because he heard Mam's voice. His legs were already pulling themselves up to spring to attention before his brain took the trouble to let him know that she was not calling him. She was talking to the Birri. Mam was fond of talking to the Birri and she spoke the language already very well, with words that were commonly used only by the juju men or chiefs like Umoké.

She was sitting on one of her own loads near the bottom of the companion ladder and at the moment she was speaking to Obai.

'But you mustn't let the white man spoil your land or take you away to work for them. What do you need money for, Obai? You have what money can't buy—happiness that the whites can't get for themselves with any money because of their bad education.'

'They cannot come to Birri if we don't choose,' said the youth. He was standing hand in hand with his friend Uli against the forward bulkhead. He spoke as if giving a challenge, with a toss of his head. Obai was as fiery as a young stag. He was also the most intelligent of the younger chiefs and a favourite with Bewsher. It was easy to see how the white woman admired him.

'If they try, we will drive them out,' he said.

Old Umoké, senior chief, who was dozing against a netful of yams, opened one little eye and smiled on one side of his narrow mouth.

'You understand, Obai,' said Mam, 'but do the others understand? Do people value the air they breathe and the water of the river? Don't they say these are things we'll always have and the others will be added to them? The whites said that and now they live in towns with bad air and no rivers.'

33

Henry listened with astonishment, and then he wanted to laugh. He looked round at the Birri with a knowing grin as if to say, 'You don't swallow this stuff, do you?'

But the Birri were gazing at the water with the wooden faces of their own juju images. Only Obai and Uli caught his eye. But they did not respond to his smile. Obai was listening to Mam with a frown as if he was anxious to miss nothing. Uli was dreaming.

Uli was a renowned dancer and fighting man. He had wide square shoulders, narrow hips and powerful legs. His sharp muscles made Obai's smooth limbs look womanly. His expression too, good-natured and tolerant, was manly beside the variable nervous looks of his friend.

Mam was telling them not to be tempted from their villages and farms even for big pay, because it would destroy their lives.

Henry grew disgusted, irritable. He tried to catch Mam's eye to let her see that she had at least one auditor who knew what was what, who had travelled in the civilization of the great Nigerian world.

But she did not see him. She was excited, eager, like a jujuman filled with his spirit which makes him sing, pray, dance. Her face was like Obai's, and Henry thought, 'Two fools, two savages. That's why the other whites won't have anything to do with her.'

'Birri is the best place for Birri to live in,' said Obai.

'It is a good place for them because the others are there too,' said Mam. 'Life is precious because there is only one life—and the sweetest thing in life is friendship, is love.'

Henry at this gave a chuckle and this time Uli smiled with him. Uli was going back to a young wife, his first, married a week before his departure. He liked love but he considered that many things were better, such as hunting or even a good war.

But neither Marie nor Obai was aware of interruption. The woman's soft voice went on quickly pouring out its difficult strange thoughts. 'Those who have children know how keen is that happiness, and in Birri every woman can have a husband and a child. But the white priests, the Christians say——' and she went on for a long time telling the Birri how wise were their laws, how good their customs; and how bad the white man's laws and customs were, how stupid and wrong their religion which spoils the happiness of this life in order to make people ready for another which doesn't exist. 'The white men's god is a lie—don't you believe in him.'

34

Uli's attention had wandered. He was gazing at the river.

Old Umoké had shut both his eyes. The loud, regular beat of the stern wheel dashing upon the water like a mill, the trickle of the waves against the low gunnels, the thud of the engine, the drowsy murmur of conversation, which filled the stifling tween-decks with all those noises as appropriate to a ship as the smell of oil, rubber, tar and wet planks, gave to these people sensations of luxurious peace in which they visibly stretched their limbs. The screaming anxious mothers of the day before lolled among their packages with half-closed eyes and sleepy smiles. Their babies sprawled between their shining thighs like puppies. The grandfathers blinked at the children, the glittering water, which slid past in endless smooth undulations; at the far bank of the river and its forests marching past like armies of ragged infantry, with occasionally a flag or an elephant. Their faces were like the surprised, smoothed-out faces of young children at a play, and it was only those who had dropped off to sleep who showed the compressed mouths, the mournful wrinkles, the agonized or broken-hearted expressions of the old.

'You Birri know that this is the only life and it is full of beauty and happiness if we know how to live it,' Mam was saying, and the words made the eyelids turned towards the water sink a fraction closer over the sharp eyes. They liked the woman's words because they sounded good and because they were intended for praise. They half closed their eyes like cats scratched behind the ears. But what the words meant exactly they did not trouble to ascertain. They were more interested in a boat that had put out from the Birri shore some time ago, simply because it was a Birri boat. Whose was it? So and so from Kifi or such a one from Nok. It seemed now like a short thick needle rocking on a crucible of melted glass. The eyes narrowed to slits gazed all at the one point. There were two men in the boat which was now as thick as a match. The current of the Birri reach is strong. The steamer was rushing towards the boat like a motor car. One of the men in it was wearing a hat. A voice murmured Bewsher, but nobody agreed or contradicted because all had decided some time before that this must be Bewsher. The dugout now lay across their course, they were charging down upon it; the boatman, a thin Birri fisherman, and Bewsher, who was wearing his best Cawnpore hat and a khaki necktie, could be seen grinning towards them. The steamer veered in the current and they were

35

hidden from sight. Henry and the Birri leapt up together and rushed to the side, Captain Osho was heard bellowing angry orders on the deck above; Mam, having asked with surprise what was the matter, ran up the ladder.

'We're over him', cried the Birri, suddenly laughing and chattering with excitement. 'Didn't you feel the blow when we struck?'

# IV

Eᴠᴇɴ ᴏɴ ᴛʜᴇ ᴜᴘᴘᴇʀ ᴅᴇᴄᴋ it was thought at first that the dugout had been sunk. The height of the deck above the water and the bluff cut of the bow made it impossible to see anything close beneath it. The prospectors ran to the rail. Even Allday left his chair. Marie, arriving breathless and green and leaning over the rail as if she was going to be seasick (in fact the idea of an accident always made her feel a little sick), was just in time to see the dugout come flying like a surf board over the bow wave and bump hard against the curve of the starboard quarter. It was about fifteen inches wide and not so many feet long. A lithe little Birri at one end, stark naked, seized one of the lower deck stanchions and grinned upwards in triumph. The white man made a leap at the bulwarks and came down on his stomach. For a moment it was not certain whether he was going to dive inboard on his head or tumble tail first into the Niger. The legs kicked furiously. Then black hands seized him by the shirt and he disappeared abruptly like a bundle of merchandise.

The dugout was already far astern pitching madly in the wake while the boatman, riding it like a horse with both his legs in the water, baled it with a sweeping motion of his arm which was itself a gesture of joy and mastery. The water thrown from his calabash was part of this dance—its glittering curves sprang up, scattered and fell, in time with the dancing boat, the swaying body of its rider, the swinging arm.

The man knew quite well what a picture he was making, for in the middle of one plunge, when the boat seemed to jump clean out of the water for three parts of its length, and stood on its nose, he turned his face towards the spectators on the ship and grinned at them. The sun could be seen flashing on his teeth which thus formed another and central point of radiance in the midst of the broken diamonds all round.

The whole affair gave Marie such a shock of delight or rather

37

half a dozen shocks that she forgot her ostracism and turned to the nearest persons who could share it with her. These happened to be Gore and White. Gore had not seen the dugout approaching. He had craned forward and put out his long neck between the rails only in time to recognize Bewsher's legs, sticking out from the lower deck. Bewsher had ostler's or jockey's legs, sinewy and fine and a trifle bandy. The right was decidedly the bandier. At the end of his long powerful body they resembled the crooked antennæ of some agitated insect as they sought desperately for purchase in the air.

'Wasn't that just beautiful?' cried Marie, opening her eyes wide and using a tone which Gore had heard before. It was a caressing note, as if the girl wanted to embrace the circumstance which had given her such pleasure or perhaps the whole world which provided her with such wonderful moments. In fact, her expression, her flush, her bright eyes, the gesture of her hands seemed to include Gore in the grateful embrace.

Unluckily he had received at the same moment a different kind of shock. The last person he had wanted at that moment was Bewsher.

'What's our friend Bewsher chasing after now?' muttered old White on the other side.

Gore gave Marie a quick distortion of his lips which for him took the place of a smile when that social grimace was absolutely required of him, and then turned to the senior. 'I don't know, sir, I was going to meet him at Kifi.'

'This new plan in Birri, is he taking it much to heart? or perhaps you wouldn't know.' Gore was only thirty, with four years' military and five years' civil service, so White spoke as to a little boy.

His intention of course was to give him a hint that Bewsher wanted looking after. But Gore was accustomed to such hints and at the moment he had no time to attend to them. He murmured that he had scarcely had time to know what Bewsher thought of it and quickly made for the ladder.

Bewsher had been dragged on board by the Birri. He was now standing among them in a characteristic attitude, looking as someone had said, like a country parson in the middle of a Sunday School treat. And though, with his broken nose, his curly hair, his high shoulders and his general air of recklessness and nonchalance

38

Bewsher was more like a boxer or a steeplechase jockey than a parson, it was true enough that there was often something of the enthusiastic vicar about his eye and mouth. To Gore himself, who was a high Churchman, the long upper lip, the lively grey eyes and the sensuous eloquent mouth were typical of a high church father. You knew at first sight of Bewsher that he was a man with a cause, and that he was prepared to tell you all about it on the least excuse. He fixed you at once with a glance which enquired, what's this fellow good for, that is to say, as a proselyte, and at the same time, his lips had a half smile as if he had decided beforehand that you were good for nothing, that is to say, as regards irrigation in Birri or the folk lore of Nok.

This was very understandable, for everybody in Kunama Province except Bewsher had long ago decided that the Birri were the biggest nuisances and the rudest savages in the country.

Bewsher was forty-three or four and looked older. Alo is not a healthy division and in fact he had been told not to come back again. No one could imagine why he wanted to come back except perhaps to annoy the brass hats.

It was the fashion to pity Bewsher. At least six other men of White's standing had commiserated him to Gore. Members of council looked sympathetic as soon as they heard his name and said 'Poor old Monkey B. Is he still in Alo? That's a sad case.' His own resident Alabaster at Kunama, a large handsome man who looked almost as important as he felt, had a wonderful speech about him beginning, 'Poor Bewsher, one of my oldest friends—oh yes, we were in S.A. together—the yeomanry—and then out here. We came over to the civil side in the same year. Brilliant fella too. One must admit that he's done for himself. But what I always say is that when a man had been seven or eight years in the back bush he loses his sense of proportion.'

But it seemed to Gore, stuck on the third step of the stair while a sleepy woman on the first finished holding out her sleepier baby, that Bewsher was one of the happiest men he had ever known. And why not, he had no envy and he had his cause, his hobby, above all, his attachments. Did your private gentleman with his family house and his country friends envy the rising politician or any other kind of careerist?

You only had to look at the man now, chaffing that dog-eyed youngster about the Hausa ladies at Kunama and firing off his questions.

Had they seen the Resident's motor car? What about the machine for making clean water (the condenser). What about the pump and the fountain?

It was exactly the parson welcoming his choir school home; and the apes looking out for the signal to laugh or to be intelligent were just like schoolboys playing up to the master with a good deal of their tongues in their cheeks.

The same smile, half paternal and half mocking, with which Bewsher chaffed his Birri favourites, was turned towards Gore when that young man at last pushed his way within earshot.

'What have I been doing now?' he asked. It was his humour to pretend that Gore had been sent to keep an eye on him. He was probably right.

'I don't know, sir. I thought you were at Kifi.'

'I was going there when they told me that the boat was passing. Look at this.' He handed a wire form to Gore who read, 'Jukes' party left to-day. Also Hasluck anthropologist for Birri. Please give all facilities. Resdt.'

'Are they on board?'

'Yes, sir.'

'And Cottee?'

'Yes, they meant to land at Kifi.'

'It's Cottee I want. I've got a summons for him. He's been prospecting in the reserve.'

Bewsher said this without any animosity, and he added now in a thoughtful voice, 'What I ought to do I suppose is to warn them all off—just tell 'em they can't land.'

This was so outrageous a suggestion that Gore treated it as a joke. He went back to Cottee's case and suggested that it was not very likely that the man had been trespassing.

'Oh yes, he has—he's marked out his boundary right from Nok village. It includes all their best farms. Have you seen the E.P.L.?'

An E.P.L. is an Exclusive Prospecting Licence which having been registered gives a prospector sole mining rights within an area defined upon it and not exceeding eight square miles. The Jukes party held two such licences for a full eight miles each, one close to

40

Nok, another ten miles away at the mouth of the Elema river. Gore said that he had copies at Alo.

'And Cottee's claim is on the north bank of the river so that it can't be in the free area.'

'Oh yes, sir, a lot of Nok has been thrown open—the river isn't the boundary.'

'Quite so, but Cottee was over the boundary, so I'm going to run him in and his E.P.L. is waste paper. The question is, can I kybosh the whole scheme at the same time?' Bewsher put this question in a most friendly way, as one brigand to another.

Gore took care not to show what he thought of it. He said only that the prospectors had spent a good deal of money on their expedition and that one at least of their licences was in order. They would not easily be prevented from using their legal rights. As for Cottee, he was sure that there was some mistake about the boundaries and, of course, compensation would be paid for any farms that were taken into a mining lease. Probably a good deal more than they were worth.

Bewsher reflected a moment and then said, 'After all, they brought out their ruddy Gazette notice when I was on leave so that I shouldn't know anything about it, so they can't complain if I don't know anything about it.'

Gore said nothing to this. Bewsher was one of the queerest of the old gang who had ruled Nigeria like independent despots, but he wasn't a fool. He must know that he couldn't play fast and loose with the whole imperial government.

He looked thoughtfully at Gore. 'You'd rather fancy a mining camp in Birri—have you ever seen one?'

'No, sir, but I don't see how we can stop it now.'

'If the E.P.L. is invalid.'

'Don't you think that's rather unlikely? The new Nok boundary may be wrong in the Gazette of course, but the notice was drafted from your own map. It must have been. There isn't any other showing the villages.'

Bewsher was obviously taken aback by this suggestion. For a moment he was ruffled and said that he didn't care what the notice said—but he was not going to have Nok turned into a slum.

'But, sir, if the tin is really there, and I gather it's a very rich field.'

'Tin,' said Bewsher, slightly raising his voice. 'It's not a question

41

of tin. There's tin for everybody in Pahang, let alone the plateau. You know as well as I do it's not tin they're after but brass. They're going to float a company and make a pot. Why not? I'm not blaming them. All I say is that they could do it just as well in Kamchatka or South America. There's no reason on earth why they should come to Birri and smash up my whole show.'

'But really, sir—of course it's not my business.'

'Then you'd better let it alone.' This was decidedly angry. But Gore, though he did not like his position any more than he cared for Bewsher's policy, which he thought impracticable, or his methods, which he thought undignified, stood where he was. He was just as obstinate as Bewsher in the pursuit of his different ends.

The noise of the wheel and the waves slapping the bulwarks had prevented the last exclamations from being heard. Gore perceived this lucky fact with something that was as much like thanksgiving as his mood of the day before had been like prayer. But natives are quick to perceive everything about them. What they enjoy is the stream of life, and all their senses are concentrated upon the movements and sounds, the gestures and voices about them. Now from all sides the doll eyes, brilliant in their black settings, were fixed on the scene. All knew that the white men were quarrelling, that Bewsher was being defied. In the background spectators were standing on the baggage. Nearby the group of Birri stared at their master with calm and critical faces—the faces of children at a circus who watch to see if the lion tamer is really going to be eaten.

Old Umoké, the chief, young Uli standing in front, had exactly the same expression, as if they had paid for their seats at the show.

42

# V

GORE CATCHING SIGHT of these Birri eyes was disgusted. He told himself again that the Birri had no manners and actually moved across Bewsher to make his body a screen against them. But at the same time Bewsher himself noticed the spectators and at once returned their stare, gazing round him with raised eyebrows and an expression which seemed to say, 'Isn't that just like 'em?'

He was not only amused but at once recovered his temper. He called out something in Birri and several voices answered. Obai, very excited, made a little speech.

'You see this, Gore—they want to know what's happening. Obai here thinks we're selling their country to old Jukes. What shall I tell him?'

'I wish I had a map,' said Gore, sticking to business and refusing fantasy. 'We ought to be sure about Cottee. But there ought to be a copy in the mail, with the Mines File, and that ought to be waiting for us at Kifi.'

'If I said it wasn't safe,' said Bewsher, still seeming to plead and at the same time smiling as if the whole affair were rather a joke, his own schemes, Gore's fears, and especially this last plan. 'After all, it isn't. The Birri don't like strangers at any time, and when they see 'em collaring eight miles of farm land——'

'Not all at once. But I believe Jukes would be quite reasonable about Nok—provided of course that it's all right about Cottee. I mean, that nothing gets his back up.'

'Your idea is to wangle these fellows into Birri in the hope of avoiding a clash.'

Gore was silent. Bewsher said in a mildly interested tone, 'Do you believe in wangling? Where does it lead to exactly?'

He might have been a bishop reprobating some compromise with the birth controllers.

'Really, sir, I shouldn't like to say that Cottee's E.P.L. was on the wrong side of the line—without seeing the map.'

43

Bewsher waved his hand. He looked more sad than reproachful. 'All right, all right. But God help you if you're wrong. These fellows don't go a yard beyond Kifi except homewards, which is the worst road in Africa. That's what you've wangled for your tin-opening friends. May they bless you for it.'

Gore said no more. He knew how much a victory of this kind depended on a quick breakaway. He went away so quickly, that Bewsher had no chance to repent.

The young man had reason to rejoice, and, though rejoicing was impossible to Gore, he did feel a kind of relaxation of nerve, which for him was a considerable pleasure. Peace was assured in Birri. For he was confident of his point about the map. The only difficulty had been to get Bewsher's leave for the prospectors to land.

In fact Bewsher did not even show himself on the upper deck. He stayed among the Birri talking to the chiefs and the boy Obai for the rest of the afternoon. Whenever Gore peeped down the hatchway he saw him in the same position, perched on a pile of bales among the deputation, with a pipe in his mouth and his hands clasped between his knees.

The prospectors were meanwhile busy with their papers and Marie had gone to sleep in her long chair, or rather half-way out of it, for one of her arms had slipped under the side member and her hand palm-upwards was resting on the deck.

Gore himself dozed over his book until six o'clock, when Cottee woke him for a drink. The ship was now approaching Kifi, which appeared like a kind of dark bluish mouth in the forest from which a brown tongue covered with small fissures lolled into the river. Three or four broken huts and stacks of cut wood on the far side of the opening took the place of large irregular teeth. These were boat-men's huts and an old rest-house; Kifi village lay further back and Bewsher's rest-house was nearly half a mile away in its own clearing.

It was twilight. The sun had gone below the tops of the trees and the trees themselves, the river, the Kifi mud bank, the ship and the faces and dress of the passengers leaning on the rail were all coloured like different shades of smoke. The engine was stopped and the ship was carried forward with the current like a moving picture.

Jukes, Cottee, Marie standing beyond them with a lock of hair hanging down her forehead and a look of surprise and bewilderment on her face, as if she had waked to find herself dreaming, appeared also insubstantial and flat, like photographs of people and events taken long ago in some outlandish spot that nobody ever heard of.

This was one of those moments when peace seemed like an actual ingredient of the air. Just as in a battle the air itself was a rapid vibration, all conflict, now it was all rest.

Gore enjoyed this sudden quiet which followed upon the stoppage of the engines so much that he did not trouble about his packing. He knew that it would not take long and that the ship must stay at Kifi till the moon rose, possibly all night if Captain Osho did not care to risk his thin plates among the snags.

He continued therefore to lie in his chair, with his long feet on the second rail, to gaze at the flickering tree trunks which passed now quite close to the ship's side, in a kind of trance, and with an expression comically like that of Marie's, twenty feet away; his eyebrows raised, his eyes fixed and blank; rather a foolish expression in fact, though his sensations were actually very pleasant. In half an hour he would be alone in the marine rest house and safe from annoyances for that day.

He was therefore very much startled and looked almost lunatic when Miss Hasluck suddenly appeared beside his chair and remarked in an apologetic tone, 'I'm very sorry to trouble you, Mr. Gore, but is it true that nobody's allowed to land here?'

'What——' He scrambled hastily to his feet. 'I beg your pardon.'

'Mr. Bewsher has turned us all back.'

'I'm awfully sorry.'

'And he's fined Mr. Cottee five pounds for going to Nok last month. Could he do that to anybody?'

'If Cottee went into the reserve——'

'But Nok isn't in the reserve any more, is it? Not by your Government Gazette.'

'Not the village certainly—I'm extremely sorry about this, Miss Hasluck. I'm afraid you'll have to go on to Alo. I won't be getting back till to-morrow, but you'll be staying with me, of course.'

'But that's very kind of you.'

The lady's sudden warmth of gratitude embarrassed the young man, who was in fact highly irritated by the prospect of sharing his house with anybody, much more a female. But orders were orders. And solitary young women (in Gore's mind) ought not to be left

45

alone in unguarded rest-houses. Murmuring that it was the usual thing, no trouble at all, he would see that she was expected, he put on his hat and retreated down the hatchway.

Here there was none of the turmoil that he had feared. The natives were stirring, but only in the normal restlessness which always seized upon them at any arrival whether they intended to disembark or not. The whole low-roofed chamber, very dark and lit only by greenish reflections from the sky and the water, was full of the movement of bulky heavy bodies as if the bales and boxes themselves had woken up and were uneasily coming to life. The voices were not yet excited, but one woman less sleepy than the rest was calling anxiously, and each call was more urgent and a little louder than the last.

Gore peered about and soon distinguished Bewsher by his high shoulders and his crooked legs silhouetted against the water. He was leaning on the gate in the starboard rail. Apparently he had moved across the deck to prepare for landing and to judge by the spears, waving round him like corn-stalks, had brought the Birri with him.

He was talking to the prospectors in a most amicable manner. In the general quiet the whole conversation was perfectly audible at the ladder three yards away.

'I'm very sorry about it, of course, but I don't want you to get your throats cut.'

Jukes, whose back was turned to the ladder, said something about an appeal, to which the other answered still more politely, almost effusively, that he would be delighted to state a case.

The prospectors were behaving very well. There were no raised voices. Allday began to shout but stopped himself when the others looked at him. Cottee seemed more scornful than indignant.

He made some remark about the affair being more of a knock-out than a washout which was probably intended for a pun. Bewsher laughed heartily and then asked him if he had his cheque book handy.

But just then the wheel once more began to turn, crashing against the water in reverse, and at this signal the whole mass in the lower deck began to work—the crescendo of noise was like a falling house; a couple of thumps, a yell, and then an uproar of grinding, roaring, screeching and thundering.

Gore suddenly perceived Cottee at the bottom of the ladder and discreetly slipped away to collect his loads.

The ship had stopped. The gang planks were down and battle was joined between the Kifi traders (there is a Hausa settlement at Kifi) wanting to embark and the Birri rushing towards their homes and their wives. Even Captain Osho's voice was drowned.

Gore let half an hour pass before he returned below. He had no intention of meeting the prospectors, even the good-natured Cottee, at this moment.

But he had no sooner dived into the crowd, which was now beginning to find its new places and whose volume of noise had diminished to that of a third form after the holidays, then he heard Jukes' voice.

Jukes and Allday were standing beside the head of the gang plank. It was necessary for him to pass them though not to notice them in the darkness.

But the bitterness of the voice touched a spring in Gore, a kind of doctor's bell, which obliged him in spite of his inclination and even his judgment to offer balm.

'I'm awfully sorry about this muddle,' he said, stopping with one foot on the plank. 'I'm afraid it's put you to a great deal of trouble, not to speak of expense. I do hope it will turn out all right. But of course you do see that'—and then he went on to explain that the Gazette notice was ambiguous, etc., and that its publication had come at an awkward time. 'As you know, Mr. Bewsher has been trying for a long time to federate the different sections of the Birri into some kind of a political unity, and this last year or two he's had a good deal of success. But you can understand that any trouble now might upset the whole scheme.'

'By trouble, meaning us,' said Allday.

'Of course no one wants to shut up Birri permanently. Mr. Bewsher's plan is to develop the whole district as a unity. As soon as the political foundations are anything like firm. And federation might go through any day now. Then there'll have to be some sort of agreement about the laws affecting strangers—they practically haven't got any at present.'

'So if we come back in ten or twenty years——' said Jukes.

'Good heavens, no—in less than a year.'

'In less than a year,' said Jukes in a mild voice. 'But unfortunately we'll be broke in less than a year—much less. It's cost us rather more than our capital to get this far. I know of course that you young gentlemen don't understand business—but nobody's going to pay us a guaranteed monthly salary for doing nothing. I fancy that's Mr. Bewsher's idea, too. It's quite natural. I'm not blaming you—you don't know any other kind of life. I quite realize that you've got to amuse yourself with something, and this Birri game is better than golf or spillikins.'

Gore murmured something that sounded apologetic but was not meant to be intelligible—a polite noise, and went ashore.

He had deserved that, he reflected, as he looked for his boy and his loads. There was nothing that could be said to that last statement of Jukes, because it was true. That looked like his loads. He strolled towards a dugout which had mysteriously emerged round the bow of the steamer, from the outer or port side  But the headman in charge was wearing a hat and Gore's Hausa boy never wore a hat. He turned away and made for the rest house. Jukes had hit the nail. Not perhaps that spillikins was the best word, unless the art of Lenin and Mussolini could be described as spillikins. But it was the same word no doubt that Jukes applied in his own private thoughts to the occupations of the poet and the painter, while they in their turn were certainly inconsiderate of the private citizen, poor devils with wives and families, with fond earthly loves and large financial responsibilities. His sympathy was with Jukes.

He found Bewsher in the rest-house walking or rather springing round the floor in the highest spirits. It was obvious that he was extremely pleased with himself. He greeted Gore with a smile which challenged the young man to be peevish. But Gore had no intention of provoking an argument. That would be a total waste of time and energy.

'Have a drink,' cried Bewsher. 'Here, Sam, drinks one time and—you're dining with me. Why of course you are.' He bustled to fetch glass and sparklet bottle. Bewsher was famous for his hospitality. His invitations were always to stay as long as you could and he was extremely particular during your stay that you ate, drank and amused yourself entirely at his expense. But to-night there was something even tender and womanly in the kindness with which he

48

urged Gore to make himself comfortable and take another spot. It was as though he had betrayed and wounded Gore by his thoughtless actions.

Gore, however, managed to excuse himself from dinner on the plea of getting the mail ready for immediate answer. He wanted a little solitude.

It was not till he was half-way out of the door that Bewsher introduced the subject that was in both their minds. 'I'll want you to concoct something nice and diplomatic for the Resident about the unrestful condition of Birri. You might send a youngster called Obai along. He will give us any evidence that may be required.'

'Yes, sir.'

'By the way, I forgot about that Yank. I suppose she's all right.'

'Oh yes.' But as he spoke he remembered the boy in the hat and the mysterious dugout full of loads which, it seemed, were not Bewsher's; for Bewsher's were already in the rest-house. And he was seized with a doubt. Certainly Marie had seemed a mild enough little person, the last to break into forbidden places. But he remembered her anxiety to get into Birri. His doubts became very strong indeed. He took care, of course, to show nothing of them in his face. But Bewsher was one of those people who had an extraordinary knack of following and detecting another's thoughts. He said at once, 'She hasn't given you the slip, has she?'

'Oh no——'

'Better go and see. She'd be worse than Jukes—and poor old J. has some excuse. It's his job.'

'Yes, sir, I'll go at once.'

Gore then walked down to the village, sent for Obai, who was nowhere to be found, and called out in a low voice, to a bank of trees and a dead wall, 'Miss Hasluck.' She did not answer. So he was able to report to Bewsher after dinner that he had sought the lady without success. She must have gone with the boat.

It seemed to Gore that Bewsher had made quite enough political trouble and trouble for himself, in that day, without risking international complications. Luckily the man was quite satisfied with this assurance. He was in the mood to be easily satisfied. His general demeanour was still that of a Grand National winner or the sporting bishop, who at a county meeting has just croqueted his adversaries right off the field. When he walked he was the jockey; when he stood

49

with his head on one side, he was the bishop. There was a slight element of the frivolous or sporting about Bewsher's most serious political operations, or his attitude towards them, which, quite as much as his independence, had spoilt his chances of promotion, and at the same time made him so excellent a hand with pagans.

Gore did not find Obai because he was already several miles away along the Nok road. All the Birri deputation had set out for their villages as soon as they landed, to carry to their people the important message from the Resident at Kunama, the King of Kings, the Lord of Bewsher himself. He had told them that the welfare of the Birri was his highest care, that no one should be allowed to take a foot of land from them and that the opening of Goshi market to traders from outside would all be for their advantage. As for the white people, who were living at Goshi (the Mission), they were harmless people, good people, who would cure their diseases and teach them many useful things.

How far this message could be believed was another matter. General opinion was that the big judge was a big rascal. Henry had pointed that out and Henry was probably to be trusted because he was not only a Birri but poor and unfortunate. But they did not have entire confidence even in Henry and when he came to wish them good night and offer them gifts of whisky and tea Obai would not accept them.

Uli, who would have liked to accept them, submitted to his friend's ruling only under protest. He said even twenty minutes later as they passed in single file through flickering brown and green shadows from the forest, 'That drink is good.'

'It's not a Birri drink but a white man's drink. Therefore we should not touch it.'

Uli laughed and said, 'That's what Bewsher says.'

Obai frowned. 'That doesn't make it a lie.'

'No, no—beer is better for a Birri,' said Uli hastily, who did not like to quarrel with anybody; and then again for half an hour or more they loped over hard ground as silent and agile as hunting dogs, with long and short steps to fit each variation in the surface.

Uli kept shoulders and body rigid as he darted onwards. The skill and activity of his hunter's progress was all in his flashing legs.

50

Obai, slimmer, lighter in colour and bone, was more erratic in movement. His feet did not place themselves with the same unconscious foresight. But they never stumbled, for at the last instant, when they were actually coming down upon a root or a thorn, Obai would make some astonishing leap or twist in mid-air and pass on safely.

Uli was enjoying the journey as he enjoyed every journey in his own land. His eyes darted here and there among the trees, noticing the smallest indications of human or animal passage, his ears were alert to the minutest sounds, all his faculties were rejoicing. He, too, was keenly conscious of this delightful time, in the cool of the evening, when he was home again in Birri among his own trees, under his own sky, among his own spirits.

It was delightful to be Uli, friend of Obai; it was delightful to have such a body, such arms and legs, full of energy, it was delightful to go home to a wife. It was such keen pleasure that often his walk became a dance as the muscles of his legs dancing by themselves made a spring forward.

Then he drew beside Obai who was flying ahead, his eyes and mouth open like a jujuman full of the spirit. Uli had meant to smile at his friend and make some joke about their women but Obai suddenly caught his hand and began to sing—

*'The spears of the Birri are thicker than corn.*
*Their women more lovely than the cotton trees, more fruitful*
*than the palm.'*

'Which Birri do you mean?' he asked.

'All the Birri are brothers.'

'Bewsher says so.'

'But it is true, true,' cried Obai, suddenly growing angry and excited. 'Why do you laugh? Don't you see that Nok and Kifi and Goshi and Paré are all one kind of people and Hausas and whites and Yorubas are another kind.'

This was one of Obai's whims. He was always catching some nonsense from Bewsher. Once it had been a medicine for fever and another time some absurd tale about the guinea worm coming out of water. Now for months it had been this talk about the Birri being brothers and one people. People laughed at Obai, although he was the leader of his class.

51

But Uli was his friend and did not laugh. He was indignant at the charge.'

'I wasn't laughing.

'But you don't believe.'

'Yes, I believe—of course I believe,' cried Uli. The words meant nothing to him.

'Aren't you proud to be a Birri?'

'Yes, of course.'

'The bravest and wisest people in the whole world.'

'That's certainly true.'

'Our country is the richest in the world, our women are the most beautiful.'

'True, true—yes.' Uli opened his stupid eyes to their widest. For these things were undoubtedly true. Obai took him by the hand. He was quivering with excitement. 'And we are Birri.'

'Yes,' cried Uli. 'We are Birri.' They rushed forward hand in hand through the forest crying, 'Birri—Birri.' Obai seemed to defy an enemy, Uli was laughing. He was going home. He did not care what he sang.

# VI

Nok, like all african and old English villages, is a collection of houses scattered without plan and facing every way. There are no roads but only irregular spaces between the houses. The largest of these is the market or assembly place which divides the village into two parts, the old ward, standing on a low mound formed by its own rubbish, and the new or river ward which is again five or six foot lower than the market-place. This site, in three broad steps coming down to the river, is itself beautiful, and its beauty is increased by some young palms and shade trees planted here and there by Bewsher's orders twelve years before and protected since by his name.

Now at night the bright doorways of the upper ward seemed like a decoration of lanterns and the palms rising into the moonlight were like fountains of quivering silver water playing into the dark blue air from an irregular pile of dark rocks. Two coils of winding river, sunk deeply between their banks, caught the moon only on one almost vertical reach which seemed to join the village with the forest a hundred yards away. The forest front in its blue shadows was like some enormous building whose façade extended into the darkness on either hand.

The glow of fires among these dark shapes, the sparkle of lanterns, the murmur of voices and laughter, the soft beat of drums practising a phrase suggested a festival in a water garden.

Uli, who had seen a festoon of Chinese lanterns and a fountain (the Resident's spray hose) for the first time at Kunama in the last month, and heard that these things were admirable, had now something new to astonish and delight him in his own village, and he thought, 'I shall tell them about it—about the tree of water.'

Uli was full of a young traveller's vanity, but like all the Birri he was passionately attached to his own village. Like all the Birri and unlike the Hausa and the Fulani he could not imagine life anywhere else.

Outside Nok he could only stare or laugh at the things people did and said and the way they behaved. Their sufferings stirred him as little as their vanities. But in Nok he was moved by everything that happened; he, too, suffered, enjoyed; his nerves seemed to extend beyond him throughout the whole village and the fall of a roof would cause more commotion in his spirit than burning and massacre in Alo or Kunama.

Already before reaching his house Uli was smiling at the darkness as if at his family, because already he was with his family. Nok was their body and its air their spirit.

Suddenly they pressed round him all talking at once, cutting him off from Obai. His mother and his sister could not find means to express their delight except by touching him and uttering shrill cries of astonishment such as can be heard from the trees when the birds gather in the evening. His young wife Enuké, however, did not smile. She stood gazing at him with her round anxious eyes which seemed to say, 'I mustn't forget my cue.'

Enuké had been well brought up, and like most Birri women was punctilious in doing things in the proper old style. She knew how to play her part in the complicated scheme of Nok society. But as she had not yet performed the duties of a married woman for very long she was still, though completely trained to her part in all its mysteries, nervous in performing it.

She was a short, very black girl of fifteen, deeply pitted, like nine out of ten Birri, by small pox. Her back was hollow and she had small high breasts which were considered a defect. For a woman should be able to feed her baby to two years old. Her head was like half a coconut, her nose was so flat that its tip was depressed below the wings whose open nostrils curled from it like fine shells. This well-shaped nose and her great mouth were her chief beauties and atoned for her unusually deep pock marks. Only the largest mouths can show the natural modelling of lips in their fine detail.

But she had not been much sought after, and Uli's parents had obtained her at a remarkably small exchange value.

'What you want in a wife,' his mother said, 'is a girl who has been properly brought up and has a good temper. A woman's work is hard and difficult and bad for the temper. That girl Enuké is not sought after because she is thin and doesn't make a noise at the feasts when the men run after her. But so much the better in a wife.'

Uli had agreed carelessly because he had to agree. He had to take what he was given. But now he was thinking very much of Enuké. It was as though she had grown into him during his absence, like a planted seed. His eyes were drawn towards her even while he did not want to look, even while it was rude and impolite to show her public attention, and seeing her scared eyes and lips parted in shyness, seeing her dodging in the background among the humble young ones, he felt for the first time the private sympathy between them. He and she were mixed up together. He wanted to be alone with her, not because she was a woman but because she was a partner with him and they had a lot of important things to talk about. Where to make the new corn store, whether to buy a new water-pot.

But meanwhile his family were pouring out their questions and he must answer.

'What is the news, Uli?'

'Nothing but health.'

'But the big judge—what did he say?'

'He says all is well.'

'He says so,' said one of the brothers.

'He says so, but who believes it? The Birri are not fools,' said another.

'The big judge is a big liar,' said Uli, swaggering among them and laughing. This laugh, strangely enough, was also concerned with Enuké. It was as though Uli, sure of the closest attention from that quarter, rose to his part. He was very successful. Everybody approved a remark so epigrammatic, so neat and so likely to be true of a foreigner.

The drums in the market-place suddenly burst into a tune and the whole party began to move towards them. Uli, still talking, close-pressed among his family and his friends, found himself under the palm trees in the market-place. This was the place of honour. Chiefs were all about him and he could hear Obai's high voice close to him speaking very fast about Bewsher and the big judge.

He did not listen to these words or to anyone else's words: the sound of the Birri voices was the music of his pleasure just as

55

Enuké's proper conduct was the ground of it. He was so happy, so content that laughter seemed to rise in him for no cause. It was not he that was laughing but some part of him which belonged to Obai, to Enuké, to his sisters whose voices he could hear twittering among the women behind him, to everybody in the village, to all the Birri gathered there; something that laughed in them and then he too was obliged to laugh. This happiness belonged to them all; it was their happiness in Nok. Now the beer came round, passed from hand to hand in calabashes; and an old chief spoke words of welcome. Then Obai made a speech saying that now thanks to Bewsher they were safe, that Bewsher had saved their country from the Yorubas and white men, that Bewsher was truly their father, that now all the Birri must join together as Bewsher had told them, under one great chief and one great law to be a nation like the Yorubas and the Hausas.

Chiefs in Birri had little authority. Anyone could become a chief by paying the price to the other chiefs and giving a beer feast to the village. Obai too was talking nonsense. Who had ever heard such stuff about unity, about nations; about one law and one juju? Even the word for nation made them laugh for the Birri had no word for such an odd thing and Obai used one invented by Bewsher himself meaning the all-Birri. It made you laugh. All the ideas of Bewsher made you laugh, when they were not a bore or a nuisance. At the word all-Birri in the last sentence of Obai's speech the girls began to titter and some man shouted out, 'The all-fish.' Then somebody else catching in a moment the notion of this new joke called out The all-goats! and everyone began to laugh and shout The all-parrots! the all-calabashes! the all-pipes! the all-noses! the all-navels! and so through all the parts of the body which made one of the best jokes ever heard in Nok. The laughter waked the birds high up in the trees, set all the dogs barking and caused the monkeys half a mile away to enquire of each other, What is that?

When the people laughed, Obai grew angry and shouted. Then Uli, seeing that his friend was serious, got up also and shouted at them. Unexpectedly the laughter faltered and grew thin. In a moment only three men were laughing who hated and despised Obai, declared enemies like the head of the eight age class, a young man known as the Fish; or the women who had come to laugh at everything.

56

Then dozens of voices began to shout at the Fish and he, too, became silent. Obai finished his speech about the all-Birri and even dared to say that Birri villages should cease fighting among themselves, and when he sat down, everybody applauded. They began to laugh again, but they also shouted congratulations.

This was a great triumph for Obai and surprised everybody. It was seen that he was becoming a big man. This visit to Kunama had made him suddenly important and confident.

It was not time for the feast. The drummers had not yet eaten. When Obai had finished speaking, people began to move about and talk; the women went to fetch the calabashes of food and beer.

Uli, like Obai, was now surrounded by a little crowd who wanted to ask him questions. The boy was delighted with himself and at every moment he uttered a loud laugh full of conceit. 'Here, let me go,' he shouted. 'I want a drink.'

'So Bewsher is all right,' said a serious-looking old farmer.

'Bewsher, who knows what he's after—something for himself.' Uli remembered that this had been a successful remark.

'But I thought you were speaking for Obai?'

'Obai, yes. Obai's a good man. He speaks well, doesn't he? Hi, where's that beer.'

A calabash was quickly passed to him and he poured the sour liquid down his throat in a cascade. This, too, was a piece of swagger, expressive of his joy in being free again, and also in being a notable person. He put it down empty. 'Ah! you should taste the Hausa beer—that's the stuff.' He uttered another guffaw.

Then suddenly he wriggled out of the crowd and made a dive at a woman. She bolted with a squeal of alarm and delight. It was Enuké.

This was not a very decent or polite act of Uli's. Later on perhaps, when everybody was drunk, it would have been in order. The little group looked at each other. Then one of them said, 'These boys— they don't know how to behave themselves nowadays.'

Everyone agreed with this statement, and in fact it was true. Manners in Nok were deteriorating.

Enuké might be a serious young woman in household matters. No one could be more serious about scouring a pot or scraping a floor. But in love she was still a coquette. She made Uli play hide-and-seek half-way round the town before she finally allowed him to see her going to earth in their own hut.

But then she was ready for him, her forehead pressed down on the stool. Uli caught hold of her to turn her round. Enuké did not understand this procedure. She fought like a demon, crying in terror. 'No, no, no. It's bad. Let me go.'

But Uli was reckless with his traveller's conceit. He'd show the little fool, educate her in the foreign art of love, face to face.

And in Uli's dexterous powerful hands Enuké was as helpless as a young kid. He gave her windpipe a pinch so that she was half choked, just enough to make her confused and weak, he twisted her hands apart and jerked up her heels. She fell under him on the ground, and on her back, two things forbidden to a Nok wife.

'There,' he said after a while, 'now, you see, you little fool. All that fuss about nothing.'

He rolled away from the girl and put his arm under her head to be kind to her. He was full of tenderness towards her because he had hurt her and abused her. She had taken it so well. She might be an obstinate little fool but she was a good wife, a good girl. No one worked so hard as Enuké.

Enuké lay flat on her back and did not move. She seemed to be dead. Uli was a little alarmed. He bent forward, peering in the dim light of the embers and said, 'No shamming?'

Enuké leapt up and dived out of the door. She did not utter a sound.

Uli was frightened. Suppose Enuké went to his mother, to the other women, or worse, to her brothers. If she liked to complain to her brothers they were bound to protect her and avenge her. They would beat him or fine him. Moreover, all the women would be disgusted with him and it was dangerous to offend the women. They had their secret clubs, their secret knowledge, and they were very revengeful. They would curse him, poison him, spoil his crops and the hunting. What a fool he had been with his new ideas.

He crept to the door and peered into the dark compound. Where was she? In some other woman's house?

One of his brother's wives was sick. A stick had been laid across her door and she had not gone to the feast. Perhaps Enuké had run in there. He called her name in a soft cajoling voice. But his brother's wife answered irritably, 'Why don't you leave Enuké alone—beating her like that.'

'Can't I call my wife?'

'Yes, but don't beat her. She's a good girl—better than you deserve. Suppose she told her brothers about you.'

'I'm not afraid of them or you, you silly fool.'

The woman gave a cry of surprise and indignation at this rudeness. Uli swaggered into the street roaring for Enuké.

But his stomach felt empty, his knees weak. A figure suddenly passing between two houses made the shout fail on his lips. For he thought, 'Suppose he knows—suppose Enuké has told.'

He did not shout again, but ran quickly from one corner to another, whispering, imploring. Now he knew that he was a fool and a criminal and the loneliness which falls upon the pagan sinner was already spreading outwards from him. No one would support him against the law, against the juju. That was impossible because he was in the wrong. How had he done such a thing?

'Enuké, Enuké,' he implored in the darkness. The movement of a rat made him leap and fly.

But what good was it to seek Enuké? He had sinned. He had broken the frame of things. He could not escape punishment any more than one who jumps off a high tree or swallows poison. And already his body felt weak, his legs slack. What would befall him, blindness, impotency?

'Uli—Uli——' A friend's voice shouted from his own house.

Uli bolted towards the forest.

Enuké had run home to Lower Nok and her brothers came to look for Uli, who was not to be found. But this interesting scandal was overlaid at once by the sudden appearance of the white woman in Nok rest-house. Obai said that she was their friend, but why, in that case, did she ask so many questions? And what was she doing in Nok so far from her own country?

Bewsher was coming at the end of the month and it was agreed to ask him what the woman wanted. But the same day that Bewsher arrived two other white men came and began to measure the fields. The Nok people were taken by surprise. The crowds that had come from neighbouring villages of the tribe to see Bewsher stood in a close packed mass staring at the three white men in the middle of Obai's yam field.

There was Bewsher with his early morning hat, a grey felt with its curly brim turned down, his hands in his pockets, seated on his one leg stool (shooting stick) with his legs stretched out and his curly pipe in his mouth. There was the Stork with his red-rimmed eyes and a drop of sweat on the end of his beak, standing beside a mysterious engine of gold and glass on three tall legs. There was the pink-faced Redhead in beautiful white breeches and long laced-up boots.

'But what is it, what is it?' somebody asked.

'They've come to take our farms.'

'They're putting magic to stop the yams growing—then they will say that the land is no good and take it from us.' This was from a young spearman in the front row, one of Fish's party. He spoke very fast and used idiomatic terms such as Bewsher would not understand.

Everybody in the crowd said, 'And what about the snake in the brushwood?' This was one of Bewsher's names.

'He's sold us.'

'Well, what then?'

'What then,' cried the young warrior, turning round, 'we're going to finish with him. We're going to finish with all these foreign vermin. To-night, these three. To-morrow, the Goshi lot.'

'Why not begin now?'

But no one raised a spear. No one even spoke loudly or looked indignant. It was felt that this matter was complicated, it required reflection.

The three white men did not notice the gradual increase of the crowd or the arrival of armed men, because they were deeply concerned with their own affairs. Besides, all the Alo carriers were standing like a wall as close to Bewsher as they dared. In Birri they felt rather like fat sheep exposed to forty thousand wolves, and Bewsher was the only wolf tamer within sight.

Gore and Cottee had come to check the boundary of the Reserve. They had hoped to perform this task, and to decide upon a course of action before Bewsher's arrival. Bewsher was not due until the next day.

But Bewsher was one of those people who always turned up when he was unexpected and at a very inconvenient time for the opposition. It was an art, typical of the pagan man, which had thrown innumerable war-plans in Birri out of gear.

On this occasion it was Gore's scheme that was jeopardized. Gore, after extraordinary efforts of hospitality and tact at Alo (he had used all his whisky and port for six months ahead), had persuaded the prospectors that it would suit them far better to make peace than war. On the one hand they might get damages, but they would have a very bad send-off in Birri where Bewsher's influence was paramount. What about their labour, their supplies, their water rights, compensation cases?

Now suppose they agreed to give up the Nok claim, already of doubtful validity, and Bewsher on his side gave them his full support and assistance at the Elema site in Lower Nok, or Jukes' Meadows, as Cottee had christened it, how would that do?

At first it had done very badly. Cottee's claim, it appeared, had rich prospects. But after a week's reflection it had done better, and after a fortnight, it had done well enough for consideration. They would like to know exactly how they stood about Cottee's claim. If it were really invalid, of course they would be very glad to overlook Mr. Bewsher's high-handed proceedings. Even if it were not, they might be prepared,—but first hadn't somebody better go and look?

Gore, in fact, was pretty sure of the prospectors, and he had received a most encouraging letter from Bewsher, in these terms:

*My dear Gore,*

*Thanks for your efforts to save me from the consequences of my youthful folly. I gather that the new scheme is this. If I stick out, I shall be sacked by the S. of S.; if I don't stick out, I shall be eaten by Lower Nok. This is a great improvement on the former situation by which I had the choice of sacking myself, or being barbecued by Upper Nok.*

*But on the whole Lower Nok have the better teeth, and peace with dishonour is always an attractive prospect. You ought to grow your hair and go into parliament,*

*Gratefully yours,*

*E. B. B.*

This from Bewsher was practically an acceptance. But now the man was wavering, and while this was a matter of trifling interest to

Cottee, who was pretty confident that the Government would support his case, it was very depressing to Gore.

'But sir,' he was saying, 'if Cottee's E.P.L. turns out to be all right.'

'Even then, I shall have to sound local opinion. If the chiefs say it won't do and appeal to Kaduna—they could easily send a deputation to the Governor—I believe we should have to meet them.'

'I suppose they'll do what you suggest,' said Cottee.

Bewsher smiled pleasantly at him and tapped his pipe with his finger.

'If you put them up to a deputation——'

'Why, damn it,' said Bewsher, suddenly angry, 'how the hell would you like a lot of Birri apes digging in your back garden and telling you to take compensation or leave it.'

'It isn't a back garden, it's common land. And even in England, land is often taken over under compulsory power.'

'Not for private profit.'

'I didn't know you were a socialist.'

'Who said I was a socialist?'

'Well, if I——'

'What the hell!' Bewsher turned deep red, gave another suck at his pipe, and then said calmly, 'It doesn't seem to me that we came here to discuss politics. I thought you were doing a survey—and if you've ten miles of it, you'd better get busy.'

'More like twelve,' said Cottee.

Gore stooped down and put his eye to the six-inch compass. His orderly and a boy shouted at the crowd. 'Get out of the way, you fools. Stand back there.'

The surprised pagans sullenly gave ground.

'What's the bearing?'

Cottee looked at his paper. '320. 15 for 580 yards—that's my boundary.'

'Is that your mark with the white rag?'

'Number four cairn at South-East corner.'

'Is that corrected?'

'Oh, I suppose so.'

'The Gazette gives our boundary at 318 and that puts you just over—but have a look for yourself.'

'That's all right, old man, I'll take your word for it.'

Gore made a note in his pocket-book and picked up the tripod. He looked round for a carrier and his eye fell on the indignant young warrior. His indignation made him appear the most alert of the bystanders. Gore thrust the tripod into his hands. 'Just carry that, will you?'

A look of dismay at once replaced the intelligence and purpose on the firebrand's countenance. He looked with trembling horror at the complicated magic in his hands.

Gore and Cottee were already strolling away. Bewsher, who had watched the taking of sights with professional interest, burst out laughing and said 'Chicken-feet (and this was actually the man's nickname), a great honour is conferred upon you by the judge Gore. Do not fail in this important piece of work and glory will be yours.'

The man looked round as if to say, 'Help me, friends.' But no one stirred to help him.

'A great honour,' Bewsher repeated.

The dejected Chicken-feet, turning in his toes even more than usual, hastened after Gore.

Bewsher picked up his peg and turned towards the village. As he did so a voice from the back of the crowd said clearly, 'Death to the whites.'

It was one of Bewsher's principles not to ignore such remarks. He stopped at once and said, 'What's that?'

The voice answered in a louder tone, 'Drive them away, master.'

'They're doing no harm, I'll see to that.'

'What are they doing then? What is the woman doing?'

'They are visitors come to admire your country, and intelligent, well-mannered people like the Birri know how to welcome their guests.'

He strolled on towards the town. Some moments passed before he understood the puzzling remark about the woman. He had heard she was somewhere about in the Nok district. He felt a strong movement of annoyance. Damn it all, wasn't it enough to be pestered by these tin-openers without having odd females planted on him? At least Jukes and Cottee had reasonable objects in view, but a journalist on the make—it was a bit too thick.

In the market-place the shout of 'death to the whites' was rising on all sides. The chief of the agitators was the Fish. Fish was called so because he had a fish spirit. This was perceived by his mother when he first began to move about the ground because he did not crawl or push himself forward with his legs like other babies but wriggled and waved his hands as if they were fins. Now he had a face and body like a tiger-fish with a big head and long jaws. He was stupid and ferocious like a tiger-fish, and also he had a way of darting here and there. You saw him going before you, then his backside gave a jerk and he was off to right or left, slipping his narrow bony flanks among the green leaves as if they had been water.

The Fish was leader of the eighth class (men between the ages of 24 to 27), a position he owed chiefly to Bewsher. Like most young warriors he had been a friend and supporter of Bewsher's. But lately he had begun to shout against the aliens. He had a grievance against the mission because his wife, after many beatings, had run off there and he could not get her back. He was angry with the whites at Goshi, with Bewsher who was their friend, with all these strangers who had interfered in Nok and his matrimonial affairs. Now as usual the man was foaming with greedy rage. He attacked even his friend Henry who was standing in his usual place near the chief's trees, in his green hat and a new pair of khaki trousers.

'What are they doing here, your white men?'

'They want tin.'

'It's our tin.'

'Very well,' said Henry, who was now a dignified person and condescended with greater men than Fish.

'Yes, and you're another of them, you thief, you spy, in your white man's hat. You Bewsher's pet,' screamed the Fish. His long chin and neck darting at Henry like a snake made the big cook start back. But at once he recovered himself. For he was now a man of property. He spat and answered with nonchalance. 'I'm as much a Birri as you. Everyone knows that, and I don't belong to Bewsher but to the woman. Kill him whenever you like. But the woman's things are mine.'

The Fish had already darted away shouting at some friend in the distance whose thick, stupid voice came from the upper ward as if out of the middle of the bright morning sky. 'Y-e-e-es—it's me-e-e-e.'

The ground was filling. Women were already seated in rows on the upper bank which was their grandstand on any occasion of ceremony. An old chief, the blacksmith, was bawling something which no one could hear and no one wanted to hear. The women too, astonished to see the young men armed, were beginning to utter shrill cries. The market-place had now come to the boil. Everyone was shouting at the top of his voice. Old fathers of families, astonished, frightened and disgruntled by this new nonsense on the part of the youngsters, were calling to their sons. 'Come here—put down that spear—do you want to get us all murdered by the soldiers?'

# VII

In birri there is nothing of what we in America and in Europe call civilization.

This was from Marie's first article of which she sent a copy to Gore. At that time she was almost as pleased with it as her publisher in America, who belonged to the most modern school of anthropologists and believed in the Golden Age, the noble savage, and all the other resuscitated fancies of Rousseau. 'The independent spirit of the natives and the rarely enlightened policy of the District Officer, Mr. Eustace B. Bewsher (Marie hoped that Gore would show the article to Bewsher) has preserved the primitive culture of the tribe both from the so-called education of the mission and the development of finance. The result is that the Birri are probably the happiest and wisest people in the world. To pass from what we call civilization into this obscure district of Nigeria is like going out of a lunatic asylum where the keepers are crazier than the patients into a spring morning of the Golden Age.'

'Among the Birri you do not find anybody who is tired of life or troubled about his soul. You do not find any uplifters, prohibitionists, Calvinists, Marxists, Freudians, nymphomaniacs, sadists, yogi standing on their heads or fundamentalists sitting on their tails, to tell you what you ought to do and to curse you, murder you or poison you if you don't do it. This simplifies life a whole lot and leaves the Birri time for such primitive pastimes as dancing and singing, making poems (any Birri will make you a poem and the Birri vocabulary is four times larger than that of the average college graduate) hospitality and happiness. It will shock a great many civilized people to hear that the Birri are not only happy but seek happiness for its own sake. The idea of being miserable in the world in order to get into a better one has not reached Birri. They'd think this a funny proposition. These people live in friendship, dignified, self-controlled, contemptuous of the grabber, the buffoon, the envious and the boaster, accepting death like sleep. Their sympathies are as quick and true as the instincts of animals, they feel as suddenly as dogs that know across a room's length when you think of them. They feel your look and turn at once their smiling faces like flowers to the sun.'

Marie stopped at this point and smiled. The smile was highly cynical. The last sentence seemed to her a little too poetical. 'Wa-al,' she thought, 'they'll like it in the office.'

It was at this moment that she looked up and saw Obai and one of his younger brothers coming across the rest-house compound. Their smiles when they saw that she had noticed them gave her a keen sharp pleasure, and she was ashamed of her timid doubts about the article. Let it be as poetical as she liked, it could not convey the quality of life in Nok, the quality of this air charged with noble and simple feeling. She went out to greet her friends.

'Health to you, brothers.'

'And to you, Mam.'

'What is the news?'

'A strange white man has come to take the fields. Also Bewsher and the little white judge are there.'

The Birri, following Hausa practice, called Gore the little judge because he was the junior official; either that, or the Stork.

'But what do you mean, take your fields?'

'Henry says so—for the tin in the ground.'

'That's what Henry is doing. I wish he would sometimes do some work. But what does Mr. Bewsher say?'

'He has always told us that no one shall touch our country,' said Obai.

The other gave a short laugh which seemed to express his doubts of this promise. Obai said angrily, 'And I believe him.'

The other instantly looked alarmed. 'I—I—no——' He did not care to differ from the young chief.

'Bewsher told us to put his loads in this house. I said, But Mam is there. So he said, Then put them under a tree.'

'I expect he was angry.'

'Yes, he was angry.'

Marie was annoyed by this accident. She had not expected to be taken by surprise in the rest-house. Neither did she want to meet Bewsher for the first time under the disadvantage of having put him out of his lodging. Her feelings towards Bewsher were compounded of admiration for his Birri policy, fear of his resentment against herself and inbred suspicion of the autocrat, the imperialist. But she saw at once that it was necessary to face him. Apologies were due.

She picked up her hat and asked Obai to lead the way.

Obai had great pleasure in doing so. For in spite of his loyal declaration of faith, he had felt, like most people in Nok, some qualms of doubt. Mam, he knew, would find out the truth for him.

Bewsher was expected in the market-place. His chair had already arrived and Obai made directly for the judgment tree. But both he and Marie were at once surrounded by the furious mob.

For a few minutes Obai kept a space round them by the force of his anger, and Marie was more amused by this sudden unexpected collapse in her popularity than frightened by the danger to herself. She knew, of course, that the Birri did not like strangers, and that they were not at all squeamish about murdering them, but she had not thought of herself as a stranger in Nok.

It was not until a sudden rush threw her against a wall and swept Obai completely away that she did for a moment expect to be killed, and then she did not feel frightened or angry so much as resigned. It wouldn't matter much. What turned up from the bottom of her mind was that very pessimism which always disgusted her.

But this was a short moment because almost at once she perceived that the rush which had carried her off her feet was not an attack but an eddy in the crowd. The people were pushing each other back. A space was opened in front of her and she saw Bewsher climbing into the market-place from the lower ward. She recognized him at once by his shoulders and his legs which were all she had seen of him on the steamer, the legs at the time of his arrival and the shoulders in the dark of the between deck while he parleyed with Cottee. She had barely time to make sure that her hat was straight before he was holding out his hand.

'Miss Hasluck, isn't it?'

'I'm afraid you think I've no right to be in these parts.'

Bewsher smiled and said nothing. The effect therefore was polite agreement and this slightly disconcerted Marie.

'It's not very healthy here,' he said then.

'I've been in worse climates.'

'I mean here and now. Your lion-faced friends got up on the wrong side this morning. Do you mind keeping pretty close to me for the present?'

At the moment it seemed to Marie that the riot was over. An alley of devoted subjects stretched itself before Bewsher up to the tree of judgment where two chiefs were at the moment fussing over his chair, dusting the seat with their hands and scraping the ground to make its legs stand level. She smiled and said, 'I'll say you've had a very calming effect.'

'Judging by the front rows,' said he with a look that was almost a wink, and he turned round, walked slowly along the line, calling out to his friends, slapping a shoulder here, a back there.

Marie, walking behind as she had been commanded, thought that he looked more like a half-intoxicated publican on the spree than a distinguished magistrate. Gait and conversation were in keeping. He rolled along like a drunken sailor throwing out jokes which, from all she could hear of them, she was not meant to hear. And when the Birri laughed, he too laughed.

When Bewsher reached the chair of state he offered it to Marie, explaining that he was going to talk, and at once began to bellow at the mob in a surprisingly loud voice (his usual tones were rather suave and mellow, parsonical) a long speech about sanitation.

This surprised Marie very much, because it was obvious now even to her inexperience what Bewsher had meant by his reference to the two front rows and his command that she should stay close to him.

The murmur and commotion at the back of the mob were growing again; shouts were heard, in one corner there was a kind of battle between the rebels and some of Obai's party. Bewsher had to shout to make himself heard. He was explaining the advantages of the Hausa well-latrine, or bottle-necked salga, over the local ditch (or nothing) and offering the expert assistance of a Hausa to build a sample.

For a moment there was silence. The strange word and proposal had caught attention. But it was obvious to Marie that the attention

69

was not favourable. The faces of the women assembled as in a grandstand on the banks on the right and upper side of the market-place afforded especially a most interesting study of conservatism in all its kinds, ages and emotions, alarmed, wooden-headed, disgusted, suspicious, contemptuous, outraged in its finest feelings or merely wondering.

'And this learned Hausa,' said Bewsher.

'Death to the Hausas,' shouted a voice.

'Will be free this present day——'

But now a chorus of yells burst out; the decorous front rows were pushed aside, a cascade of armed men poured over the chief's heads. The Fish, armed with the long spear of a war chief (he had no right to it) was seen within a few yards of Bewsher, tossing up his arms, and bawling something about the mission.

Obai, who was standing with the other chiefs behind Bewsher's chair, now darted forward and began bawling at the Fish. He, too, tossed his arms, waved his spear. Bewsher looked at Marie with that same expression, a joking grin, which she had seen on his face at their first meeting, and remarked, 'The debate is now open.'

Fish and Obai had been joined each by his more energetic followers. About a dozen were shouting, waving and hopping on Fish's side and seven or eight on Obai's.

They were now balancing their spears in preparation to stab. Bewsher walked forward into the middle of the market-place, knocked up one of the spears and said in Birri, 'Now that's enough; tell me about this——'

The spears were lowered, and Fish in a high angry voice, jerking his chin and eyes from one side to the other, began to explain his objection to the mission, to the whites, to the woman (with a chin jerk at Marie); what did they want, why did they come, why did the mission take their women, why did the woman ask so many questions?

Bewsher was filling his pipe. He put a match to it while he listened. The whole action, the deliberate movements, the blink of the eyelids, the dropping of the match seemed to say, 'Now we're going right into this—there's no need to fuss.'

'They've got my wife at that mission—she says she won't come back—and this woman here (another jerk at Marie) she tells the girls they can lie down to have a baby—that's a wicked thing—it's done so that harm will come—we don't want any perverted white bitches——'

Bewsher smoked calmly, his eyes fixed on the ground. But at the last word, Obai, suddenly losing his temper, spat a furious insult at his enemy.

The men stood too close together to use their spears, but every Birri in war dress carries a stabbing knife, nowadays often a Sheffield cook's knife ground to a double edge, at his belt or strapped to his left forearm. Fish whirled upon Obai with a scream of rage, jerked out this knife and swung it up behind him for the cut which can disembowel a bullock.

Bewsher put up his foot in its big shooting boot and gave the man a push on the right buttock which swung him round. But the Fish, recovering his balance, instantly made a jump towards Bewsher, and crouched a second time. His arm hung poised for a full swing which is rather like that of a discus thrower in a more upright plane.

There was a sudden commotion. Some of the bystanders, terrified of seeing the blow, turned to rush away, others, the younger ones, were pressing towards it. Some of them burst out laughing in their excitement, like schoolboys running to a fight.

Bewsher himself was startled, and very much alarmed. He lost all his equanimity and uttered a yell of wrath that could have been heard half a mile away.

This yell did not frighten the angry savage, but it surprised him. Bewsher had a big voice and he used all of it. Fish, disconcerted, lost his head for an instant, and in that instant he had time to recollect that the visitor in front of him was Bewsher and that Bewsher was an odd specimen.

It was doubted by many Birri that Bewsher could be killed at all, and it was of course quite uncertain what would happen if he were killed. What would his spirit do? How could it be laid?

These considerations, which had saved Bewsher's life several hundred times already, occurred now to the Fish, not of course as arguments or reasoning but simply as the feeling produced by contact with mystery, with oddness. Bewsher was sacred. So that the right and usual thing, which he proposed, the avenging of an insult, became all at once the odd and wrong thing. Fish's expression changed in a second from reckless ferocity to stupidity and bewilderment. The knife and the eyes faltered together. Instantly Obai had the knife and Bewsher was shaking a freckled hairy fist in front of the man's bony chin.

'Would you, you bastard? By Christ, I've a good mind to put you down and give you twenty-four—by God——' he turned half round as if appealing to a friend, 'Did you see that?'

This was in English, and Marie heard it. But the Birri jostling in front of her to see the fun had already pushed her away from the scene and she did not resist them, because the last thrill had been momentarily a little too much for her. She had confidently expected to see Bewsher's entrails tumbled out, and though the vision had lasted barely half a second, it had been remarkably clear.

Bewsher did not seem to be talking to anybody in particular. It was perhaps a rhetorical appeal, to Heaven. He was still highly disturbed in his feelings and in a very bad temper.

'What the hell has bitten you fools,' he roared in English, and then in Birri, 'You Nok people are the most damned blockheaded set of apes in Birri, by God you are. Haven't I told you a thousand times that the mission is a good place where your wounds and your sickness will be cured? And it's not coming here. What in God's name are you worrying for? The mission is at Goshi—Goshi— and it's going to stay there. You can go and bother it, if you like— but it can't come and bother you. By God (this was an English parenthesis addressed to Fish, who stood now with a very sullen expression, half turned away, about five yards off) you pig-faced bastard, I've a good mind to run you in to Alo. Do you hear?'

The Fish, suddenly furious again, bawled, 'What about these new white men? You tell us that. What about them? What do they want?'

'Hold your tongue,' Bewsher roared. 'What about them? (but of course he didn't know what to say about the new white men, for if he accepted the compromise they were certainly coming to the district. And his hesitation was obvious to everybody). What stupid nonsense has got in your heads now? Not one foot of your farms will be taken from you—do you hear that, and these white men don't mean you any harm either. They are simply tin men. They want tin—

72

but I'm not going on talking to you, for a bigger lot of wooden-headed, uneducated, ill-mannered, ungrateful, sons of bitches I never met—no, not even in Hausaland——'

But Bewsher's flow of curses was gradually exhausting his indignation. The insults were becoming literary, far-fetched. It was obvious that the man was beginning to amuse himself with his own inventions. All at once he broke off and said in a mild voice, 'And now if you don't mind stepping back a little, I'll go and have some breakfast.'

'Death to the strangers,' bawled Fish from ten yards away. He was looking over his shoulder with the expression of a savage dog still in two minds about a bite.

'It's a pity the Fish is a fool,' said Bewsher, 'because his face is also not much good.'

But the joke was not well received except by a few of the chiefs and Obai's people, who set up a laugh. Louder than these were cries from all sides, 'What about the new white men? Death to the strangers.'

'Well, I'm damned,' said Bewsher in English, and then he shouted, 'What's the news of the beef?' That was to say, 'Is there any news of game.'

'The strangers, the whites,' shouted a dozen voices.

'Beef—beef—you pudding faces. All that's over—I'm not going to talk to you all day. Lions—leopards. What have you got? But you look pretty hungry. What about a hippo?'

At this a kind of tremor seemed to pass through the whole mob. It was plainly heard in one voice which now asked, 'Hippo?'

But again the chorus bawled, 'What about the farms? What about the aliens?'

The crowd was thickening round Bewsher as streams of young men and women kept pressing forward from the flanks. For a minute or two Marie could see nothing but his hat, and heard nothing at all. The rebels were noisy again. She saw Obai rush down the hill. A gust of Bewsher's voice broke out towards her, bawling, 'Meat—meat—meat,' with an intonation which sounded exactly like the cry of a cat's meat man. Probably it was an intentional imitation.

Then Obai with a gun, Sam with four labourers carrying a chair hammock, came panting up the hill. Obai flung himself on the

73

crowd to break a path for them, leaping like a stallion with his arms stretched up and his chest thrown out. He, too, shouted 'The hunt—the hunt.'

Two minutes later Bewsher came rocking up the market-place in his chair. His gun was between his knees and he was still bawling, 'Me—at——me—at——meat.'

There were at least a dozen shoulders to the hammock poles and those who could not help stretched out their hands to touch it. All round the young boys leapt and danced, laughing up over their shoulders at the hunter, the meat-giver.

Bewsher was still calling out 'Meat, meat,' but he was also roaring with laughter. His eyes had almost disappeared, his whole body shook. He looked like a Silenus, not a pink Rubens, but a brown Poussin, borne up on a green chariot by black cupids.

The chair swayed wildly and he burst into language such as even Marie was not acquainted with.

But suddenly he caught sight of her under the tree. This produced an entire change of expression. It was obvious that he had forgotten the woman. He looked extremely blank. Then he roared at the carriers. But the enthusiastic amateurs who had taken charge of the chair were not under discipline. They gave a cheer and galloped in a fashion which caused the passenger to grab at his hat. Carriers and chair dived into the gap, leading down the flank of the hill towards the river-road. Behind streamed men of every age, young warriors with spears, old men, little fat children. Uli, darting past and seeing Marie, gave her a leer in which every one of his teeth expressed the same aspiration. In five minutes she seemed to be alone in Nok. For even the women, debarred from hunting, had hastened from their grandstand to the other side of the hill in order to watch the hunters set out.

A frightened-looking boy came running towards her. He looked like a nervous wreck just about to fall down in a fit. 'Master say,' he panted, 'sorry he no can stop. He say better for you go way now to Alo or Kifi because people here very bad people. Dey fit to kill you.'

'You can thank him very much and say they're much more likely to kill him,' said Marie, walking off.

She had recovered from her little attack of bourgeois and

unpagan nerves. She walked along with the expression, cheerful and a little surprised, of one who has had a novel and interesting experience.

As for leaving Nok, she had no intention of it. For one thing, she meant to see Mr. Bewsher again. She knew now why everybody, even Mr. Gore, spoke of Mr. Bewsher with a peculiar intonation. He was a very interesting man.

# VIII

GORE AND COTTEE did not return till nearly eight o'clock and both were depressed. Gore had found it easier to get on with Jukes than Cottee, who had been in a pernickety temper for weeks past; and he made the mistake, on this occasion, of remarking that they might run into the Hasluck.

Cottee, already at nine o'clock hot and blowing, took this for an innuendo. Why shouldn't they? he asked. Did people think he was smitten? He wasn't caught so easily. If Gore was so interested, let him go in and win by all means. She was at any man's service who knew the way to her, a little soft sawder and a touch of the romantic. She was at the right age and she had the temperament.

But as soon as Gore agreed that the lady might be a little too exotic for a wife, he became extremely sentimental and said mournfully, 'Of course I ought to jump at her.'

'Why don't you?'

'The trouble is that I've had such a damn good time.'

'Why stop?'

Cottee brooded over twenty yards of path. 'D'you remember Pauly of our year—he went into the Church?'

'Was that the man who always stood about the lodge in breeches and pumps when people were going to lectures?'

'Yes, the worst kind of horsey snob. Well, he's in the Church now. I called on him in an awful hole down East and do you know I rather envied him.'

'He's married, is he?'

'No, no, no. It's his job.'

'Yes, it's a good job.'

'Mind you, Pauly didn't have any more vocation than you or I. Less. It was just luck. He got caught by somebody—I rather fancy it was through the Magdalen crowd. But of course it didn't matter how he started—the job's got hold of him and carries him along.'

'But he must have believed something.'

76

'No, no—at least that was part of the luck. He just ran into somebody at the right moment. But it doesn't matter what he believed—and now he hasn't time to worry. The point is that he's got involved—like you, you old tramcar—in your blessed service that keeps you so worried and saves you from getting rich. See the dignity of the great Gore—get out of the way, you Rolls Royces— but it's only because somebody stood you on the rails and turned on the juice.'

There was a short silence. Gore did not bother to follow the argument. But he was mildly surprised at Cottee's next remark that that was why he ought to jump at Marie.

'Settle down, what?'

'But that's just what it isn't. Marriage isn't settling down—it's getting mixed up with things—things that you can't get away from because they matter too much. It's the bachelors that settle down— like bla'mange that hasn't come off.'

'Well, if you think it would make you happy.'

'Oh! you historians.'

Gore had in fact been an historian at Oxford, third class by hard work, and Cottee a philosopher, second class on style and caffeine. Cottee's insult was an old favourite meaning blockhead, plodder. He mopped his face and groaned, 'Happy. Like old Jukes—five children and one foot in the workhouse—and Marie wants children. She told me so.'

'Really, that's rather interesting.'

'Which would you rather be, Jukes or Dollar?'

'Dollar,' said Gore promptly. He was confident that this was the answer expected of him. But Cottee stopped and glared at him in disgust.

'Do you mean that?'

'Oh well, Jukes is happier I suppose.'

But even this further piece of insincerity did not save the situation. 'Happier,' said Cottee disgusted. 'My God. Have you ever looked at Jukes? He's in hell. But that's the whole point! It's not a question of happiness at all. It's simply what sort of a person you are—and whether you could stand yourself.'

'People can generally stand themselves whatever they're like,' said Gore consolingly.

'So much the worse,' said Cottee with a voice so tragic and a look

77

so gloomy that Gore felt inclined to laugh, a temptation which he resisted not only for the sake of diplomatic relations but because he was respectful of a serious emotion.

'I wonder what her people are,' said Cottee sadly; 'probably rather impossible,' and then immediately, though Gore took pains not to let him catch his eye, he became ruder than ever on the subject of Government officials, 'I suppose the real purpose of this little jaunt is to provide you with a claim for fifteen shillings bush allowance.'

'That sort of thing,' Gore agreed

Gore's patient kindness was due partly to the fact that half the Nok claim, and that the richest half, was found to be on the wrong side of the boundary, a discovery that did not improve the prospector's temper.

'I don't give a damn,' he said. 'It's poor old Jukes with his school bills and his wife living on bread and margarine that'll get the shock'; and he added, 'I wish I did give a damn.'

All this accumulated bitterness and fatigue overflowed when after the last hour's march, by lantern light, over a jungle path of the roughest kind, he found that there was no one to receive them in Nok, no sign of a billet, of his servants, of a bath or a meal.

'The rest-house system of this charming country is the finest example of Government management in the world—you take a monopoly, charge the highest possible price for the worst possible service, and then pat yourselves on the back for doing anything at all.'

Gore apologized. The rest-house, a small one, about half a mile out of town, had been left for Bewsher. But he had given orders that the rest-house master was to find other accommodation for their loads and beds.

They were standing at the corner of Nok market-place. The three tired carriers who had borne the kitchen box, office box and chairs all day, squatted like frogs behind their loads, silent and dejected by this last unexpected hitch at the very moment of arrival. Gore supported himself on one leg and his polo cane, with his hat falling off the back of his head. His face, shining in the lantern light, appeared sharper and thinner. His nose, prodded forward as he drooped, seemed absurdly long, foolish and patient; it infuriated Cottee as he walked up and down and cursed the Nigerian administration and

78

exclaimed that thank God in any case the thing would be finished that night.

Meanwhile the young Birri who had carried the compass was hurrying about in search of the rest-house headman, bawling out angrily that this was a scandal, an insult, to treat important persons in this way. All day they had been engaged on most important Government business (he held up the compass like a standard) and now they had to stand about while worthless headmen neglected their duties. But his white men would not stand it—and so on. This young man was now, in his own estimation, a Government official and an expert surveyor, and the slight to Gore and Cottee wounded him in a particular manner.

'If Bewsher's in the rest-house I don't see why we shouldn't tackle him now and finish this stupid business,' Cottee said.

'I think I'll just make sure of a bed.'

Someone in a group of bystanders called out in Birri, 'Go away, white men,—we don't want you.'

Marie's Birri lessons had been wasted on Cottee, who preferred flirtation, and Gore didn't know any but the greetings. He answered the shout with a polite, 'Good evening and good health.'

'We want the damn thing settled for good,' Cottee said, 'it doesn't seem a *very* difficult problem.'

'Death to the strangers—death to the whites.'

This was from several voices in the crowd which now jostled round the two white men. Their eyes and teeth glittered ferociously in the lantern light, but the small boy who held the lantern was equally contemptuous of the Birri and ignorant of their language.

'It's as simple as A.B.C.,' said Cottee. 'There's my E.P.L. and there's the ground. Hi! not so much noise, young feller, it's very nice of you and all that, but three cheers is enough. What's happening, anyhow?'

'Looks like a bean-feast of some kind,' said Gore, gazing round at the fires, the shouting excited mob.

'Death to the whites.'

'Hullo, Uli, what's all the excitement?' Gore had recognized Uli's face overtopping the front row.

Uli shrank away from the white men and uttered another nerve-shaking yell. But it was his own nerves that were shaken by Gore's sudden recognition. Gore's calm melancholy look and languid attitude were those of a creature different in every way from himself, one above danger, all powerful, all knowing. Was it safe or even right to annoy him?

'Uli?' Gore raised his voice. 'What's all this—a wedding?'

Uli gave up his attempt to wriggle backwards into the mass.

'A wedding?' Gore tried Hausa.

Uli, looking at the ground, muttered in Hausa that Babban judge Bewsher had shot a dorina and they were going to play.

'That means no sleep to-night,' said Gore mournfully. He loved his sleep.

'What's that?' Cottee asked.

'Bewsher has shot a hippo and they're going to have a binge. They'll be drumming all night.'

'The end of a perfect day.'

The rest-house chief was struggling through the crowd, crying out apologies.

Gore, with a very depressed mien, waved towards him. The small boy, aged about twelve and not four foot six high, rushed at the crowd crying in a shrill treble, 'Way there, you pagan rubbish.' He himself was a Christian from an Oyo family, an honest, clean, decent small boy like many Christian small boys before the age of puberty. 'Get out of the great lord's way, you filthy pagan animals.'

The crowd gave way between the double onslaught, and the two white men passed into it.

'But what—what about?' Uli as he squeezed himself back spattered out this question into Gore's face, which leaned over him as if from a window. 'What about—what they say——'

Gore had come to a halt. He looked down at Uli with patience. It was his silly job to answer silly questions at any time of day.

'What—what—I don't understand,' said Uli, wildly. His thick lips sprayed Gore's chin and neck, as his eyes stared upwards with an imploring expression.

'What don't you understand?'

Uli made a desperate effort to put his question into words. 'It's—it's—I don't—about it——' but it was too much for him. The question it seemed was not a thing you could take in one hand, like a spear shaft, but a whole mass of things, a forest, a web of foliage and tie-tie.

It wasn't only about farms, about the juju, about law, nationalism, about strangers, whisky, war, money, Christianity, trade, soldiers, and the rights and the powers of the white men and the authority of their Gods, it was about himself too. Where was he, what was he? What had happened to him? Had he committed a sin worthy of punishment? or would nothing happen to him if he escaped from Enuké's brothers. Nothing had happened yet. And Enuké's brothers had not caught him. Was it therefore no sin?

'Spit it out,' said Gore in English.

But now everybody's eyes were fixed on Uli, and he was seized with panic. He expected to hear 'Hi, you Uli, what abomination have you committed with our Enuké?'

He turned and plunged head first into the crowd.

'Drunk already,' said Gore sadly as he strolled after the chief. 'This is going to be a big noise.'

'Death to the whites,' Uli screamed; 'death to the strangers.' He wanted to kill somebody, he wanted to cry. Somebody stopped and looked at him. Instantly he darted away, silent and terrified, into a dark corner.

But there, among a crowd of people, chatting in subdued voices (they were the Alo carriers keeping out of view) his agony burst out of him like the yowl of a mad dog. 'Death to the whites.'

The carriers were instantly mum.

'May they rot, may they be blinded and impotent. May they swell up and burst with rottenness.'

One of the carriers gave him a push with the sole of his foot that sent him staggering into the firelight. He fell on his hands and beat his forehead on the ground. This was the punishment that had fallen on him. The punishment of those that broke the law of things—this confusion in his head, worse than pain. He was going mad. And he had no friends. He dared not tell anybody what he had done. Uli began to sob, grinding his teeth and uttering long high moans through his nose.

Nobody paid any attention to him. There were plenty of drunken men and women performing stranger antics.

The drummers had been sitting under the judgment tree for the last half hour with the big drum, a large wooden object of the shape and size of a beer barrel, standing in front of them. The other drums,

81

one shaped like an hour-glass so that its drumhead strings stood free, the other like a long thin cylinder, were lying between their owner's knees.

The drummers were foreigners, Goshi men. But in Birri, as in old Europe of the dynasties, artists were privileged. They moved freely from village to village even in wartime, sure everywhere of a welcome and the best entertainment. Goshi and Nok were at war at that moment about fishing rights on the upper fork of their common river, but the Goshi drummers were completely at their ease, full of the tenderest meat and the best of beer, under the chief's tree.

Even those voices which now began to call out, 'Play—play —' were respectful and tentative rather than commanding. The drummers continued to laugh and talk, but the youngest and smallest, without looking, gathered up his little cylinder, and put it under his arm. Then, still chattering and showing his scarlet gums as he laughed, he took his long hooked drumstick and began to tap on the skin, a regular light beat.

At once silence spread through the noisy market-place and all heads were turned towards the tree.

The second drummer, with the hour-glass, was now tucking away his instrument. He tightened the skin by pressing the strings with his elbow and began to throw little broken phrases staccato into the regular beat. The drums were now speaking; they said 'Don't be in a hurry—don't be so impatient.' They were reproachful. The big drummer took up his two sticks, one a heavy curved club, the other a light cane, and made them quiver over the top of the barrel.

But the result was scarcely perceptible, a kind of purring music which carried away the tenors like boats on a current. Already girls and men were forming into long lines for the first figure of the spring dance and now a hundred voices called together, 'The dance—the dance.'

The drums were shocked by this outburst. They were surprised. They stammered like frightened children. 'What—what—but what is it? Can't—can't—just understand,' and then ran off in alarm, 'I'm frightened, I'm frightened—I'm frightened.'

At the same time while their thin hands fluttered in the air, the drummers continued their after-dinner conversation. The big drummer was telling a story, and the other two were listening with the closest attention.

82

Some of the old people sitting on the bank were laughing and applauding the drummers. But the youngsters were still screaming for the dance.

The little drum and the big drum stopped. The hour-glass faltered. 'We don't know how—we are too shy—yes, very, very, very shy'—and he faltered into silence.

Then some of the young warriors broke line and rushed towards the tree. Whereupon the big drummer, without even looking round, raised his big stick and sent out a thunder louder than the shouts of the whole village.

'Bam—bam—bebom bam—dance—now shall you dance. No you *must* dance (the must was sharp and clear) you can't help it, you shan't stop it. Without thinking, without ceasing.' The little drum was saying, 'This foot—that foot—bend the knee—this way—that way—shake behind.'

The long chains were coiling round the wide market-place, round each of the four great fires, two of men, two of women, locked close together, so that each was like a single animal. All the legs on the same side moved together, and the knees crooked into each other like the belly scales of a snake. The heads bobbed slowly round the fires and uncoiled again towards the middle of the ground, like beads pulled on strings.

Uli was second in the row of the young warrior's line, behind Obai the leader. The drums had commanded him and he had risen from the ground. Their music had compelled him with a voice that was part of his own brain as Nok was a part of his body. And their rhythm darting into every part of his mind like an electric charge had already made patterns in that chaos, patterns of movement, of action. Now he knew what to do, how to act, and what he was doing was easy and right. His toes were curled, his ankles flexed, his back hollowed, his chin raised, his buttocks protruded, his stomach drawn in, his elbows held stiff, his palms turned up in a style that none could better.

Obai was next man in front, his own half-brother next behind. He had been running from both for the last twelve days. But now he could feel Obai's back against his chest, stomach and thighs and Obai's forearms over his forearms, and against his own back the warm flesh and rolling muscles of his own brother. And it seemed to him that he belonged to them once more, he was theirs and they were his. They supported him and moved him; he supported them and moved them. They were all parts of one creature whose slow regular motions arose from a will not his own. This creature which was full of an enormous power and lust, of languid voluptuousness, of drunken wantonness, held him like some old chief who had seized upon a young girl. Now it was playing lazily with him. He was soothed. His head lolled from side to side; the words of the song drawled from his mouth.

> '*We do not care for you maidens,*
> *We are going to the hunt.*'

But soon it would twist him, hurt him, make him mad. Let it do so. He gave himself up to be used. That was what he wanted. Not to think, not to be responsible.

Gore and Cottee had been placed in adjoining huts close to the river and at some distance from the village. This apparently was by Bewsher's own orders. The huts were extremely small and dirty, but Gore, finding himself surrounded once more by a wall and seeing his own belongings, his own lamp, table, bed and bath, stretched himself out in a long chair with profound satisfaction. He was especially glad that the place had been too small to hold two guests.

He lit a cigarette and then, after a minute, reached out for the nearest reading matter. Gore could read anything, and found anything better than nothing. His hand fell on an old Sunday newspaper and his eye on the outside page of advertisements, Hotel advertisements. He had read everything else. But this was a good piece of reading because it took his mind straight from Birri and this stinking mud hut to those scenes where his existence most nearly approached happiness, enormous drawing-rooms, twenty foot high and completely empty for most of the day, dining-rooms as large as an ordinary house, red-carpeted quiet lounges, long hushed corridors full of white doors and bare well-warmed bedrooms with h. & c. and plenty of clean towels. In a good hotel a man enjoyed all that civilization could offer in comfort, cooking and peace, without trouble or responsibility. It was his fortress and his palace. He need not talk to a soul and he could read the newest illustrated papers and two novels every day. Thank God that in another eight months be would once more feel silk underclothes next his skin, down cushions under him, know that an efficient staff, three or four large empty rooms and a porter were standing between him and the rest of the world.

For the moment he must be content with an hour's peace. Thank God Cottee had not asked him to dine.

His boy came in. 'You have chop here, sah?'

'Of course, and as soon as you can.'

'For one, sah?'

Gore hesitated. A struggle took place in his breast. Then, like a criminal under the press, he groaned. 'Go and ask Mr. Cottee if he'd like to dine.'

'Mr. Cottee go for rest-house, sah.'

'What?'

'He go see Mr. Bewsher.'

Gore rose silently to his feet, gathered up his pile of papers and went out. His expression appeared perfectly calm, but it caused the boy, who knew him very well, to withdraw discreetly and rapidly out of his way.

Gore left the village at a leisurely pace. His air was rather, 'I suppose I must go, but I'm not going to hurry myself.' But in another half minute he was whirling along at top speed. The idea that the compromise might be lost by a few seconds was too much for him. It was a good compromise. It didn't deserve to be wasted.

The new rest-house at Nok was the regulation quarter mile from the village. Gore covered the distance in less than three minutes and he was extremely glad that he had made haste when he saw Cottee just in the act of entering the rest-house. He actually ran across the last twenty yards. But Cottee was still blocking up the doorway and as Gore also stooped to go under the low eaves, he turned and grabbed him by the arm. 'H'sh!' he whispered. Then with something like a giggle, he pulled him slightly to one side, so that looking through the inner door past the side of a half-drawn blanket curtain he could see the interior. It was in strong lamplight, which illuminated with especial clarity the faces of Marie and Bewsher. The former was seated on a box, the other on her bed and their noses were not six inches apart. The lady, looking up from the bed, and therefore turning up her eyes, seemed to mix devotion with a much less respectable sentiment, while Bewsher, stooping forward with his hands clasped between his knees, wore a crooked grin and a kind of sidelong squint (his head was also very much on one side) which should by themselves have been enough to make any nice girl run home to momma. But the remark which came to Gore as he took in this scene was from Bewsher who was saying in a most professional tone, 'But when you say pagans, do you mean the Munchis or the Jukuns or the Birri or the Kukuruku?'

Cottee had taken a firm nervous grip of Gore's arm and seemed inclined to be waggish; he was muttering something about a real case. But Gore did not see any excuse either for humour or peeping. He called out, 'Are you there, sir?'—and then after a second's pause, ducked past the curtain.

Bewsher was still on the box. It was Marie who had hopped to her feet. In that second she had reached the farthest corner of the room, so that she was found looking over her shoulder with an air of surprise and pleased anticipation.

'Why, Mr. Gore, how lovely'—she ran forward to seize his hand in both of hers. Apparently she thought that Gore was a very old friend. 'Now isn't it just too good—we'll have a real party.'

'What's that—the map?' said Bewsher. 'I thought I said after dinner—put it down over there—you don't mind, Miss Hasluck? Hullo, Cottee, you look as if you wanted liquid nourishment.'

'Poor Frank!'

She ran to call Henry, to pull out the chairs into the compound, to make a fire.

Bewsher also showed cordiality. That is to say, as soon as he was reconciled to this uncalled-for interruption, he took up two bottles of whisky and a sparklet bottle and guarded them from loss or damage until the table had been brought out of the house. At the same time he smiled hospitably on the young men, and said several times, 'This is very nice—quite a party.'

All this time Cottee was displaying those signs of pique which had already alarmed Gore. As Bewsher was preparing solemnly to put a match to the sticks, he said loudly not three yards away, 'That's quick work—she's nailed him in an afternoon.'

Gore turned quickly to take a chair from Marie. She was much concerned about the short foot-rest.

'You have a special foot-rest on your own chair, don't you?'

'But this is perfect—really and truly.'

86

'She knows the way to fetch 'em.' This was Cottee just behind.

'But no, you'll be like Harold Lloyd just holding on for dear life.' Marie ran back to the house.

'All the same it's rather disgusting with an old goat like Monkey— it's a bit too barefaced. I wonder he doesn't see that she's pulling his leg.'

Gore slipped away again. For in fact he was extremely pleased that Bewsher and the Hasluck had hit it off, whatever their motives. It was going to save everybody a lot of trouble.

# IX

HE DID NOT FEEL so sure of this when Marie, having seen an empty chop-box adjusted to his chair, said that she did not approve of compromise even about being comfortable; and of course it soon appeared that the meeting of the two pagan enthusiasts had been a very bad thing for peace. Bewsher, who was still crouching at the fire, rearranging the sticks and blowing up the flame, looked up at her and said, 'Hear, hear, neither do I,' and then at once began to make rude remarks aimed at Cottee's direction about the effects of civilization on the Birri. Kifi had got it badly.

'No doubt they wanted it badly,' said Cottee.

'Like bootleg whisky—and it's about as much good for them,' said Marie.

'And your idea is to shut them in a museum.'

'Oh come,' said Bewsher, 'Miss Hasluck doesn't mean that—she only thinks the Birri might be getting rather more than they bargained for in what you call civilization—and so do I.' Bewsher said this in a most genial manner. He always became more genial at the prospect of a fight, either because he enjoyed arguing or more probably because it annoyed the enemy.

'And so you put them in a sort of human zoo—Mappin terraces for interesting pagan specimens.'

Bewsher answered that the funniest animals were not to be found in any zoo, a remark which alarmed Gore so much that he put himself between the antagonists.

But, luckily, at this critical moment Marie diverted Cottee's anger by declaring that he was talking pure nonsense. The Birri were perfectly free to come and go as they liked. They were indeed the freest people she'd ever known—and certainly freer than wage-slaves anywhere. Nobody even tried to make them do what they didn't want to. There was not a policeman in the whole country; policemen weren't needed. Cottee turned on her. 'Marvellous—all God's chillen in fact.'

'Not at all. They're a primitive type even for West Africa. It's simply that they're taught right from the beginning—to like the right things'; she looked at Bewsher for approval; 'to be proud of doing the right things—and ashamed of the bad ones.'

Bewsher inserted another stick into the fire (he was proud of his scientific fire-making) and said that they certainly were a sporting lot. 'A friend of mine called Obai once went out on foot to meet a leopard that was dragging away one of the village goats and killed it with his spear. A boy of sixteen.'

'Did Obai do that?' said Marie, walking round the fire to him.

'That's why he counts for something in Birri. You know him, do you?'

'According to you a lot of performing mice are free—or boys at school,' said Cottee.

'But that's not fair.'

Unexpectedly Gore came to her assistance by remarking that, practically speaking and from a political point of view, he supposed that the Birri's kind of freedom was the only possible kind; and this effort to guide the discussion from the dangerous particular into the safe general was for a moment successful. Cottee said that Gore was the regular Jesuit, and Bewsher that it sounded as if there was a catch in it somewhere, but Marie was delighted, and for two or three minutes the party seemed to forget their animosities. They provided themselves with drinks and chairs. Marie herself, in spite of the enthusiastic mood which was so alarming to Gore, consented to sit down, though on the extreme front rail of her foot-rest, and to light a cigarette.

'The Birri are the happiest kind of people,' she said; 'we have nothing to give them but disease and lies and poverty and envy and vulgarity. They're doing no harm to us—they're not asking for anything from us—quite the other way. But we just can't help spoiling this beautiful thing. Why can't we? Why can't we be satisfied with making all America and Europe fit for millionaires to live in?'

'What I want to know is who invented this wonderful education?' Cottee asked.

'It's traditional—it's just grown up—isn't that so, Mr. Bewsher?'

'More or less.'

'So did the Chinese, Indian and Tartar not to speak of European and American——'

Marie replied that of course the education had to be of a certain kind; you had to bring people up to like the right things, the natural things.

'The natural things,' Cottee pounced on her at once. 'What are the natural right things. I'm interested because I hear so much about natural education nowadays. Who decides what's natural and what isn't? Some kind of a god?'

'Why no, it's just nature.' But she was obviously disconcerted. She saw Cottee's point before he made it.

'Nature or God, it's all the same if it makes the rules. So Birri is really the kingdom of heaven. It doesn't need a government because it's been put on the right lines for ever.'

Bewsher, who was sitting between them smoking a large curly pipe and admiring his fire, remarked that in fact there was very little crime in Birri. Marie at once appealed to him. 'Mr. Bewsher, you agree with me that Birri is run by traditional custom—it *is* a system of natural rights and duties and obligations——'

Bewsher took his pipe out of his mouth and looked enquiringly at the excited young woman. 'Natural?' and then after a pause, 'You mean family feeling—that sort of thing?'

'Which is apt to be anything but affectionate in a large household,' said Cottee.

'I mean the whole system—the co-operative idea of it.'

Bewsher said that he was afraid Birri didn't run itself if that was what she meant. It had to be kept up to the mark.

'But you told me yourself that chiefs only administered customary law.'

'Yes, but it's a whole man's job seeing that people learn the rules and keep them and pass them on—administration is just people doing a job.'

'A job that takes a lot of doing,' said Gore.

'Now in Kifi at this very moment the whole thing's broken down because the chiefs were too slack and the youngsters too uppish.'

'That reminds me, sir, I heard from Kifi——'

Gore began to talk business. The new irrigation scheme in Kifi had broken down again and the chiefs were complaining that it was unworkable.

This intervention was highly successful in diverting Bewsher's interests. It was curious to notice the man's change of voice, attitude, even expression when he came to a particular and practical subject. 'Are they, by Gad?' he said. 'That means Kifi to-morrow. And what about the new Upper canal?'

The discussion became technical. This Kifi scheme was in fact one of Bewsher's darlings on which he had spent a good deal of his own money. It was intended to be the foundation of a most elaborate structure which had so far not got beyond foundations and a pigeon-hole at Kunama; the famous Birri co-operative society, about which so many jokes were made.

Bewsher, in fact, was one of those enthusiastic disciples of Plunket who are apt to make themselves so boring in mixed company, especially to the ladies. Everybody in Nigeria had heard him on the subject of individual ownership of land as a product and necessity of better farming, and co-operation on the Irish model for marketing and supplies.

But of course in these ideas as in most other respects the man was against the prejudice of his time, the vague communism which floats through all the official Nigerian mind, impregnated with the idea that individual ownership of land is not indigenous to Africa.

'Nor among the Anglo-Saxons,' Bewsher used to say.

But it was necessary to admit that co-operation and individual ownership had not yet got very far in Birri. The Kifi people were still doing their best not to understand the cultivation of onions.

Cottee dawdled round the fire to mix himself another drink and said to Marie, 'So your Birri is not the Noo Jerusalem after all.'

Marie did not answer him. She was still looking at Bewsher with a surprised and indignant expression.

'That's what all you people want, isn't it—the golden city. You want to get rid of politics and all that horrid machinery which is always going wrong and frightening the children—all these complicated diplomacies and Leagues and Unions and Empires and Alliances so that you can go back to natural obligations and natural rights, isn't that the word—back to providence.'

'But it's you that want to smash up the Birri machinery— machinery that really does work.'

'Not a bit of it.' Cottee was irritable with the woman. 'All I say is

91

that it's out of date and ought to be scrapped for something more modern. I want to improve the government, you want to abolish it.'

'What nonsense, Frank.'

'You're just an anarchist like so many others from your side; only you don't know it.'

'Anarchist!' said Bewsher, startled, turning. To him the word suggested bombs.

'Don't listen to him, Mr Bewsher. He's got some silly notion that Americans are always against the government.'

'I didn't say so. I said they didn't take kindly to the idea—or why is the world full of American anthropologists looking for the golden age—in Achill and India and Malaya—trying to find some form of society that runs itself without a government—that doesn't need any of these nasty policemen—I beg your pardon, cops—or anybody giving orders—or any wicked district officers and cruel judges.'

'Or residents,' said Bewsher, who was enjoying the battle. He loved an argument, especially upon such imposing subjects as these. He stretched himself at full length and puffed a large cloud.

'Is it the protestant strain?' said Cottee. 'Is it because when every man is in direct communication with providence he doesn't see that he needs government or what governments are for except to do the devil's work. We have that in England too. The real primitive protestants are always getting up against the government. And look at the Doukhobors, or the Hussites, I believe the Doukhobors even protest against clothes.'

'But then I'm not a real primitive protestant or a Doukhobor,' said Marie.

'Well, I wonder—you were bred that way—and here you are trying to leave everything to providence—nature, I mean—it's the same thing in this case.'

'That's silly.'

'Nature looking after everything and making the world safe for Beudy (caricaturing Marie), truth and goodness for ever and ever while you sit in your armchair and admire the view.'

'Do tell us some more.'

'Like Mr. Bewsher looking after the noo——'

'Don't say that again,' cried the lady, and suddenly it appeared that she was extremely angry, and that she and Cottee were having a quarrel.

The effect on Gore and Bewsher would have amused Cottee had

he been in a mood to enjoy anything—Gore's sudden lengthening of face and furtive, alarmed glance, and Bewsher's solemn countenance as he rose up from the bottom of his chair, not too suddenly, and gave his putteed shins a rub. He also took a peep at the lady and then, after a pause, remarked in a pensive tone as if his mind had been far away from the subject of discussion. 'I heard a good story to-day about old Umoké, he's our senior chief, Cottee. It appears that when the old boy arrived in Kunama, Alabaster told the Emir to be polite. The idea was to smooth him down. So the Emir invited Umoké to court and at the same time sent him a present of a nice new gown. But Umoké sent a return invitation for the Emir to call upon him and a return present of a gin bottle full of something like old motor grease, with this message, "This medicine is an infallible cure for the mange, craw-craw, and leprosy. If my brother of Kunama will condescend to use it, he will soon find himself in a condition to appear as decently naked as myself." '

Nobody laughed, so that Gore, who had heard various versions of the story before, hastily produced a loud ha-ha, and said, 'That's very good.'

'Not bad, I thought,' said Bewsher. 'The old boy meant to keep his end up and he did.'

'My sympathies are rather with Kunama,' said Cottee in a very provocative tone.

'Would you like to get an invitation from a millionaire accompanied by a clean shirt and a white tie?'

'I should be a snob to refuse them if I hadn't any of my own.'

'But Umoké has his dress suit—he never wears anything else.'

'If he was really nature's gentleman, supposing that such a creature could exist, he wouldn't have insulted his host in a particularly cheap manner.'

Bewsher looked at the young man for a moment with raised brows. It was obvious he had a lot to say. Bewsher could be extremely voluble and eloquent in defence of his Birri, especially on a point like this. For he gloried above all in the Birri pride, their refusal to be put down by the self-righteousness of the more sophisticated peoples who surrounded them on all sides.

But after a moment's reflection, he said politely, 'Oh! of course, it's only a small point.'

'Is it though?' It appeared that Cottee's temper was growing

93

worse. His face was red and his voice began to rasp. 'I don't think so. It seems to me typical of the Birri—and a spirit that's much too common everywhere in Nigeria. I don't say, of course, that the chiefs here are encouraged to think themselves little gods almighty and to keep their people back from any kind of development. But it's not a policy I admire.'

Bewsher refilled his pipe and lay back in his chair from which now his voice murmured in propitiatory accents that some pretty good kinds of people had gone easy on the trousers.

'Greece,' Gore suggested.

'But they could have had 'em if they'd liked, and I'm not talking about clothes. The idea in Birri seems to be to prevent 'em from getting anything new at all, and especially the things they want.'

Nobody answered this.

Gore, who was sitting forward, continued to stare at the fire, which threw deep shadows into his hollow cheeks and eyepits and throat. Bewsher was slipping gradually into the bight of his chair. Already he had disappeared below the level of the table.

'Don't let 'em have any money to play with in case they buy the same sort of things that we find indispensable—clothes and metal pots and hats and so on. It's a funny idea at first sight.'

'It is,' Bewsher agreed.

Gore turned to Marie and asked her if she had ever read Mr. Bewsher's Memorandum in Birri development. She turned her face towards him but her answer was so vague that she had obviously not listened to him. And he, supposing her more interested in Cottee's attempts to quarrel with Bewsher, gave up diplomacy for the present, took a long drink, lit another cigarette and stretched himself out in the shadow to his full length. The movement itself was a prolonged sigh.

But in fact Marie had not been attending to the argument. She had been too angry with Cottee and then with herself for losing her temper. Hadn't she heard him say exactly the same thing three or four times before? What did it matter what he said?

But it mattered a great deal what Mr. Bewsher said, and Bewsher's voice, half amused and half polite, when he had asked 'Natural?' had made her suddenly uncertain of her whole position.

Marie was liable to these fits of doubt, and dreaded them. They

94

had a physical effect upon her nerves. She felt sometimes as if the actual ground had wavered and sunk beneath her. It was for a moment as if the most solid objects were illusory, as if there was nothing secure, nothing fixed, permanent and trustworthy in the whole world; no peace, no refuge.

And whenever this happened to her some eager traitor in her own mind said, 'Of course, you fool—and well you know it.'

She did not listen to the traitor, whom she recognized for an enemy, and neither did she allow herself to feel lost. The result, as she knew, would be such depression as frightened her, suicidal misery. And the cure was easy because in actual fact (she could tell herself) there were plenty of things in the world that you could be sure of. The difference between selfishness and unselfishness was a fact as obvious and much more solid than a rock; and so was the difference between Frank Cottee and Mr. Bewsher. For one was always thinking about himself and the other did not think about himself at all.

Whether Frank Cottee was right or wrong about the Birri, he was wrong in himself. Whatever he might say about the blessings of civilization he knew perfectly well that the kind he was going to introduce was not a civilization at all. It was really and truly anarchy, a mess, a muddle. That was certain. Cottee was clever, but he was outside things. He didn't really feel them. He couldn't see that what he proposed to do was a crime which must be prevented. And that was the most certain thing of all. For it was the most horrible kind of crime, to debauch and ruin a whole people for profit; it was like deliberately, just for one's own pleasure, infecting children with a filthy disease. Whatever Mr. Bewsher said or did he would always be more right than Cottee, just because he did feel that, he did see that enormous fact, as big as a mountain. And he was prepared to ruin himself to prevent the Birri being degraded and exploited. That was why a man like Mr. Bewsher, even if he was not very clever or well educated, was worth a million Frank Cottees, and that was why he must not be allowed to give way.

When Marie reached this point in her cogitation, returning to her first enthusiasm, she felt such restless excitement that she could not sit still any more, and jumped out of her chair. To excuse this sudden activity, she sent Henry for small chop and made up the fire, vigorously heaping up the sticks.

From the far side of it, she looked through the smoke at Bewsher. She had a compelling need to look at the man again, to study him, to see if in any way he answered to her idea of him as a heroic figure. She wished very much that his nose and his legs were straighter, that he had more dignified manners, more respect for his own position. Did he indeed know what a great position it was? Did he understand what he was doing? Was he really a brave man moved by the noblest sympathies or only rather a stupid and obstinate one determined to get his own way? A little of both, no doubt. And she was making a fool of herself as usual. But at once she despised herself for criticizing him at all. The defender of Birri.

Her glances were quick and stealthy because she did not want to be seen by observers like Gore and Cottee. Either of them would penetrate her feelings in an instant and she hated the thought of Cottee's cynical or condescending grin as much as Gore's indulgence. But nobody paid the smallest attention to her.

Gore had sat up and turned himself sideways towards Cottee. He sat crouched on the chop-box with his elbows on his knees, his cheeks in his hands, his cigarette pointing upwards from the centre of his pursed up lips.

Bewsher had sunk almost out of sight. His hand was behind his head and a powerful forearm, projected into the firelight, glittered with fine golden hairs. The soles of his boots, the other most prominent objects in view from this aspect, were thickly covered with large nails polished by sandy roads to the brightness of silver. She noticed that the left had several nails missing and a hole. Pipe smoke rose from behind successive ranges of his knees, stomach and chest in small clouds as if a concealed howitzer were firing there.

Cottee was sitting forward like Gore and talking. He was smiling all the time, but he was obviously very angry. 'Co-operation,' he said, 'was all very nice. Let 'em co-operate by all means. He quite agreed that they were probably ideal material for co-operation. But that wasn't the point. What he was talking about was the whole policy of segregation, the idea that civilized dress and amusements were bad in themselves. It wasn't even a justifiable policy. Natives who wore trousers and went to the cinema instead of hunting lions mightn't be so picturesque as the naked savage, but they'd be happier—they wouldn't want to go back.'

A puff of smoke came from behind the knees and Bewsher's voice said cheerfully, 'That's true. They wouldn't go back.'

'Of course I'm not up in these things,' said Cottee, 'but it does seem rather strange that we won't let these poor devils have any of the comforts and conveniences that we couldn't do without ourselves. I think sometimes it's due to a kind of prejudice—like that of the old squires who tried to keep their labourers in smock frocks and wouldn't let them learn to read and write. I wonder is there any connection between that old ruling class and the modern one. (This was a very obvious shot at Bewsher, whose people owned land in Somerset.) Why, we don't even teach them English. We behave exactly as if English books and English ideas would poison them.'

Bewsher said nothing and did not move, but Marie, roused out of her meditations by this spiteful attack on the man, hastened to defend him. 'That's just not so, Frank—it isn't prejudice at all. And English means missionaries and traders.'

Cottee overbore her with his louder voice. 'The French don't make that mistake. They think that they can't do anything better than give people French civilization, French literature, French art. Ask a Senegalee how he likes being a conscript and he'll tell you, "C'est pour la patrie." Ask one of our apes who he's fighting for, and he'll probably say H company, or Captain Stoker.'

'Absolutely true,' said Bewsher. 'By Gad, yes.'

'We're losing our Empire simply because we don't know how to keep it together. Just encouraging people everywhere to be rebels.'

'Not rebels but themselves,' said Marie indignantly. She had moved to the table to pour herself out another drink. From this point behind the table she had a good view of the top of Bewsher's head and the curl of his pipe.

'Thank you, ma'am,' Bewsher murmured.

'It's a good thing the Romans didn't work on those lines or there wouldn't be any European civilization at all, what, Gore?'

Gore, who had been looking on with the patient but alert air of a private detective expecting a bomb answered that all these questions —it seemed to him—depended so much on the details.

'Yes,' murmured Bewsher. His heels slipped on the canvas-covered foot-rail and shot out a couple of inches—an accident which caused a shower of sparks to fly up from his pipe as he was jerked another inch or two into the sag of the chair. But after a moment's reflection, he completed his remark, 'Our system is different. I wonder why.'

'We haven't got a system at all—no sort of principles. None of the people we send out have the faintest idea of what they're for.'

'I suppose not,' said Bewsher.

But Gore could not allow his District officer to pass over such violent exaggeration as this. 'Isn't it one of the chief principles to leave people to run their own affairs as much as possible. That's actually laid down in plenty of instructions and memoranda.'

'That's not a principle at all—it's just lack of intelligence. We don't know even what to do with an empire. We can't even guess what it's for.'

But Marie was ready to defend even the Empire against Bewsher's enemies.

'Why,' she cried, 'isn't it the only league of nations in the whole world that really has worked?'

'Thank you very much, ma'am, you're the best Englishman of the lot of us,' cried Bewsher sitting up like a jack in the box and reaching for his glass.

'The commonwealth of nations—I call that just the grandest kind of idea. And why shouldn't Birri be a nation too. Nations don't go by size.'

'To the Birri nation,' said Bewsher, raising his tumbler.

Marie hastily reached her own glass across the table to clink with him. 'The Birri nation.'

'And Ireland and India and all our other grateful pupils,' said Cottee. 'With which let us couple the name of the U.S.A.,' said Bewsher, taking another sip, and bowing to Marie across the table he called out 'Speech,' and collapsed again into the bottom of his chair.

'Well, you certainly taught us how to shoot at Lexington.'

'Where was that?'

'Does it beat you again?' said Marie laughing.

'Yes, and now we're encouraging the Birri to shoot—the only question is who'll get it first,' said Cottee. 'Bewsher or the rest of us?'

Marie shivered and said that this was silly.

'Let me get you a coat.' Bewsher threw up his legs, brought them down with a swing and came up all standing. 'You have to look out for chills in these parts.'

Gore shouted for Henry but Bewsher was already half-way across the compound towards his bed, which could be seen dimly, like a large green meat safe, under a dunia tree. His crooked legs carried him away so fast that Marie's and Gore's protests missed him by ten yards. He came back at equal speed with an old-fashioned British warm, very short and roomy, like a pea-jacket.

At the same time Henry, answering Gore's call, came rushing from the rest-house with Marie's own coat, a brown garment with a fur collar.

Both were held up before her at once. She laughed and put her arms into the sleeves of the British warm. 'Let me feel what it's like to be British and Imperial,' she said.

'Take care then that you don't feel like playing hanky panky with boundaries,' Cottee remarked, ostensibly to her alone. He had turned his back on Bewsher. But he spoke loudly enough to be heard ten yards away.

Gore and Marie both started talking at once, Marie about another drink, Gore about the plans for the next day, but Bewsher, who had also turned red, like Cottee himself, tapped the young man on the arm and said, 'What about the boundary?'

Gore said hastily, 'I brought you all the papers, sir.'

Cottee did not like to be unpopular, but he was not to be intimidated. He looked down at Bewsher and answered, 'I said that in that coat she'd be trying to do me down.'

'Yes, yes, of course—the licences.' Bewsher was perfectly charming. 'H'm—well, the fact is—I've been talking to the chiefs and they say—I'm sorry, Cottee—but they're quite clear—that it would be absolutely impossible to start work on either area for the present. Their young men are quite out of hand.'

'I should think so,' cried Marie. 'Why, look at this morning——'

'But dash it all, Bewsher—this is—it's impossible. You can't do it. The place is open. If we choose to come, who's going to stop us?'

'As for that, we'll see what the Resident's got to say when I send the chief's message to the governor. But of course I shouldn't hesitate to read the riot act if there was any danger of a row.'

'Riot act?'

'Run you in, if you like.'

Cottee stood speechless. Marie put her hand on his sleeve and said with a comically maternal sympathy, 'Don't be cross, Frank. It really wouldn't be safe for you. You don't know——'

'Of course I don't accept this. Not for a minute.'

'That's all right. What about chop? Stay and feed.'

But neither Gore nor Cottee had any desire to stay and feed. It was noticeable also that Marie herself, the hostess apparent, for all her natural hospitality, had not asked them to stay and feed.

They took their leave, Gore's lantern boy came running to conduct them into the narrow gully of the town road.

'This will just about finish the old moss-back,' said Cottee, striding out in a most dramatic rage.

Gore quite agreed with him, but he did not say so. He was regretting very much that Bewsher was a bachelor, susceptible especially to ladies of doubtful reputation, and that he had allowed Marie to slip through his fingers at Kifi.

In fact, Jukes and Cottee made their appeal before the end of that week and Alabaster immediately sent down orders that Bewsher was to come into Kunama. Mander, A.D.O. Kunama, wrote to Gore, 'It appears that Monkey has finally done for himself. These pagan men all go the same way home, in the cart. Why is it that the back bush conduces so strongly to megalomania? Is it true he threatened to arrest Cottee for the crime of trespassing on his own property? Alabaster says that the damages might run into four figures. You can imagine the fuss in this office—it's strange that a man of our Resident's figure and deportment should have the temperament of fidgety Phil.'

But the peremptory command and three or four urgent wires that followed it, being sent on to Bewsher in Nok, did not even receive an acknowledgment. The man had disappeared into the most inaccessible parts of his domain.

Of course this old trick of the district officer at war with his Resident did not improve Alabaster's temper. The wires poured in; and when at the end of another week, nearly a fortnight from the time of the unlucky evening at Nok, Gore received the following note, delivered by the hand of a savage whose dialect and tribal marks surprised and amused even the Birri interpreter, he found a good deal of difficulty in carrying out its orders.

*Dear Gore,*

    *Alabaster is throwing fits about the tin-openers. Send him the enclosed wire and make him understand why Kunama is out of the question just now, and also that there's not the least to worry about the situation here. Jukes Cottee and Co. will crumple as soon as they realize that we're standing together. As for his suggestion to station troops in Nok, look up my memorandum of 1912 or thereabouts, when old Tinbelly Grote trotted out the same happy thought. I fancy I can't improve on the wording.*

*Yours sincerely,*

E. B. B.

*P.S.—Please send the following stores,*
    *One case, A2 assorted small chop, sardines, etc.*
    *One case milk.*
    *One case, B3 coffee and flour.*
    *One case, sauterne.*

The wire read:

'In pursuance instructions your wire 17.72 re facilities Hasluck am conducting Hasluck tour Paré investigate juju. Already valuable results view future religious developments Birri. Propose report to you course of next month, D. O. Alo.'

# X

On the third day of the feast the beer and meat were finished. On the fourth two small children ventured out of the compounds and paddled gravely in the ford. Fish was smoking his pipe on the bank, a string tied tightly round his forehead showed that he suffered from a headache. Of three women huddled together in a listless group under the shadow of the nearest hut, two had strings and the third had an eye swollen to the size and colour of a mango. Two boys on the far shore wandered listlessly far apart. An old man was trying to lift himself out of a thorn bush at the foot of the bank; groans burst from his lips as he tried to bend his stiff, bruised limbs.

But his expression was resigned and patient. All these people had the same look of calm resolution. They had exhausted all their desires for that time, they had spent every possibility of enjoyment and they felt the spiritual repose of paupers. There was no more escape from daily responsibilities.

The old man having at last propped himself upon his feet lurched off, bent double and uttering still louder groans, towards the fishermen's huts. He was going to mend a fish-trap. One of the women put her hand to her head, scrambled to her feet and tottered through a doorway. In a few moments the sound of pestle and mortar was heard in Nok for the first time in three or four days, no one knew or cared precisely how many.

Little else was heard in the village for that day. The men, as one by one they crawled out of huts and holes, went away silently to hunt, to fish, to bring yams from the farm stores. The women were relighting their fires, refilling their water-pots, grinding their meal. There was little talk, and that was business-like. Meanwhile it was known to everybody that the sixth, eighth and ninth classes and half the seventh were plotting an attack on Goshi mission under the Fish. The young men went into training and separated themselves from their wives. They ate no food prepared by women which might convey to them some of women's weakness. They had even sent for a juju man to take an oracle and choose the best day for the battle.

All this was done against the will of the nominal rulers of the village. But since more than half and nearly all the best warriors were with Fish they could not do anything. Their government had always depended on consent.

Now that these youngsters, inspired by some evil spirit, excited by all these changes, this confusion brought by the damned whites, had taken it into their heads to go to war on their own account, nobody knew how to stop them. The situation was quite new.

All the elder men in the village were bitterly opposed to the Goshi war. 'Fight Kifi or Goshi if you like, but not the whites.' They said, 'You young fools, do you want to bring soldiers to burn up the whole town and shoot you with guns?' But the young men, now that their rebellion was known and also successful answered with contempt that if the soldiers came they would kill them. 'Bullets won't go through trees—and how can any soldiers find the Birri in the forest?' The fact was, of course, that the young men were not going to listen to any arguments. They did not want to argue, they wanted to fight above everything else in the world. Also they had nothing much to lose in a war with the soldiers except their lives. Who cares about risking his life? The more the risk, the more the excitement and the glory to be won.

It was the old papas and mammas with their beloved houses, with sons and daughters, grandsons and grand-daughters to feed, to teach, to guide, to preserve, who had much to lose. Naturally they were full of warnings and fears. But Fish and his men despised the old cowards.

It was only Obai whose opposition was troublesome. Obai was backed by some of the best fighting men in the place. Obai said, 'These people are under Bewsher's protection. Before we attack them we should tell Bewsher that we don't want them in Birri and that they must not interfere with our women.'

'We told him and he did nothing.'

'I'll tell him myself that if he does nothing we will fight. You know that Bewsher is a joker (Obai used a word in Birri meaning, a not serious person, a putter-off with jokes), but he is our friend and we must treat him fairly.' Obai, as usual, was furiously excited. 'We

Birri are not beasts to betray our friends. We are not like the Yorubas and Hausas whom nobody can trust. We do things in the open,' he shouted, and when Fish argued with him, he called him a snake and a fool, a bastard and a Yoruba and wanted to fight a duel with him.

But Fish was too clever for Obai. He caused a message to be sent that Obai must get at once to Paré, the juju town, to confer with Bewsher's head chief Umoké about the All-Birri. Obai set off at once, and the same evening the war party also set off.

It is thirty miles from Nok to Goshi, a single night's journey for a Birri war-party travelling light. But Kifi lies between, and Kifi, always deadly enemies of the Nok, turned out in force to block the road. Two men were killed and seven wounded in this unnecessary fight which obliged the expedition to make a detour of forty miles and put back its arrival at Goshi for two days.

Fish's plan was to stay in Goshi village, which had promised help, till dark. Meanwhile a few chosen heroes going unsuspected from the village among usual visitors to the mission would hide in a certain store-house till night time; then kill the whites in their sleep and set the roofs on fire. This was to be the signal for the main body to charge either from Goshi or the bush, or on both sides at once, storm the mission compounds, massacre the Christian natives, and take the women prisoners.

Henry had provided all information. He also undertook to receive the killing parties at the hiding-place and afterwards to guide them to the quarry.

Henry, in fact, promised every assistance except in the actual throat-cutting. He pointed out that in any little war with the English soldiers which might possibly follow the attack, he would be more useful to his countrymen as a spy in Alo than a warrior in Birri. He must therefore be above suspicion, and he even refused to accept any share of the profits except the property of his own mistress, which might be considered his already, and five pounds in silver.

There were to be three parties of three men each, one for Mr. and Mrs. Dobson in the main building, one for Miss Dorothy Dans next door, and one for Marie who might be in either place. Fish himself would keep watch with Henry and give the signal for the main attack.

Unluckily Goshi village, taking alarm from Kifi, had blocked up its gates, and when the Nok approached fired at them with new-poisoned arrows. An enthusiastic youth belonging to the fifth (he was just sixteen) who volunteered to go forward and explain things to them, had barely got so far as 'Brothers of Goshi, we are all Birri——' using in fact some of Bewsher's talk, when he received a sling stone in the face which broke his jaw.

Fish was obliged to withdraw his men into the bush where they lay all that day. The wounded boy cried out so much in his pain that the leaders, seeing the other youngsters growing dispirited, took him aside and cut his throat.

And though volunteers, attracted by the rumour of loot, now began to come in from neighbouring villages, including twenty from the Goshi hamlets, the Nok leader did not trust them and placed them at a distance. The only useful recruit was Uli, who suddenly emerged from the forest in full war dress and offered his services.

Uli was a tried campaigner and he had planned his arrival very well. Men on the warpath do not enquire into the domestic character of an ally, and in fact, the worst characters are often the most welcome comrades in battle. They have more enterprise and despera-tion. This was at once proved true of Uli, who carried out two dangerous scouting expeditions during the afternoon.

In this critical time mature warriors like Fish and Uli were electric with power. Fish could not stay in one place for a moment. His little red eyes glittered like a wild pig's. He darted here and there, over to the Goshi party, down to the outposts, encouraging, abusing. Uli did not seem to exert himself. He lounged about with a broad impudent grin, quite new on his good-natured face. But it was not insulting the Birri, it was defying the world. He was like a rogue leopard ready for anything or anybody. He did not stand still even among his Nok brothers, but was always moving away, turning sharp round. He was watchful in every direction.

The new plan suggested by Uli was for a single scouting party of three men to go forward at midnight, when, according to Henry, the whole mission would be asleep, and set fire either to the chapel roof or the mission house according to the most desirable line of attack. The main body under Fish would then charge in two converging wings, the Nok party on the right.

Uli volunteered to lead these scouts and he was at once accepted on account of his experience, and also his knowledge of English, which might enable him, if challenged, to give a plausible answer.

Goshi village and mission stood about a mile apart in a large cleared plain three miles wide and at least seven in length. The mission was nearly two miles from the Kifi bush on the east, and lay, as Henry had described it, open on every side. The buildings, two large finished houses and one not yet roofed, a thatched chapel and a row of huts for the servants and pupil teachers, were not even fenced. The compounds occupied by refugees, orphans, patients and a shifting population of visitors and disciples were surrounded only by mat walls and a thin line of scrub, intended to keep hyenas and thieves at bay.

The Goshi Elema river on the east was too far to give protection and could easily be avoided by the attacking party. Uli led his men for some way along the shadowed bank of this river before turning towards the mission. The thin moon, just risen above the trees, gave barely light enough for him to pick his way on the ground which appeared to have a thicker layer of darkness attached to it like a mist. The air itself was bright and clear. Goshi village could be seen a mile away like an island on a sea of grey smoke; and the mission buildings were like a fleet of square high ships becalmed in an estuary. The huts which protruded here and there were buoys and fishing boats, the forest walls, stretching out of sight on each hand, were like a rocky coast.

Lights were still to be seen in the missioner's house and the compounds. But Uli and his men advanced with confidence. They knew how difficult it would be for anybody looking out from a lighted room to see their black bodies.

Uli made directly for the mission house which he had visited once before and knew well. It was a large building designed for the Dobsons by Bewsher himself according to his favourite model. It consisted of a large earth platform or stoop raised two foot above the ground and about seventy foot long and thirty wide, the whole covered by an enormous roof of thatch on palm posts. Under the roof and therefore in perpetual shadow an inner flat-roofed house of mud, fifty foot long by twenty foot wide, well provided with tall windows, contained three rooms. At each end the stoop was ten foot wide and thirty broad, at the back and front it was about five foot broad.

The lights, some of which had moved, showed that there were people still awake both in the mission village and the big house. But everything favoured Uli. No sentry challenged, no dog barked. The back verandah of the house proved moreover a most excellent hiding-place. It had been divided into stalls full of mixed stores and fenced with zana mats. Behind the stoop, an alley of mats, leading to the private latrines, such as village headmen are wont to build for a white woman, gave cover from the servants' huts. Moreover, the back windows, for further privacy, had also been stuffed up with mats. Uli and his scouts had only to creep into these stalls and poke their fingers through the mats to see everything within the rooms, themselves completely hidden. The peep-holes were smaller than their eyes. But what they saw surprised them very much. The room was not occupied by the Dobsons, but by Marie and Bewsher.

This was surprising because Bewsher was supposed to be at Kifi. According to the Goshi recruits, his carriers had been sent from the village that afternoon. It alarmed Uli's men who had not bargained on meeting this dangerous and powerful adversary. It caused in Uli himself a feeling which put in verbal form might be represented by the question, Will it pay me better to do a heroic deed or play the traitor? For Uli with all his desperate rashness and ferocity had perpetually at the back of his mind, like other men in his situation, the thought, 'I've got to look out for myself for no one else will.'

Meanwhile there was nothing to do but wait on circumstances till Bewsher should go away or go to bed. And at the moment he was already undressing.

He did this slowly, pulling off a garment with deliberation and stopping with a face half eclipsed in his shirt, or one leg in his shorts, to continue to talk with the woman who was sitting in a green canvas bath at the other end of the room.

The pagans looked with curiosity at the woman whose whiteness fascinated and also disgusted Uli. He did not at all like the variations of colour in her flesh, and wondered how any man could bear her. She was sitting with a pensive expression, holding a large sponge in her lap and sometimes dribbling water down the front of her body.

Her eyes were fixed on Bewsher and now and then she said something agreeing with him or anticipating him. But it was plain even to Uli that she was not really listening to the man so much as enjoying his talk, his gestures, the faces he made while he described what he had said to the Resident and the Resident had said to him.

Uli had seen a hundred times such a conversation between some Birri warrior and his favourite wife, even the same expressions, the same gestures. Thus had Uli found himself eloquent with Enuké and felt in her presence justified of his deeds, and so had Enuké gazed at him apparently attending to his words and actually thinking perhaps, 'What a nice face he has, how strong he is, how brave,' or perhaps—'and he likes me—all this talk is because he likes me very much. He belongs to me.' That is the kind of thought that delights a woman.

Uli, like every negro, was a student of expression, of voice and gestures. He had lived all his life in community and the most interesting and important study available to him, after the ways of beasts, was the looks, the ways and the secrets of his friends and comrades. His penetration into character, his power of detecting mood and anticipating a thought was probably greater than a white man's. It amused him very much to see in Bewsher's looks the swelling valiance of the bridegroom, and in Marie's the watchful pondering joy of the bride.

In their curiosity the pagans had not noticed the rising of the moon over the mats behind them. Their heads were now to be seen, while they dodged here and there to different peep-holes, as black-polished balls against a surface of bright dun, not only from a quarter of a mile across the open compound but from the servants' huts behind the mission house. The mats were six feet high, but Uli's head, raised by the stoop, was more than seven and a half from ground level. The Birri were therefore inexpressibly startled to hear a shrill woman's voice exclaim in English, 'What you do dar, you trash.'

They whirled round together and saw an Ejaw maid standing in the alley. She herself recognized them, at the same moment, for Birri. A look of terror transfigured her, she opened her mouth and turned to run. But Uli had not lost his presence of mind. With an immense silent leap, he flew over the mats like a leopard and as it seemed, in a continuation of the same movement, an upswing with the body and arm after the downswing of the leap, struck up with the knife in his right hand. The woman's shriek ended in a kind of grunt as the point of the knife having divided the stomach, with a momentum which carried Uli's hand into the opening of the body, passed three inches beyond the diaphragm.

As Bewsher appeared in the back verandah three shadows slipped along the alley and round the corner of the house into the shadow of the front. That again was a stroke of Uli's bush craft. He had taken flight apparently in the worst direction—towards the open front of the mission house; actually the safest, into the deep shadow.

From that shadow it was easy to pass into the next, that of the chapel, and under cover of the empty chapel they darted away across the open plain.

At first the dead girl was not seen in the shadow of the mats. Dobson, the missioner, coming out of his room with a lantern and meeting, to his mild surprise, Bewsher, in pyjamas, also with a lantern, asked what had happened. He looked in his sober brown dressing-gown and gold spectacles like a little plump lama from Tibet. His pale round face and rather flat features wore their invariable expression of benevolence and repose. Mrs. Dobson, on the other hand, tall and beautiful, dressed in real Chinese embroidery, seemed like a Valkyrie, rather a sleepy and languid valkyrie but completely pagan. She was sure, she said, that it was only a hyena, the nasty creatures always waked her out of a really good sleep.

'It sounded more like a lady's protest against the friendly pinch,' said Bewsher, who had an indescribably rollicking air. 'Where's that brown girl of yours, Mrs. Dobson—and where's your Henry, Marie—he'd pinch anything.'

'Yes, Henry's a Christian to the finger-tips,' drawled Marie. She had just appeared, huddled in her overcoat. She, too, had a reckless and wanton air which made the Dobsons glance discreetly at each other as if to ask, 'What do you think?'

Bewsher gave a loud laugh at Marie's joke, and then quite unnecessarily touched the breast of her coat, pulling the lapels across. 'What about that fever, my dear.'

Marie smiled, looked up and down, wet her lips with her tongue and turned slowly scarlet; she might have been a shy schoolgirl threatened with a kiss under the mistletoe; in fact, the scene was such that in other circumstances would have charmed the Dobsons and especially Minnie Dobson. As it was the lady blushed, and Dobson clearing his throat said in his mildest voice, 'I was wondering if I ought to see what's happening over there.' He looked towards the compound where lights were showing and excited cries could be heard.

His remark was in tone a question. Bewsher, thus obliged to turn his eyes away from his young woman, also noticed those signs of panic in the compounds, and said, 'The sooner the better.' He jumped down with an abruptness which made Marie look a little surprised. She smiled at Minnie Dobson as if to say, 'These men.'

Dobson, who had already descended, gravely leaving the scene of embarrassment for the scene of duty, was ten yards away when a boy came darting towards him from the corner of the stoop, shrieking that the wild Birri had come, the bush Birri were after him.

Bewsher made a leap at him and grabbed him. 'Wait a moment.' He talked to him as to a young horse in a reasonable tone that was in sharp contrast with the tiger spring. 'But those weren't the Birri, you know——'

Dobson turned back. 'What makes you think that, Tom?'

'I saw um—I saw um—dey go for back of chapel, in der war hats.'

'That's the third time this week that Tom has seen the wild Birri in their war hats and tails,' said Miss Dans, flying in from the compound.

She was a little woman, very like Marie, to whom she was related. But her looks were disfigured by large black-rimmed spectacles very unsuitable to the small flattish nose and prominent eyes which she shared with Marie, and she had nothing of that play of expression which made some people, like Bewsher, think Marie pretty. Miss Dans was tight-lipped and austere. She was also extremely efficient, the real housekeeper of the mission and Dobson's right-hand man. Miss Dans disdained dressing-gowns. Her thick white pyjamas and black boots were like a uniform. She carried a bottle in her hand and was followed by a hospital boy with a basket full of dressing and bottles.

'Why, what've you been doing, Dawl?' Mrs. Dobson asked her. 'It's too bad the way they get you up.'

'That fool Susan dropped her baby in the fire, and Gar'ba here,' she turned upon the hospital boy, 'was half-way to Alo before I could find him. He's worse than Tom with his wild Birri. If that coat is all you've got on, Marie, you'll be in hospital to-morrow. You can't play at pagans in Goshi—the Goshi night-breeze brings the fever out in *real* pagans. Mr. Dobson,' she called to Dobson in the compound, 'I have to tell you that three more fever patients have run away from hospital since ten o'clock—that's seven to-day,' and she vanished into the house with a hop.

Bewsher was laughing at Marie. His laugh meant, 'Your friend Dorothy gave you a nasty one that time.' But he said, '*Yellow* fever, I suppose. Like poor Tom's case—but look here, Tom, you're very ill, you know, seeing things that aren't there.'

'I tell you sah, dey here—Goshi people shoot em dis morning— all de people know dey live for bush.'

'If Goshi didn't drink so much they wouldn't waste so many arrows,' said Miss Dans, suddenly reappearing with another bottle. 'Last week it was my best nanny goat.' She went off at top speed towards the hospital compound.

'It's too bad the way they pester Dawl,' said Minnie Dobson, in her soft drawl, the voice of an odalisque, 'she's just too good to them.'

Tom was still protesting. His eyes bulged, he was weak with terror. 'Lemme go—sah—dey coming—dey fit to kill everybody.'

'But look here,' Bewsher remonstrated.

'I suppose it is just possible,' said Dobson, 'that there are Birri about—if they had this fight at Kifi.'

It was the Kifi fight which had brought Bewsher south from Paré.

'Kifi gave them a beating whoever they were—and not even the Nok would attack the mission.'

Marie had descended in order to stand close to Bewsher. She was smiling at his confident air, and now she murmured, 'Why wouldn't they?'

'The village perhaps—if it's the Nok they've been at war with Goshi since the year dot. I shouldn't be surprised if they had a return match at Goshi. But Goshi can look after itself, none better.'

Marie said that if the soldiers were wanted Tom could go on his bicycle.

'Soldiers?'

'Isn't that what they're for?'

The two men looked at her in surprise, and then Bewsher said, 'It's all right, you know, they're not coming here.'

Marie was equally surprised. The fact was that she had scarcely been attending to this affair, and her remark about soldiers had been small talk. She answered in the same absentminded and amused voice that it was all right for her. Women were loot. It was the men who had to be nervous when the Birri went on the war-path.

'What I'm nervous about are the lads of the village,' said Bewsher, twirling on his heels towards the compounds, and he shouted, 'Sam, bring them lantern and them big torch.'

'It's under the pillow,' said Marie, causing Dobson to retreat a stop or two as if from an intrusion.

'And we'll leave you to hold the fort at this end—but don't go beyond the chapel.'

'I thought the Birri had all gone away.'

'Thank you, Sam.'

'And don't you go beyond the compounds,' said Marie.

Bewsher made no answer to this. The two men with Tom gesticulating between them walked off towards the village.

Marie looking after them, saw Bewsher suddenly bursting into speech, wave the lantern abroad in a vigorous gesture which nearly put it out. Then he stopped to find out what was wrong with the wick and she thought, 'That will keep him happy for another five minutes.'

Marie set out at once to make a wide circuit into the forbidden ground beyond the chapel. Her excuse was to explore it, but she knew that the Birri would prefer to lie in the forest rather than the open ground and the high bush was half a mile away, far beyond arrow shot. Meanwhile she wanted to be alone. She did not care to face any of the Dobson party without Bewsher.

They disapproved of this immoral woman who had seized upon their dear Bewsher, and at each visit their disapproval increased. This was the third time she had been made to feel uncomfortable.

She had warned Bewsher that she could not bear another, but he had insisted, declaring that she was only suffering from conscience, that the Dobsons had never guessed anything. Besides, they would be careful.

Monkey's notion of protecting her reputation had been to call her Miss Hasluck at supper and shout out of her bedroom window at breakfast-time, 'Hi, Marie, what have you done with my pyjama legs?'

It was no wonder that the Christians looked askance at her, and that Doll Dans made spiteful remarks about pagans. She was the biggest scandal in the province.

She moved forward slowly in the pale moonlight, picking her way among half-burnt tufts of grass and low bushes, smiling at the incident of the pyjama legs. Her smile was derisive, with pursed lips, as if to laugh at herself as well as Bewsher. This was exactly its intention. She treated the affair as a joke for the very reason that it had such powerful effects upon her. The smile was her defence not only against disappointment, against expecting too much happiness, but against sentimental excess. She called up before her eyes Monkey's broken nose, and crooked legs, his shrewd grin, his rolling walk, his love of a doubtful joke; she pictured him as she had seen him fussing absurdly about his underclothes and flying into a rage because breakfast was not ready, talking bad Birri and pretending to understand answers that were double-dutch to him, listening in bliss to the gramophone playing 'Home Sweet Home,' or 'Pack up your Troubles'; or making his approaches towards herself with a kind of lickerish crooked smile which brought out very strongly his resemblance to a blond chimpanzee.

Or possibly he was most ridiculous in the maternal aspect, when he looked at her tongue or took her pulse, mixed her a dose, rubbed the skin off her back with embrocation made from his own recipe or waked her three times in a night to change her sheets. Monkey as nurse could be exasperating. He had all the worst faults. He was tyrannical, restless, anxious and experimental. He had probably made her single attack of fever three times worse. She would take very good care not to be ill again while he was in the camp.

She wanted to regard these aspects of the man because if she thought of him simply as Monkey she began to feel uncomfortable and could not smile any more. The very episode of the embrocation which had enraged her at the time now made her feel sentimental. A dangerous emotion made her throat swell and her eyes fill.

In the same way she assured herself a hundred times a day that Bewsher's declarations of love were all humbug, directed to the usual end, and that having obtained what he wanted, he would soon grow tired of it. This was just a little flirtation by the way, temporary in its very essence. It would never have begun had he not gathered from somewhere, some gossip or other, the notion that she was easy of access, that she did not expect any permanent relation.

And his first approaches had been exactly like Frank Cottee's. Probably all Englishmen made illicit love in the same way. The difference was in the man behind the gun—and the end was the same everywhere. If you gave them what they wanted they went off without a thank you, and if you did not, they went even more quickly; that is, unless you were a platinum blonde or had a hundred thousand dollars.

Bewsher would go; probably he was already planning to get away. Three weeks of one woman day and night, of almost incessant talk on every possible subject were enough to exhaust any man's constancy. In her experience a single week was usually enough, and a much less crowded week than three days with Bewsher.

It was true that she had been useful to the man. He might laugh at the lion-faced Birri and say that the lion's expression was due to a single-minded contemplation of raw meat, but he had put her Nok folklore into a special report and he was paying her out of government funds (Special Services) for her work on the Paré juju. That would take another fortnight. But after that? And at any minute he might be relieved, disgraced; he was even expecting it himself. Then indeed he would not want to be bothered with a woman.

'It's a wonder that it's lasted so long,' she reflected, shrugging up her shoulders in a chilly draught; but she was reasoning with the strong conviction that this was not at all a temporary affair for Bewsher any more than herself.

'Why?' asked the derisive mouth of a dejected-looking thorn bush fluttering with rags. 'Because you want it that way.'

114

But hadn't Bewsher said good-bye four times to her that very evening when he should have gone to Kifi and at last failed to go at all.

'Poor boob. It was because he had one of his good ideas and wanted to tell you about it.'

But already argument seemed like trifling, like a piece of cowardice. It was wrong to doubt the man who loved her. It was ingratitude and meanness.

She turned aside looking for the faint tracks which marked the path from the back of the chapel to the Nok road. She had been making for the boundary ditch of the mission simply because she needed an objective and by way of the boundary she could join Bewsher at the compounds with the excuse of reporting all clear. But she was now following the plan without conscious volition. Her eyes looked for the path but she had no ideas about it, much less of possible Birri. She was telling herself that she ought to be ashamed of her cynicism. Wasn't that the most contemptible kind of vice, the smoke-cloud of the defeated and the coward. Why should she be afraid of her happiness, why should she be astonished at it and try to depreciate it when she had always known that it was natural and right, something that everybody ought to have, that everybody was looking for.

That was why the Dobsons were so stupid (she drifted across something like a path and moved quickly forward) they were disapproving of the very thing which they themselves were trying to bring about, because when they talked about a state of grace that was exactly what they meant. They were even stupider than Alabaster who could not understand that the Birri's way of life might be happier than his own even though they were naked and always at war—that the quality of life had nothing to do with any special kind of lawfulness or dress or religion. Two Birri arm in arm might be much better off than the most civilized kind of people, who had been brought up in mutual distrust and watchfulness and jealousy instead of sympathy. And their happiness was more secure. It did not rest upon being cleverer or richer than other people but only upon liking them (all signs of a path had disappeared and she strolled at random). This happiness which seemed so extraordinary to her; this

115

new kind of experience in which she moved awkwardly and doubt-fully like a child at her first party was not a holiday, an escape from daily endurances, but life itself. It could not come to an end because it was natural and real, the right kind of living. To love and be loved.

A piece of broken ground, the washed-down ruins of some huts stopped her way, and she looked up at the grey moon, the grey fields, the smoke-grey wall of the forest behind the falling sheets of dusty light and without any thought of them felt the mysterious physical excitement which acknowledges a grand beauty. Her being felt it as the dreamer acknowledges the cathedral overhead by a quickened sense of man's privilege and God's eternity. It was real, this life (she began to find her way among the ruins. She could see the ditch now, marked by tall bunches of grass like the remnants of a fence) it was more real than any other kind of life because now when she looked out from it, from this secure delight and trust, all things fell into their harmonies, the flesh was reconciled with the spirit, the mind with the heart, egotism with sacrifice, self with other self. When she took Bewsher in her arms she did not give or take, she entered into a completeness without limits or division, without description or laws. It was the life of life, the centre of being.

She gave herself up to confidence, to security, to delight with the same feeling of luxury with which she indulged her passion for the man.

She had reached the ditch, a broad shallow hole, and began to cross it before she remembered that it was her destination. She looked about to find out where she was.

Something behind a grass tuft caught her eye. It looked like a crouching man. For a moment she was startled; then walked over to examine the place.

This was partly bravado. She was punishing Monkey for his doubts about her courage. He ought to know by now that he need not coddle her in the bush. She was well tested.

Suddenly she noticed a light far away apparently on the edge of the forest. It flickered among the trees. She stared with mild curiosity. It certainly was a lantern. Its flame was almost brown. Could the Birri be walking about with lights or had some traveller chosen this evening to go to Kifi? If so he would receive a very unpleasant shock from one war-party or the other. For pagans, however respectful of the laws of war concerning non-combatants and travellers, were always liable to shoot first and look afterwards. They were entitled to shoot.

Another light flashed, a cold diamond of light, and immediately winked out. Then again it pierced the twilight with a narrow sharp ray which revealed two or three vertical streaks, the stems of trees. Somebody was using a torch. The notion of the Birri carrying torches to their war gave her a shock of surprise mixed with the kind of amusement with which one watches a promising child show unexpected acquaintance with grown-up manners. It was certainly a magnificent torch, it contrasted very prettily with the smoky lantern. Again it flashed among the trees. It was always turned away from her. In fact it must belong to somebody on the cleared ground, some Goshi scout or the mission watchman. If so, the man was a fool. But what a torch! It must be the twin to her own.

But hadn't Bewsher said something about her torch? And the smoky lantern?

Suddenly surprise and curiosity were driven out of her by a shock of revelation which was like a heavy blow. She was seized by a terror quite new to her. She was shaky, faint and sick with fright, and at the same time quite unable to reason with her own panic or form any clear notion of what she ought to do; a sensation more unpleasant and humiliating than any she could have imagined.

Her rush towards the mission-house was half involuntary, a reaction.

Mrs. Dobson was moving across the stoop towards her long chair with a cushion in each hand. She gazed at Marie as if a little surprised by this display of excitement and agitation. 'Why, Miss Hasluck, I was just wondering where you were—what light did you say?'

Marie shaded her eyes to look past the mission compounds which were now blazing with lights and fires. 'Isn't that a light moving along by the edge of the high road?'

'I expect that's Mr. Bewsher—he said he was going to have a look around.'

'I thought so—just the kind of fool trick he would play.'

'But you don't think there are really any Birri around?'

'Why not? If they were at Goshi village last night—and if they're anywhere around now they'll be over there at the edge of the high bush.'

Mrs. Dobson said in a soothing voice as if speaking to a frightened child, 'I'm sure Mr. Bewsher is quite safe with his own Birri.'

'That's a comfort if you can believe it,' said Marie, whose panic had given her a sharp look as well as a sharp tongue. 'But I don't. I know the Birri and Monkey is just the man a war-party would kill. He's the very biggest kind of game. The chief that get's Monkey's brains to eat and Monkey's finger joints to hang round his neck will be a hero for the rest of his life, and every good Birri wants to be a hero. But if they do get him, they'll probably go away. So that you needn't worry.'

Mrs. Dobson, full of sympathy and understanding, begged her to come and lie down. She was just going to make some chocolate. But Marie, ashamed of herself and angry with Bewsher, went to her room.

In a moment she was out again on the stoop, looking towards the village. But it was impossible to distinguish any of the figures which were now whirling about the walls and the open ground like swarming bees. There was certainly a panic. Another group, carrying bundles on their heads were hurrying towards Alo.

What suddenly decided Marie to send for help was the arrival of Obai. He had come forty miles from Paré in the day but he was now anxious to fight the whole of Fish's war party. He was full of rage and contempt for them. 'It is only that fool Fish—he wants to be a war chief.'

'But where are they now, Obai? When are they coming?'

'Who knows? At dawn perhaps—whenever they like. I'll be watching. I'll give you warning.'

Obai apparently thought that the warning would be sufficient. No doubt his idea was that Bewsher and the other whites being warned would come and blast their enemies either with guns or pure magic.

But Marie sat down at once to write to Gore. She explained that in the absence of the men and the emergency of the moment she ventured to let him know that the Birri were expected to attack any time, etc., etc.

As a matter of fact some time before she had finished this note

Bewsher's voice was heard outside shouting for a stretcher and at the same time a tumult of native voices shouting and shrieking.

But she finished her letter and handed it to Tom and saw him mount his bicycle in the dark front compound between house and chapel, before she went to the bush.

The maid's body had been found. It was now lying on a stretcher, the entrails roughly stuffed in and secured by a bandage, while Bewsher, Dobson and Miss Dans were clearing a way for it through the crowd of hysterical women and jabbering terrified boys who surrounded them on every side.

The sight filled Marie with indignation, a general moral indignation rather like that perpetual simmering wrath inspired in Miss Dorothy Dans merely by the thought of wickedness and cruelty, alcohol and the Roman Catholics. She pushed through the crowd and accosted Bewsher. 'And now perhaps you'll believe that poor Tom wasn't seeing ghosts.'

'According to Obai, it's the Fish who has been playing the fool.'

Obai, hearing his name, stepped forward with a grand gesture and delivered an energetic speech in the Nok dialect. He defied the Fish and all his men to come on at once. For he was Bewsher's friend and he would glory in destroying his enemies.

It was in fact a very good speech of the kind that used to have the most powerful effect at public meetings and before battles and on the stage. It was also sincere. Obai had performed already an heroic journey to defend the good Bewsher against the bad Fish, to prove that the Birri had honour and intelligence and gratitude. He said so and he meant every word of it.

'Very nice, Obai,' said Bewsher in English, inclined to chaff these grand attitudes and at the same time pleased with his pupil's eloquence and fire. He looked round with a smile which would put off criticism. But the fine sentiments had a fine effect on the crowd, who cheered, and on Marie, who warmly assured Obai in his own language that he was a hero and that he need not be afraid of the Fish gang; when the soldiers came they would get a lesson.

'Soldiers,' said Bewsher. 'Who said anything about soldiers?'

A great many voices in the crowd at once said something about soldiers.

'But I thought you were all Christians,' he chaffed them, appar-

119

ently in great surprise. 'You don't want *soldiers* to protect you—what do you say to this, Dobson?'

Dobson slightly inclined his head towards one shoulder, smiled, shut his eyes and said nothing. Mrs. Dobson, who now appeared in a white flannel coat over her wrap, carrying a large grey scarf, proceeded to drape it carefully round her husband's neck.

At the same time and in the same affectionate manner, she remarked, 'You wouldn't have soldiers in the mission, would you, John?'

'But Mrs. Dobson, you don't realize—we have it absolutely certain that the Birri will attack at dawn—this is Obai who will tell you himself.' Marie seized Obai by the arm to draw him forward.

Mrs. Dobson turning her beautiful placid face towards Marie, answered gently that she was fully prepared for that.

'Prepared—there's nothing prepared'—and in sudden amazement she added, 'You don't want to be martyrs.'

'I meant,' said Mrs. Dobson, with a faint blush, 'that we're in Gawd's hands, isn't that so, John?'

Marie was so angry and astonished that she could not speak. She turned livid with rage. And before she could find words rude and violent enough to demolish the imbeciles, Dobson proceeded calmly, 'Minnie's solution is perhaps a little too concentrated to be true. But I think you understand, Mr. Bewsher——'

'Of course, of course, besides soldiers are the last people we want—the last time they poked their noses in where they weren't asked they put back the clock in Birri for years. And all for nothing. It took me six years to get on any sort of terms again. I haven't time—here you, run along. He turned to the crowd and shooed them away. 'Yes, yes, anywhere. Yes, old lady, you can tell me tomorrow at the sewing-bee—now then dirty-face, where's your mummy? all right, you take hold and keep on holding. Sam, this mud-fish here seems to belong to your down-river lot—tell him if he goes on spitting in my face I'll massacre him myself—yes, Topsy, wherever you like—that happens to be my room, but you're quite welcome.

Bewsher had the art of handling a crowd. He talked without stopping so that their minds were in a whirl and at the same time he kept them moving. In three minutes the whole party of twenty or twenty-five had been dispersed about the stoop and back premises.

'It's not that we want to take unnecessary risks,' Dobson was saying, 'much less to seek—er (trying to avoid the word martyrs used by Marie) any kind of dramatic apotheosis—but simply that one has to be consistent—to one's professions.'

'Very much so, in Africa,' said Bewsher, returning and wiping his forehead on his forearm. 'You can't shake hands with a Birri one day and shoot at him the next, he gets the idea that you're not to be relied on.'

'But that's exactly what they've done to you over and over again,' Marie exclaimed.

'They haven't so much as given me a passing half brick for ten years, and I doubt if they will.'

'Mr. Bewsher has won the confidence of the most dangerous tribe in West Africa simply by trusting them,' said Mr. Dobson, 'and I hope to follow in his pioneer footsteps.'

'And by trusting God,' said Mrs. Dobson, looking at Bewsher affectionately.

'His trust was of God and in God,' said Dobson in the same apologetic tone as if he wished to excuse himself for talking shop. 'But that is why he understands that after I have been telling these people for a year that we are all in God's hands and He will keep us and guard us, they would be a little bit surprised to see me calling in soldiers to protect God's house and people at the first suggestion of trouble.'

'That's it,' said Bewsher cheerfully, 'and besides, to tell you the honest truth, I've had these alarms before and so I'm not feeling any great anxiety—except for the chickens.'

'But they are here,' cried Marie. 'We know they're here—they've been in the mission.'

'After the chickens—and made a bolt for it as soon as they were spotted. I should be very surprised if there was a single Nok within ten miles at this moment. I know the species. They hate coming out of the forest even for a county match with real arrows.'

Then just as Marie's fury was on the point of breaking in an extremely rude remark about fools and fanatics, he grinned at her and asked, 'When did you fall for the British army, Marie?'

Marie herself perceived the futility of her outcries. It was useless to argue against the conviction of Dobson, who did not care what happened to him, and the optimism of Bewsher, who was always sure that everything would happen just as he wished it to happen. And perhaps he was right about the Nok. He certainly knew their ways.

She was making a fool of herself. But luckily or tactfully Bewsher had given her an opening for escape. 'Well,' she drawled, 'I will say that if it does come to a war I'd prefer to be raped by an expert.'

Bewsher, like Cottee, enjoyed an Americanism. He laughed and took her arm. 'What you want is a cocktail.'

'As long as I've got an inside to put it into.'

# XI

Marie's note reached Gore at half-past eleven. He was not in bed because refugees had already reached the station and he was expecting news. Stoker, O.C. troops had been standing by for orders. Now he was able to put his men on the road within twenty minutes.

Gore himself was delayed. He had to send off the soldiers' carriers, a boat to seek out Bewsher who ought to be at Kifi, a wire to the Resident, and it took him ten minutes to soothe an angry Christian who demanded immediate compensation from the Government for the loss of a bed, a chair, a cooking-pot, a store of yams and a new English hat, straight from Home. Nevertheless he caught the soldiers up on his motor bicycle, at Halfway House, and though the bicycle proved too heavy for the Goshi section, three and a half miles of swamp track, he arrived at the mission very little after two. But he found himself at once in an awkward position.

The first person he met as he entered the mission house was Marie, and she confessed at once that neither Bewsher nor the Dobsons knew of her appeal for troops. Neither must they know or they would probably send them away again.

She made this surprising communication in the big central room of the house, which was full of natives lying or crouching among their bundles. The other rooms and the back stoops appeared equally crowded. A few lanterns standing on the floor threw an upward light on the grotesque melancholy faces, exaggerating hollow eyes and wide nostrils, like those of frightened animals.

'Bewsher must be told if he's here,' said Gore.

'If you like, Harry. There he is, in there,' and in fact Bewsher's voice could be heard, from the next room, saying something about juju. 'He's with his friends the Dobsons.'

Gore hesitated, and she added, 'But you might as well tell them all together. He's just as bad as they are about soldiers.'

'He said so, did he?'

'You know what he is—he thinks he can shoo these Birri around like hens.'

This was a nice dilemma for the young man. He looked at the crowd of refugees, chiefly young boys and women and children lying on the floor in every attitude of patient terror, and thought of the Birri hacking and stabbing among them.

'Yes, yes,' said Bewsher next door in his liveliest and most penetrating tones, 'but that's my point too—keep the thing fresh. Keep your ceremony, your forms (even in his anxiety Gore was amused to think of this advice being preached to the evangelical Dobson) keep all that's local and active and full of juice, just as we did in Christianity when we collared all the pagan gods and turned them into saints.' There was a short pause while Mrs. Dobson said something.

'Yes, thank you, I think I will. Half a cup. But that's the idea—Keep your juju gods, keep Ogun especially.'

Gore was peering through a corner of the door. The room within, called usually the dining-room, a tall whitewashed chamber, recalled with its deep embrasured windows and timbered roof a mediæval guardroom. It was also crowded. Natives were lying or sitting on every part of the floor. The whites were at the far end where the wide doorway, opening on the stoop, gave a view towards the Birri bush. The Dobsons were sitting at a table which supported a lantern, a number of jugs of all shapes and sizes and thirty or forty cups, glasses and tins. Dobson was nursing a cup in the palm of his hand, Mrs. Dobson, dressed now in three coats, was knitting a bright scarlet cap, and Bewsher, pipe hanging from his mouth, was walking about the stoop and carrying on the argument through the window. He, too, like Dobson, had one of Mrs. Dobson's scarves tied round his short neck, and this with its ends hanging down his back, gave him a very unusual appearance. He reminded Gore for some reason of Tam o' Shanter: there was something about his shrewd, animated, not to say intoxicated appearance and gestures which fitted in very well with the conception. He turned suddenly again to the window, causing Gore to move back quickly from his own spyhole, and exclaimed, 'Thunder is too good to waste in a religion. I wish we had him in ours—a God that can knock the chimney-pots into your eggs and bacon——'

'Hear him,' said Marie. 'Isn't he just too——' She could not find a word to express her mingled feelings about the enthusiast.

'But have they done anything at all?' Gore asked.

**124**

'Oh yes, Mr. Bewsher walked three times along the edge of the bush with a lantern so that his dear friends from Birri could shoot him if they wanted to.'

'Or to let them see he's here,' said Gore. 'But what about all this?' He glanced at the floor.

'Mr. Dobson asked them because they were frightened and they made themselves comfortable. There's a girl having her first baby in my bed at the moment. And thank God there's the soldiers at last,' she exclaimed, running towards the edge of the stoop. Gore followed her without alacrity.

The men were drawn up in a long line beside the path, at the edge of a stubble-field. A thin little sergeant, very smart in his glittering buttons and his red sash, was walking up and down with a lantern. Now he came running up to Gore with an expression very like Marie's at their first meeting that night, his eyes wide, his lips parted so that the lantern light sparkled on the tips of his teeth. He saluted with a convulsive smartness and said, 'What we do, sir?'

He gazed anxiously at Gore. He wasn't afraid of pagans but he was afraid of not doing the right thing or perhaps of being asked to do something too difficult.

'Where's the captain?'

'He go way, sir.'

The man's nervous excitement made Gore look at the soldiers who had seemed to him merely a row of uniforms and uniform faces. But there were no signs of panic. One man was dreaming, the next bored, even in the slackness of his belt and the set of his coat he looked bored; a third, conscious of the white man's eye, was striking out his chest and looking fierce. He was full of duty and courage, a good soldier. A fourth was simply a tired, stupid boy.

A fire was burning fifty yards away towards the river. Its broad glare fell on one wall of the schoolhouse, a half-finished structure near the Goshi road, and silhouetted a dozen soldiers carrying branches. Others were seen actively at work on a zariba at the side of the walls laying their branches, twigs outwards, towards the Birri bush.

'Have you got chop, sargy,' Marie asked briskly.

'No, sir.' To the sergeant all whites were sir.

She flew off at once to order the food. She seemed to dance over the ground.

Stoker's narrow figure with its thin waist and thin legs came striding out of the dark. Beside him Obai could be seen, loping easily along and waving his left hand as he poured out some eager speech.

Stoker had the appearance of an old tired man in a rejuvenated body. His face, deeply lined, was full of cynical impatience; his steps were brisk, his gestures and voice curt. He was twenty-eight but he looked and talked like fifty.

Both Stoker and Gore belonged to that select band of veterans who had seen four years in the trenches. Their attitude towards life was a mixture of pessimism and a devotion to the task in hand. It was as if they had said to themselves, The world is a hopeless mess but meanwhile one has to get up in the morning and shave and carry on with one's job and one may as well do the thing properly.

Stoker walked up to Gore and asked him in an ironical tone:

'Who's in charge here—Barebottom?' Barebottom was Obai, who stood close by with the proud look of a chief and his spear in his hand. As the white men glanced at him, he came forward, pointed towards the bush and made some emphatic statement.

A Birri corporal came forward to interpret. 'Dis man Birri chief, he say Birri come from over dar, at early morning.'

'Birri chief is he—what's he doing here then?'

This was an expression of natural doubt about Obai's character. Why wasn't he backing up his own side? Stoker and Gore both looked critically at the haughty young man. But the corporal took the question seriously. He asked Obai what he was doing here.

Obai answered with passion that he had come to fight for his friend Bewsher against a lot of bad Birri, stupid wicked people who were going to spoil the future and blacken the name of the great Birri people (the noble All-Birri).

'I don't quite like the look of you, Barebottom,' said Stoker in English. 'Too chatty by half. Here (to the corporal) don't say that. Say thank him very much and will he show these men where to get some branches for the zariba.'

The corporal translated. Obai, with a splendid gesture, gathered the soldiers together and led them away.

It was obvious that whatever Stoker and Gore thought of the

126

traitor he was extremely proud of himself. Obai, in fact, having
defied the patriotic fury of his own people for the sake of what he
thought right and honourable had a certain reason to be proud. But
it is only fair to say that patriotism even in a single village and even
in Obai's head was still an idea rather nebulous beside the solid
traditions of friendship and the obvious expedience of policy.

'You be careful of that chap, Sergeant. He's probably a spy.'

'Yes, sir.'

He turned to Gore. 'You realize this mission is about a mile
round. The fool that planned it hadn't much idea of how it was
going to be defended.'

Gore fell in at once with this essentially military attitude towards
the layout of missions. 'And that schoolhouse is masked by the
chapel group.'

'Quite so. I've got a party knocking loopholes in the chapel to
cover that side and what you call the schoolhouse is the only building in the place without a roof. I don't fancy being roasted out.'

'Don't let the missionaries catch anyone in the chapel, I should
keep out of sight from the mission house as much as possible.'

Stoker gave him a sharp look. 'Don't they know I'm here?'

'I hope not yet.'

'That's rather funny work, isn't it. Who exactly is giving me
orders? Barebottom has been jabbering about Bewsher.'

'Bewsher's here and it's just possible he might try to send you
back.'

'Aren't the Birri coming then?'

'My private opinion is——'

'That's no good to me—I want an order, preferably in writing.'

'I'm giving you an order now.'

'I'd prefer black and white, if you please, from your department.'

Gore, who knew that the man was a bundle of nerves, like himself, made no answer to this. Stoker suddenly walked off, shouting a
command to his men. They sat down and loosened their belts. The
little sergeant was seen darting away upon some errand. His legs
quivered with zeal.

But just as this lively figure was passing beyond the light of the
watch-fire, Marie was seen approaching into it at the head of half a
dozen carriers with pots and calabashes on their heads. At once she

turned aside towards the sergeant, the sergeant towards her. The two figures darted towards each other with gestures of an amusing likeness, two ardent spirits, and conferred with the most vigorous gestures. It was like a dramatic interlude by a couple of marionettes in an Italian tragedy. One expected them both to turn their arms inside out, go back at the knee, or suddenly retreat to the wings in one jump of twenty feet. In fact, their separation was as abrupt as their meeting. The sergeant, after pointing in a couple of seconds, first at the roof of the chapel then at the bush, then, turning right round, at the troops, and finally with his chin and whole body inclined upwards, at the sky, saluted with a jerk and flew into the darkness; Marie rushed back to the labourers and could be heard abusing them with great indignation for standing there and doing nothing.

'I suppose no one had the idea of sending out any pickets,' said Stoker's voice, causing Gore to turn round with unusual quickness. He was feeling apologetic to the man.

'I don't suppose so.'

'Unless Goshi had the sense. Nothing to do with me, of course. It's your funeral.'

'Are you putting out any pickets?'

'Naturally. They've been there since we came. They're lying low near those fires. I'm not going to have my men scuppered because you people can't agree among yourselves.'

'Suppose I go along to Goshi?' cried Marie who had been listening to this conversation literally on tiptoe.

Stoker was already returning to his men. He did not like women, and he ignored them if he could.

Marie's eagerness and martial excitement made Gore laugh, an extraordinary circumstance. It was a compliment that Marie did not assess at its full rate. She did not know the man's misanthropy or that her use of his Christian name, for the first time in that evening, had struck him as a piece of impudence, only to be excused in a foreigner.

It has been suggested that people like Gore marry foreigners simply on this account, that they allow them as foreigners to make a closer approach than the native, to pass under their guard in the disguise of guests who must not be snubbed. Certainly Gore, who had made no friends, male or female, in Nigeria during five years' service, already found himself, a little to his own surprise, on friendly terms with this American woman. Now he was laughing at her. And she, not knowing in the least what had tickled the queer Englishman with his peculiar sense of humour, smiled at him affectionately. She was pleased to see that he could smile.

'You like a little war,' he suggested.

'Of course not,' raising her eyebrows at him.

'Most people do—for the first time.'

'Don't you think somebody ought to go to Goshi?'

'I know you're not going because if Stoker's pickets didn't shoot you the Goshi watchmen would.'

'And what about Mr. Bewsher?'

'I think as we're in for it in any case we'll wait till the forts are Birri proof.'

'Well, I guess that is a real compromise—it suits everybody.'

'You don't approve then of the other——'

'I'm not going to quarrel with you, Harry. Not to-night. Come now,' she put her hand into his arm. 'Come and have that highball. If you know how I just prayed for you to come.'

'And the Imperial troops.'

'You can laff at me if you like, but you haven't been watching Mr. Bewsher play around with that lantern and the Dobsons leaving it to God. I won't say I like your politics, Harry, but thank goodness you're not a Christian.'

Gore, much surprised by this slander, murmured, 'Who told you that?'

But Marie answered in a reproachful tone, 'But it isn't a joke, Harry. After all, we do know the Facts,—and that Christianity has them all wrong. Of course they twist them to suit—but if you twist facts you get all twisted yourself. Don't you think so? Just look at these poor things here——'

Gore murmured some protest.

'I can see that you've forgotten what Christians are like,' said Marie. 'I'd forgotten myself. I'd no idea. When you see them on the mail boat in their waists and their sensible skirts and their stove-pipe trousers looking like everybody else you just forget that they're not like ordinary people in some school teaching kind of job. But you're wrong. Christians are different. They live in a different world, where everything is all out of shape like after an earthquake. John Dobson and Minnie and Dawl Dans are as different from you and me as Pavlov's dogs. They've got great slices of their brain clean taken out and the holes filled up with raspberry preserve.'

'Dobson seems to me pretty intelligent; isn't he a bit of a philosopher?'

'I do wish we could stop Mr. Bewsher coming here, Harry. Can't you use your influence? It's no good me saying anything. He just thinks everything I say is a kind of American joke. Do you know he's been here three times in the last three weeks? I can't understand it.'

'Bewsher reads the lessons in Church when he's at home.'

'Why yes, but he's not a Christian. He's what Frank Cottee calls Church. He goes to Church as a kind of political duty. He thinks of God as a kind of head of the religion and ethical department and the Holy Spirit is the district inspector going round the sub-offices checking up the staff work.'

She paused reflectively while Gore was trying to do justice to this statement.

'Of course he does have a sort of feeling for Jesus. I should think he feels that Jesus was a good sportsman the way he carried on with that bad team against the whole crowd and never made a grouch.'

'But that's not like Bewsher.'

'And isn't that a good religion? I just can't understand why you English are so ashamed of yourselves and your religion and your flag and everything about you. When I talk about the Union Jack Mr. Bewsher looks as if somebody had put a cold sponge down his back. What have you done to feel so shy? Nobody else does. Look at the French and the Italians——'

'You must ask Mr. Kipling.'

'If you would take Mr. Bewsher's real religion and write it down —don't you think it would be a very good kind of religion—the best kind of an ethical religion.'

'Ethical religion?'

'Yes, like the old Chinese or the Buddhists or the Greeks—a religion telling you how to behave—how to live—how to do things.'

'But doesn't Christianity do that?'

'But there's always that old God of Moses waving his arms at the bottom of it like an octopus in the tank—spitting ink into the nice clean water and grabbing the weak ones by the ankle. Religion ought to be as clear and bright as the air, a beautiful simple kind of thing—an art of life.'

'I'm afraid yours would be rather like the rules of the M.C.C.'

'What's that?'

'A cricket club.'

'Oh! but why should it be anything dull?' Gore began to laugh. But this time Marie did not laugh with him. She was disappointed and indignant at his lack of understanding. 'Why, that's the very thing it mustn't be.'

'My vicar at home tells me that religion is rejoicing—that's the essential part of it.'

'Oh! but that's beautiful. Oh yes. I like that very much. Have you ever seen Mr. Bewsher looking at his Birri?'

'That's where his real religion is.'

'And yours?' Marie looked at his long hollow face and could not help smiling. But at once she was afraid that he might be hurt, that he did not care to be laughed at. She pressed his arm and said in her most caressing voice, 'Irish or Scotch?'

# XII

I⟨T WAS ON THIS⟩ evening at Goshi that Bewsher hit upon his celebrated idea of turning the thunder god Ogun into the god or more strictly the Saint of Electricity and Vital Energy. According to Mrs. Dobson he produced it immediately after supper and it was then quite new—an inspiration. Dobson would not confirm this. He never told any tales about his guest.

But Mrs. Dobson can be trusted. Moreover, it is well known that Bewsher, when he had a sympathetic audience, a rare enough occasion except at Goshi, or perhaps with Marie, or sometimes on leave, when he happened to meet another pagan-man in a corner of the Spotted Dog or the Parson's Rest, always produced new ideas. Sympathy made him extremely fluent and excited. He also drank more when he talked with enthusiasm, and as he was normally a two-finger, two-drink man, half a dozen doubles gave much vivacity to his brain. But the idea was not really so absurd as people made out. Bewsher never proposed to import a dynamo into the Birri cult so that worshippers approaching the Holy of Holies should feel the presence of the god in the soles of their feet and the hair of their head. His incidental remark about a dynamo was a joke, one of those dry, hasty jokes which the man often threw into his stream of talk, especially when he was in good form, without sufficiently marking its humorous intention.

His real idea was that since the typical pagan worship was in itself a cult of life, and especially of this life, so that to pagans the life and passions of men extend through all being, animals, trees, even the sun and moon, the thunder god would be an excellent representative or saint of material energy, of all-pervading electrical force. As he said, Thunder is literally the sound or voice of that energy.

When Dobson objected that this peculiar religion had no ethics, he answered promptly that its ethics could be very easily provided. For instance, they would make it a sin to impair or damage the fullness of being. In fact, by that device any kind of ethic, the

132

Christian if necessary, could be injected. 'Ethics are the simplest thing in the world. Everybody knows what's good, and you can shove it into any religion. But the trouble is to get a good religion, a good sort of form, to shove it into. You can't invent a religion. It's got to grow—and here we have old Ogun well rooted in and quite enjoying the climate.'

Mrs. Dobson afterwards made gentle fun of these remarks, so it may be suspected that Dobson, in private, also found them amusing, but in fairness to Bewsher, who was in his way a kind of genius, it ought to be said that this first sketch was on his own statement a crude one, that he was never very good at explaining himself, and that at the best, he never intended to make Ogun into a god, but rather a saint. It was always his belief that religion for the pagans should be rich with ceremony and many saints, simply on the grounds that religion entered already into every aspect and moment of their lives, and that each aspect required a reminder or representative.

Thus he always wanted to preserve the sanctity of certain trees, so that they might stand, as now, everywhere by farms and paths, witnessing to the patience, the strength, the beauty, the long innocent lives of these companions to humble men, without any hint of the tortured theology which hangs about the roadside Calvary. But all this could be read in his assessment reports buried in pigeon-holes at Kaduna, in his articles known perhaps to three or four other enthusiasts of the same kidney. It is brought up here only to show that his Ogun project was not a wild fancy, but a suggestion, thrown out by a man who may have developed, like so many of the Nigerian pioneers, some odd notions, but who had nevertheless a consistent idea of what he was driving at, to preserve and develop the rich kind of local life which is the essence and the only justification of nationalism.

But the result of this happy conversation was that when he went out after supper for a stroll towards the bush, he was in the highest good humour. Gore, Marie and Stoker, who saw him approaching from a long way off with his pipe in his mouth and his thumbs stuck into his belt, perceived at once that they had nothing to fear.

Nevertheless Marie went to intercept him.

'What's this?' he asked. 'Is Dobson trying for the building record?'

'That's Captain Stoker. He's making a fort for us. He says it's quite impossible to defend the whole station with fifty men.'

'In that case he'd better go home again. Who on earth brought him to Goshi?'

'I wrote to Harry Gore that the Nok were coming and I'm very glad that I did, and I was very glad to see Captain Stoker, and you know quite well he can't go back to-night with all his men just worn out. I think it's just wonderful the way he's made that fort in an hour. And I think you'll not be rude to him, Zaki?'

The last sentence, with a sudden dramatic change of tone, was an imitation of a native offering up a petition.

Bewsher had already recovered from his first surprise. He began to laugh. 'Look at Gore there, saving the state. He looks like the second grave-digger playing super in *Macbeth*. (Gore was stalking gravely towards the fort with an immense leafy branch on his shoulder.) He's having the time of his life playing soldiers again.'

'Harry's just been splendid, and I shall be very disappointed in you, Monkey, if you don't appreciate what he's done to-night.'

'Oh, I do, I do. I'm not going to spoil their fun. It's a regular holiday for the lads. Field-Marshal Stoker has been missing the war ever since it stopped and Gore still dreams of the time when his King and country really needed him. The Heroes of Goshi. We must take their photographs in the morning. Hullo, what are you doing with that bath?'

This was addressed to a couple of carriers who were trotting towards the fort with a bath full of bedclothes, pillows, slippers and toilet boxes, swinging between them.

They stopped now with looks of alarm. One of them began to stammer in Hausa that the woman's boy had told him to take the judge's loads to the fort.

'I told Henry to move you into the fort,' said Marie. 'But he seems to have put somebody else on the job. I don't know what's wrong with Henry to-night unless he's drunk again.' Marie, who had given instructions that the loads were to be carried over in the most private and discreet manner, was greatly irritated against Henry. Now partly to break off the subject with Bewsher, partly in annoyance, she began to call for the boy.

'He's gone to the mosallachi (chapel),' said one of the labourers.

'You can just take that bath to where you found it,' said Bewsher in Hausa, and in English, 'Captain Stoker is a nice man. I like him in his brass buttons. But I never did fancy the song of the sentry by night. I'd rather get some sleep.'

Marie began to argue with him. She pointed out that now his bed was actually in the fort he might as well sleep there. She was sure that Captain Stoker wouldn't allow the sentries to call out to each other or rattle their rifles.

In the middle of this the carriers gave a shout and the whole party saw a broad glow spread over the ground like a sunrise. They turned round and there was the chapel roof on fire. The flames had already run along the ridge and made a comb of flames from one end of it to the other.

Stoker gave an order to his men and ran towards the mission house. As he passed Bewsher and Marie he shouted at them: Get into the fort quick! The soldiers could be seen already taking position behind the zariba and the click of their bolts as they loaded caused Bewsher to jump. He ran a few steps towards them holding up his hand and bawled, 'No shooting! Till you get the word,' turned round then and ran towards the fire. Marie flew after him calling to the Dobsons. As they reached the corner of the chapel, which lighted up the plain for a quarter of a mile they could see at a distance of three or four hundred yards a solid black mass like a low cloud rolling rapidly over the ground towards them. The moment the three whites appeared in the light a tremendous yell went up from this cloud which now in the mounting flames could be distinguished as being made up of a great number of charging warriors. The fire glittered on their spears. Marie was turning to run back to the fort when she saw, to her astonishment and horror, Bewsher set out at full speed towards the Birri, holding out his arms like a man trying to turn a flock of sheep, and shouting at the top of his voice expostulations in the strongest language. Beside him Obai galloped uttering a war-yell and poising his spear. And from the other end of the burning house Gore suddenly appeared, carrying a large stick, and went sprinting after his D.O. with an agility quite unexpected and rather comical in a man of his figure.

Marie herself began to run in the same direction, crying 'Come back.' The Birri were advancing so quickly that Bewsher, also running at his best speed, was among them in thirty seconds. Marie

135

and Gore saw him break the front row and fall. The Birri went over him like a wave.

Gore was swearing furiously at the enemy, threatening what he would do to them if they killed Bewsher. But his strongest impression was the folly of the whole proceeding. 'Damn it,' he thought, 'I've seen a lot of funny things in my time but this takes the cake. However, if Monkey chooses to play the bloody ass I can't exactly stand out.'

But he had barely time to excuse himself in this manner for an undignified and idiotic performance before he found himself, still mechanically uttering horrible threats and curses, among the Birri, who now proved not the solid army seen from the station but a mob loosely spread over the ground. He saw them all round him, but none very close, shouting and apparently even arguing among themselves with every expression from enjoyment to ferocity. He saw Bewsher about ten yards away beating somebody with the shaft of a broken spear, and he saw Marie, to his great surprise, rushing towards Bewsher. He was impressed by her expression of horror and amazement. She looked as though the Birri attack had been the last thing she expected.

But all this was like a snapshot taken by the light of the burning roof between his discovery that he was not dead yet and that the Birri did not appear inclined to kill him, and the terrific blow which now fell on the top of his head and seemed to drive him into the ground.

Stoker's men in the chapel had not been able to shoot because the three whites were in front of them. Stoker came running from the other side and fired several shots with his pistol. Meanwhile the Goshi Birri had already bolted, fighting their way through their allies, and the Nok themselves were wavering. The treachery of Goshi, the sudden appearance of Obai on the other side, Bewsher's indignation were too much for their patience. They ran or rather walked off in disgust, quarrelling violently among themselves. The whole expedition, they said, had not been at all what they expected.

The only casualties left on the ground were six wounded, of whom Obai had his belly split open. He appeared to be dying. But Dorothy Dans was not going to allow anybody to die in her hospital without a considerable argument. She had already rolled up her sleeves to

136

make a job of Obai, a good long job with plenty of night calls, such as she loved.

Gore, staggering about with a large bump and a splitting head-ache was not supposed to be a casualty. He was looking vaguely for a quiet corner in which to sit down and possibly to be sick. But quiet corners were scarce. In one room Mrs. Dobson was washing a new-born baby among a large crowd of shrieking children; in another Stoker was holding a kind of preliminary court-martial on the sergeant. Why had he taken orders from a civilian to hold his fire? In the third, twenty refugees and the three prospectors were all talking at once.

The prospectors had just arrived. Jukes in field boots, cartridge belt and white helmet still looked like a professor. The contrast between his benevolent spectacles and his annoyance at missing a shot at the Birri was all the more striking. He was still hoping for a shot.

'Now's the time, when they're on the run,' he said.

'That's 'ow they missed the chance in Duchi—waited too long.' Allday in a huge Stetson looked the typical forty-niner.

'I don't know about that,' said Jukes. 'They did the Duchi job properly with two companies and a gun, and Birri might turn out a tough proposition.'

'They can't let 'em off this time, whatever happens,' said Cottee.

'No, I think this settles it.'

Gore had found a soft bundle of rags in a dark corner behind the table and the jugs. Another attraction was an enamelled basin left by some native housemistress. If this peculiar sensation in his stomach did take a definite turn—— But meanwhile his head was really very troublesome. Also he felt as if he was perpetually cross-eyed.

'It is lucky for us, I suppose,' Cottee was saying in the tone of one who would prefer justice and logic.

'I believe you.'

'The upper Elema——'

'It's the 'ighlands where we'll want to make for.'

And then Bewsher came rolling in, dropped heavily into a chair, lit his pipe, stretched out his legs, stuck his thumbs into his belt and said, 'I'm sorry about this business. I'm afraid it's put the kybosh on your arrangements.'

137

Bewsher, of course, was in the highest spirits. He had every reason to be so. It is generally agreed that the attack on the mission saved Bewsher from being removed, more or less politely, from the service; and though no doubt he himself never for a moment supposed that these brass hats whom he despised so profoundly would have the nerve to drive him, he had certainly begun to feel a little uneasiness about the position. He had even asked Gore, it was true only in a postscript to a demand for another case of whisky, whether there was anything in the ordinances and especially the Native Lands ordinance which could 'be dug up for a bit of legal stuffing if high-hats turn nasty.'

But after the attack he was of course in a strong position. His letter to Alabaster, composed and dispatched that same evening, ran in his best style.

*D.O. Alo Div. to Residt., Kunama Prov.*

*Sir,*

*Your 19.46 of the 17th ult., stating that Birri was now in a state of settled tranquillity was duly received in Paré bush camp on the 27th. The contents were immediately noted, for the information of all parties concerned including chiefs.*

*2. I have to report that the Nok tribe, having fought a battle with Kifi on the 24th inst. with upwards of twenty casualties, attacked village on the 25th and were fortunately beaten off.*

*3. The same or another party raided Goshi mission this evening, eviscerated a Christian native, and burnt the chapel. I regret to say that Mr. A. D. O. Gore, whose admirable conduct on this critical occasion will be the subject of a separate report, was slightly injured and chief Obai of Nok, very dangerously wounded, in a successful attempt to prevent the enemy's charge.*

*4. Whether these events can be considered favourable to the new policy and the security of Birri for wandering parties of prospectors depends upon the construction placed upon them. At present the indications appear slightly adverse.*

*I have the honour to remain sir,*

*Your obedient servant,*

*E. B. Bewsher,*

*D.O. Alo*

And to the prospectors he showed his hand at once. When Jukes asked him why the burning of Goshi mission should alter their arrangements to visit Lower Nok, he answered with a great appearance of surprise, 'My dear Mr. Jukes—Birri isn't safe anywhere, and Nok is probably the unsafest place in all Birri.'

Jukes said that in that case it was a job for the soldiers and the sooner they got on to it the better.

'Oh—soldiers,' said Bewsher whose exuberance of joy was hardly restrained by his desire to be polite. 'That's a big question. War costs a lot of money.'

It was Cottee who showed the most indignation. Did Bewsher really expect them to stand any more of this nonsense?

He turned red and even spluttered. No trace was left of the nonchalant gentleman adventurer. Possibly he surprised himself. But the truth was that he was in a peculiar and novel position where any man can be excused for novel behaviour. The prospectors had already come to the natural conclusion that war had started and that all Birri would soon be opened to them; that was to say, the Paré highlands which was believed to be the richest mineral area in the country. No one had been to see it, and the story was very credible.

But for more than three hours Cottee had been thinking like a very rich man, not in terms of a big car and a month's razzle-dazzle, but deer forests, yachts, a cut-away with the Pytchley. Cottee argued like Jukes that either the new sections of Birri were open or they were not open, and since in fact they were open it was the Government's business to secure the King's peace within their borders.

Bewsher listened to him politely, and answered, 'The fact is that you fellows owe me a vote of thanks for stopping you from getting your throats cut. That is, if you haven't insured each other's lives.'

'I don't know exactly what you mean by that,' said Jukes, in a tone almost rude; 'as far as I know there has been nothing to prevent us from using our licences in Nok district during the last six weeks but your illegal action in preventing us. And I'll take the Governor's opinion on that before to-morrow night.'

Gore was now quite sure that he needed to be sick, but he knew also that he couldn't afford the effort. His head wouldn't stand it. As for these pig-headed fools, he did not give one damn for the whole lot of them. Let them smash each other up and Birri too.

Bewsher was on his feet bursting with delight—'And give my

respects to the Duke of Plaza Toro at the same time.' He walked to the door. Gore also came staggering to the door and called his name.

'Hullo, Gore, where've you been? I thought you were in bed?'

'Sir, about the patrol!'

'There's not going to be a patrol.'

'No, but if the Resident puts a company at Nok.'

'He'd have a war on his hands in ten minutes.'

'Why, yes, but—we want to avoid that——'

'Hadn't you better stick to your own end of the job?'

Bewsher rolled off in a fury. The truth was of course that Alabaster had already proposed several times to station the Alo company at Nok. It was a favourite scheme of his.

Gore returned into the room. His aspect startled Jukes even in his irritation and he dragged forward a chair.

'Thanks very much, but I'm just going through—sorry you missed the fun.'

'It hasn't started yet,' said Cottee.

'Oh! I don't think there'll be any developments. The Resident will avoid a patrol if he possibly can.'

Allday uttered a kind of snort and Cottee exclaimed that they were not going to be wangled. 'It's nothing to do with us whether you let the Birri burn missions or not—but we've got definite legal rights and you can't do us out of them.'

'On the other hand, we can't let you get yourselves murdered.'

'That's our business, Gore, I should think.'

But Jukes already saw the drift of Gore's casual remarks. 'You think that the whole district might be closed up again.'

'It *is* on the cards, don't you think—if the Resident won't allow a patrol. And wars cost a lot of money.'

'Now then, Gore, if you think you're going to diddle us out of that Nok claim——'

But Jukes was beginning to look thoughtful and Allday at once ceased to utter sounds of contempt and defiance. Gore produced another ghastly smile and tried at the same time to prevent his left leg from jumping about all by itself. He succeeded in looking like a head waiter raised from the dead after several weeks. 'It's awfully bad luck on you people,' he said, 'and of course the position is rather

140

complicated.' He turned towards Cottee, the most obstinate and tenacious of the opposition: 'with so much to say on both sides.'

At this moment Bewsher and Marie came in from the hospital. Marie looked exhausted, hollow-cheeked. Her eyes were like a hare's. She said to the general public, who knew of course nothing about Obai, 'He's conscious all the time. But he's never given one groan. It would make you cry to see the poor lad setting his teeth——'

Bewsher was asking if anybody had seen the boy stabbed, for if he died, by Christ, he'd like to hang somebody for it. 'Gore there, you were on the spot——'

Gore was still muttering something about the extreme difficulty of a position in which both sides were in the right, but Jukes had already walked off and Cottee, the moment Marie appeared, made a kind of plunge in her direction and was already exclaiming how delightful it was to see her again, and what a damn good thing that those brutes hadn't scuppered her and what a first-class article that was of hers about the Paré juju.

'Yes,' said Gore to Bewsher, 'I beg your pardon—I'm awfully sorry, but I don't quite——'

But just then his skull finally burst into small pieces and he fell down dead.

However, after some undetermined period, he found himself alive again, though extremely tired, on Mrs. Dobson's bed. Marie was putting a cold compress on his head and Cottee was holding the basin.

'But, Marie, it's not the money, it's the principle of the thing.'

'And interest at twenty per cent.'

'Well, if you won't believe me.' His tone was aggrieved. It was obvious that for the moment he had forgotten all about his rich hopes of Paré. 'But it's simply because you're prejudiced——'

'I guess that's the trouble with all of us,' said Marie in a tired voice, and then detecting Gore's wakefulness she stooped over him and said, 'Why, Harry, if you're still alive after Doll's brandy, you're going to live a long time. Frank, you might go and get some more of the poison.'

Cottee disappeared, Gore murmured the usual apology required by the circumstances.

141

'You may well be sorry. You're the most unpopular man in Alo at this minute. The compromise has gone through.'

Gore said nothing to this.

'And Mr. Bewsher says that if they put soldiers in Nok he'll resign.'

Gore could not say how much he approved this suggestion. He murmured only that Bewsher wouldn't enjoy life very much without his Birri.

'What I'm beginning to wonder is how much of it he's going to enjoy with his Birri.'

# XIII

THE CASUALTIES OF THE Goshi war were all light or lucky.
Gore was found to have concussion and the doctors sent him home.
Obai at Lokoja hospital made a surprising recovery from peritonitis.
The four other Birri wounded, of whom one was Uli, were on their
feet in a week. Three of them though still with large open wounds
requiring daily treatment at once vanished into the forest. But Uli
whose wound was almost healed did not want to go at all.

'You can't stay here,' said Miss Dans.

'But if I go, dey kill me dere. Dem juju fit to kill me.'

'It's that juju, is it?'

'Same man who cut me for belly for war go kill me.'

It was Uli's conviction that some emissary of the juju, perhaps a
spirit, had given him his wound.

'Then you'd better be a Christian, Uli,' said Miss Dans, using
exactly the same tone with which she was accustomed to tell him to
turn over or keep his legs flat.

'I tink so, Missy. I like that too much.'

Miss Dans announced her convert at breakfast, and Uli sat down
for instruction that same day. In a week he was not only a useful
member of the choir but he seemed to understand some of the
melodious noises that rolled out of his large mouth. But what was
more important, he was assiduous at his prayers, his lessons; there
was no doubt of his sincere devotion to Christ.

Uli turned out one of the star pupils. For Goshi, like other new-
established stations, had suffered by an influx of scallywags and
parasites; and among the others was a pretty large proportion of
blockheads, African blockheads of the impenetrable type.

'I've great hopes of Uli,' Dobson confessed. 'I believe he'll turn
into one of the most useful pupils we have—certainly when we get
forward to Nok. He really was interested in the reading this morning, his questions afterwards showed that he had taken in every
word.'

And Uli, walking gravely through the compound in his clean shorts and white shirt, was saying to himself, 'According to your faith be it unto you.'

This was a valuable form of words for the curing of evil spirits, and according to Dobson, even bad temper. He memorized them with care to add to his repertory of the Christian spells. For Uli desired power.

In fact to Uli all religion was power. He could not conceive of any other reason why a man should study, learn, stint himself and waste time on chapel going, except to make himself stronger or safer in this mysterious and dangerous world.

Thus when Dobson told him, this conduct is wrong and this is right, he understood the lesson like any child at home. This conduct will pay and this other will get you into trouble.

Atua was waiting for him in his hut. Atua was a Birri girl converted six months before when she had run away to avoid a trial for adultery. She was hospital cleaner, and it was in hospital that she had met Uli. As soon as Uli saw her he began to laugh. But Atua was jigging with impatience. She attacked him before he was well within the door.

Uli was not yet accustomed to these forward manners in women and he protested loudly, 'What are you doing?'

He tried to keep the girl away while he wrapped up his Bible in his silk handkerchief. But he was never a very good match for that enterprising young woman, and when as now he had only one hand and his elbows with which to defend his person, he was not likely to be successful. Moreover he was obliged as she knew to put the book into the box at all costs because it must not be present during the next proceedings. The book was the biggest juju of the whites, and it was very dangerous to insult it or offend it in any way. Fortunately it could not see through tin.

'Atua, Atua!' he squealed, laughing and struggling. Atua said nothing but continued her operations with merciless determination and deft fingers. As the box lid dropped upon the Bible her heels tripped him. They rolled on the floor breathless.

What a girl she was. What tricks she knew. These Christian women were like leopards. They were fiercer even than the Hausas. He wished Enuké, that ignorant prude, could see him now.

For Uli the white man's village was a new kind of universe. Even

144

the sky was new, wide and open, free like the life. These Christians at Goshi had no cares in the world, no fear of enemies and no dread of famine. When they were not eating, drinking, singing and telling stories they were making love or talking about it.

Often at night, when he played with Atua, he roared with laughter in the delights of this new kind of life, the free life which had proved even better than Henry had described it. When he was tired of playing there was always something to tell. Atua had heard a fine piece of scandal in the sewing class, and Uli related with disgust some story of the ignorance and superstition of the Nok, how Enuké had refused him, how Birri men denied themselves. He always told stories of Birri, and even when he was alone on the mission fields he would make a gesture of contempt towards the forest and say, 'Fool people.'

# XIV

Gore was on leave and sick leave for seven months of which he spent several fishing and much of the rest in armchairs with a book. He avoided members of his own service, and indeed anybody who might talk to him about political affairs, with a great deal of success. His only failure was with the newspapers. He had the newspaper vice. Thus once a day at least he was reminded of the instability of all peace and comfort, even in this little interval of his holiday.

For a few minutes each morning he felt the distress of an intelligent cabin boy who finds himself in a ship with a drunken crew, empty bunkers, rocks all round. But the knowledge that he personally could not do anything in this case soon restored his tranquillity.

Of Nigerian news he would have known nothing without Marie's letters. He had not asked her to write and he did not write to her. But Marie's peculiar doctrines of friendship made her one of those perfect correspondents who do not expect to be answered.

Her first letter was from Alo at the end of January, about three weeks after the Goshi affair.

*My dear Harry,*

*I hope your headaches are better. If they don't get better, you must try science. I don't mean be a scientist because no one could believe in the hokum of it, but I do know several people cured of migraines by absent treatment. This is a fact and after all you can't get over facts. You'll be glad to hear that Mr. Bewsher is resigning. A new Gazette notice opening Nok district came out last week and he said he would resign if it was published.*

*I don't know if you'll be glad to hear another piece of news, that Mr. Bewsher has asked me to marry him and I intend to do so. This has made me very happy because I didn't know he felt*

146

*that way. But perhaps you don't realize how it feels to be a woman when she gets a proposal from someone that really counts. (This made Gore smile.) We are going to be married at Kaduna in March and then we shall come straight away to England. I shall be sorry to leave Nigeria and especially Birri, but I feel it would be terrible for Mr. Bewsher to stay here and see all his work in Birri ruined. Also it would be very dangerous, as the Birri may blame him for the new policy and we all think there is bound to be fighting.*

*I hope you will still be in England when we come home, as I have looked forward very much to seeing you again, my dear Harry, and you can believe that I am always and always,*

*Your affectionate,*
*Marie*

Two months later she sent him a note.

*Dear Harry,*

*I was married yesterday and we are going to catch the boat train in ten minutes. Thank you a thousand times for your wire. It was dear in every sense. If all my friends panned out at tenpence a word I should be the richest woman in the world as well as the happiest. Don't forget that our London address is at Colonel G. S. Bewsher, 74 Pelham Place, Kensington. Come and see me and I will find a wife for you. You must get married. It is the latest fashion and one of the nicest for a long time.*

*Your very affectionate,*
*Marie B.*

Enclosed in this, folded crookedly and scrawled in pencil, 'For your information,' was a circular from a London finance company introducing Nok Development Company which proposed to offer Messrs. A. F. Cottee and P. P. Kemfrey Jukes £10,000 in cash and 10,000 ordinary shares of one pound each fully paid for their mining and timber rights in this rich area. Profits from tin, antimony, and mahogany were estimated conservatively for the first year at £20,000 net on the capital of £40,000, but they would be immensely increased on the opening up of the whole area.

The note in Marie's hand was followed by two exclamation marks set down with passionate energy, but Gore was rather pleased than otherwise to know that Jukes and Cottee were going to make a fortune. Now that Bewsher was safely out of Birri with his throat and his limbs intact he saw no objection to their activities.

From a soldier in the Incubator he had a comic account of the wedding. Bewsher, of course, was fair game for the humorist because he was a character of many years' standing. It appeared that Marie had also become a character. It was the thing to tell funny stories about them both and the marriage gave opportunities to the dullest. Men of the strictest honesty and simplicity of mind, who never dreamt of telling lies, embroidered yarns about Bewsher and Marie just as they would have repeated jokes from *Punch* or old chestnuts about famous characters like Rusty Buckle and Bugle Thompson. It was said that they had arrived at Headquarters accompanied by stark naked Birri carrying phallic emblems. That they had been married according to the Birri rite after a pagan dance lasting all night. That Marie, in accordance with her free love principles, had invited all her previous lovers to the wedding lunch and assured them of her continued favours. That she had been married in the celebrated pyjamas of red flannel.

Cottee, whom Gore, on his way back to duty, met in the boat train, repeated all these stories and declared them true. He had been at the wedding. But the naked Birri with phallic emblems were reduced to one man in a loin cloth carrying a bundle, which was in fact wooden phalli of all sizes, intended for presentation to some American museum. There was a dance by the Birri carriers at which Bewsher and Marie had been present, but they had not been drunk, or not very much so, and they had certainly not taken off their clothes and joined in the orgy. Marie had in fact entertained a good many bachelors including of course Cottee himself, and assured them all individually that she was not going to let marriage affect her friendships, that she loved them all even more than before, and would never forget a single one of them, and it was true that the Birri wedding rites had been carried out. But there had also been a wedding by licence in the Provincial office, and the other ceremony had been a joke played by Cottee himself and two or three more who took the bride home with drums and horns. 'In fact, it was a great show. The races were on and the whole place was crowded. I should think there were about sixty people at the lunch, and I shouldn't like to say what it cost Bewsher in drinks. Of course he was in his element, smiling like a Ho-ti and sending round the bottle. As for Marie she looked like death, with her eyes starting out of her head and her face as white as paper. But that's the way she always looks when she's really happy—enjoying what she calls a strawng feeling. At one time in fact I thought it was going to be too strawng for her. An ass of a policeman and some of the soldiers shouted out Speech—speech. But she spoke quite well and it was only when it was all over that I saw how shaky she was.'

'Did they go straight home?'

'Good God, no. Straight back to Birri.'

Gore showed no surprise. He murmured apologetically that he had heard something about a resignation.

'Quite so,' said Cottee. 'But you didn't think it very likely, did you. The only people who ever believed in Bewsher's resigning were himself and poor Marie—and I'm not sure about Bewsher. He may have written the letter but he certainly didn't let it go. All I know is that the honeymoon was all arranged, they were going to Madeira—when something or other happened in Birri—some row about the juju, and the Bewshers were off to Alo the same night. I must admit that Monkey tried to go alone and didn't mean to stay. He said he'd settle the whole thing in a week. But Marie wouldn't let him out of her sight for a single hour and they've been there ever since.'

'How is she?'

'I've not seen her for two months. I've hardly been out of the train these last six weeks—trying to get these mining people to pull together a bit. What a life.'

In fact, things were going badly with Cottee. The Elema flotation had failed and the remodelled company with half the capital was facing default on its debentures. The labourers had gone to harvest and Jukes was ill.

Cottee was yellow and fat. He was one of those men who fatten in the tropics. He looked forty-five at least and in tone and expression he had changed still more greatly from the smart young business man of six or eight months before. He did not seem to triumph over Nigeria, over Gore. He was mellow, thoughtful; the philosopher who would rather talk to you about life than livelihood.

149

He could not say what had gone wrong with the labour at the Elema; he was quite vague and uninterested about all commercial projects; but he was full of an evening spent with the Manders at Oyo. Mander had been up at Univ—he was probably the only man in Nigeria who had ever heard of Paul Nash or Gilbert Spencer. But of course Gore had met the man at Kunama last tour. He'd like Mrs. Mander—not exactly pretty perhaps, but she was keen about the things that really mattered. That was so refreshing. It had done him as much good as a month's leave to meet someone who actually bought poetry—modern poetry. She had really and truly fallen for Marie at the time of the wedding. And that was a high tribute, because Marie was anything but a highbrow, poor dear, and neither was she public school. Anything but. To the ordinary official's wife she was simply a pain.

'I wonder how she's standing it.'

'Did it give you a shock, the marriage? It did me.'

'It seemed rather a suitable thing.'

'Suitable? Bewsher the toughest old pagan and rationalist you could find and Marie the real Boston mystic, direct in descent from Emerson and Thoreau. By the way, has she been talking to you about Christian Science?'

'No,' Gore lied. He did not want Cottee to know that Marie had been writing to him. He opened his book.

'Didn't she?' Cottee looked at him suspiciously. 'All the same, I shouldn't be surprised if they caught her. Now that the nature god is a bit exploded and Birri hasn't turned out to be the Kingdom of Heaven. She certainly inclined that way when Monkey had a funny pain for a day or two in the bush and she thought he was poisoned.'

'What?'

'Oh! it was probably a dirty cooking-pot. She leaves things to Henry—but the point was that she was talking about the power of faith for the next week. She seemed to think that Monkey had got over strophanthus simply by calling it colic. And when some joker put an arrow through the nuptial mosquito net, she talked as if an arrow or two in the ribs wouldn't matter to the man. His faith would make him whole—of course—she didn't call it faith. She called it guts. But she meant faith.'

150

What Gore wanted to know was how this marriage had turned out. Was the woman happy? or as the question formed itself in his mind, was she, in Cottee's view, being treated properly? But he found it difficult to invent a suitable approach to such a delicate question, and meanwhile Cottee had darted off in pursuit of his favourite metaphysical hare. Marie, he said, was a perfect example of your inner light mystic as produced so freely by all the Protestant nations, especially in times of trouble. People who despaired of the existing state of things and wanted to find a short cut to a new one—and found it by revelation. 'You saw those Birri articles——'

'Have you ever heard her on the subject of missionaries— especially the Protestant and Puritan variety?'

'Mysticism isn't a religion, it's a temperament—a very powerful kind of temperament. Hence these tears. Because mystics need the very best religion to keep them from making the worst sort of trouble. They have such terrific force of character—look at Rousseau or Gandhi?'

Gore suddenly poked his head and several feet of his body into the corridor to call a train boy. He was always bored with Cottee on the subject of religion; not because Cottee did not know a great deal more about it than himself but because he was not religious. He had no experience of religion and so he did not really know anything about it and his words though they might be true had no importance or interest.

Not that Cottee wasn't sincere. He was always sincere in every one of his moods and wobbles. His flexibility combined with scholarship and reading made it easy for him always to be not only himself but at home with himself. He carried the furniture of two or three selves. But he wasn't settled yet and he had never been settled long enough to belong anywhere, to acquire a more than temporary and verbal significance. Perhaps he would settle someday, or, to put it into his own words, get involved. No doubt he would then quickly become a notable person, himself an experience; but at present he was only conversation.

'And the trouble is,' he murmured in his new rôle of middle-aged philosopher, detached equally from the fluctuations of tin and the vicissitudes of morality, 'that they get such poor ones nowadays.

Your young St. Francises have nothing to fill out their visions but the theory of surplus value or equal pay for equal work.'

Gore had stopped a boy. He twisted his long neck over his shoulder and asked, 'Would you like a beer?'

'That's very kind of you.'

'Two beers, please, and don't forget the ice.'

'And that's the greatest and Greekest tragedy in the history of this unhappy world.'

'Greekest?'

'That when a civilization or an old palace gets a bit out of repair or knocked about in an earthquake the people who live in it, just because they've been so comfortable and grand, have forgotten all about practical bricklaying; and the inspired odd job-man who rushes in to clean up the mess, just because he *is* a practical enthusiast, doesn't give a damn for architecture or any of those frills. Practical enthusiasts never do. They're too energetic and original and self-reliant. They go by common sense—that's to say they consult the inner light about the drains. So the poor old family find themselves making a new start in a shack with a bad smell and no bathroom—much less proportion—some tin tabernacle or Soviet Utopia.'

'Aren't you rather mixed?'

'Well, you ought to know what I mean. I suppose you'll agree that the principles of building are always the same—just as God is always the same. What Marie calls Beudy, truth and goodness are always the same. But religions and nations can be as different as cathedrals and pigsties and a long line of experienced saints and social artists working in what you might call the same school of architecture usually end by producing something rather fine and rich.'

'Here's your drink.'

'And the trouble is that we all depend on rather elaborate constructions of tradition and poetry and art and religion for our possibilities of feeling—the quality of our feelings about things, the quality of our lives—and when the old systems crash we have to start again with an extremely low quality—raw first principles like cubism and functionalism—golly, the word's enough—and communism which actually wants to go back to the prehuman era of the pack and the herd in politics and abolish religion altogether—I suppose they'll have to begin with animal religion too—mascots, favourite lamp-posts, turning three times round before you lie down and howling at the moon: or perhaps with luck they'll hit the next stage, Mah-rie's stage, what you might call neolithic.'

'Your drink's getting warm.'

'I like it warm. I want to preserve my digestion for one or two really decent meals before I die. And the luck must turn some day. What were you talking about before I interrupted you so rudely?'

'Earthquakes.'

'Exactly—and when you come to people like Mah-rie with the strongest kind of religious instincts and no theology you can expect the worst. Imagine the demons and wishfulfilment djinns that arise from their subconscious, shouting "Do what you like and all will be well. Follow your lusts and they will make you whole"—all the modern gospel. The complete nature god. The whole Shelleyan formula. Down with all creeds. Bring in the golden age. Free love and no more clothes.'

'Hardly the doctrine of a puritan mystic.'

'What about the anabaptists? Of course Marie herself thinks that she was being highly original when she offered herself to a stockbroker in a sleeping-car and came to Birri and joined the nudists.'

'What do you mean?'

'Well, you know that she used to bathe in the Elema before the whole village.'

Gore answered curtly that he hadn't heard that yarn, but it struck him as rather stupider even than the others.

Cottee gazed at him with surprise and joy. 'Oh! but it's a fact. When we set up camp in Lower Nok we found that everybody knew about it.'

'An old chestnut. They told the same story about that doctor's wife—what was her name——'

'But, my dear chap,' Cottee was beaming, 'don't you understand that it's just exactly what she would do—as a religious act—it's so perfectly in character—so perfectly period.'

'There was that other story about the pink pyjamas.'

'But don't you see—as a martyr to the faith—even if she blushed all over—as I daresay she did.'

153

But this picture was so offensive to Gore that it made him angry. For the first time in his life Cottee saw the man in a rage. He turned red and glared. 'No doubt they peeped—the Birri would.'

'But that's stupid. Don't you understand that it was a public ceremony—a rite?'

'Which nobody ever heard of before—not even Bewsher.'

'Oh! the husband is the last. Do you think he'd mind? Yes, I suppose he would. But he's bound to get some shocks, as I said; the interesting question is what kind of shocks—and how he'll take them.'

There was a pause. Cottee eyed his friend thoughtfully, and then tried again. 'How long do you think it will last?'

'Did you say there was trouble in Birri?'

'Are you jealous?'

'Good Lord no.' Gore, still a trifle pink, raised his arched brows as high as they would go and caused his pale blue eyes to protrude in an expression which asked, 'What does the ass mean?' Then he reached for his book.

'Because I am,' said Cottee. 'Very much so. The woman's simply wasted.'

'But if it's not going to last—you can hope.'

'Oh! it will last for her. She thinks him the greatest man on earth—that bandy-legged bush-whacker. She sits there looking at him as if she could eat him. It's the real thing. The grand passion. Isn't it annoying to think that it would have been just the same if you or I had been the happy man?'

'H'm.' Gore opened his book. 'Have they really been shooting at Bewsher?'

Cottee politely agreed to change the subject and asked if shooting at Bewsher were a novelty.

'They haven't done it since before the war.'

'Then I suppose things are warming up—certainly Jukes is worried. He's been asking me to get him some ex-soldiers who understand how to shoot—but perhaps I oughtn't to tell you that.'

'Not if you're smuggling in rifles for them.'

'Good Lord, no—the idea was that they'd use our spares—my Mannlicher and Jukes' Mauser pistol.'

Gore raised his book and began to read. His gestures were a trifle self-conscious. He was still feeling a little surprise and embarrass-

154

ment on account of that fit of indignation which, as he now saw, might have given a false idea. Cottee put on a pair of horn-rims and opened his writing-case. But he continued every now and then to look at his friend with a particular smile; especially when Gore was at the top of a page and might see the smile. It was not, however, that he wanted to embarrass him further but only to show his penetration, his mellow sagacity.

## XV

THE TROUBLE IN BIRRI was due simply to the first arrival of the miners at Lower Nok. Bewsher settled it quickly because the Goshi affair had given him a high prestige. He fined Nok four hundred loads of yam and made the warriors put a new roof on the chapel; so that they respected his power. But they knew also that he was a rascal and even the old chiefs did not trust him any longer. They blamed him for all the misfortunes of the time, not only for the loss of Goshi and Lower Nok but the collapse of their own authority, of all decency and good behaviour. Old white-headed men, meeting night after night, not at the judgment tree but in some secluded hut where none of the youngsters would look for them, uttered groans of distress.

'What next—we'll all be destroyed.'

'It's Obai and Bewsher and Fish.'

'And that Henry—he's the worst.'

'These conceited young fools will get themselves into fine trouble and serve them right.'

'But unluckily their trouble is our trouble, for they are our sons.'

It was well known that Henry had assisted Fish and Uli to plan the mission attack; that he had fired the roof which guided the charge upon a line covered from the soldiers' guns.

Some wished to denounce him to Bewsher. But again this would have risked a war. For Henry was more popular with the young Birri even than the Fish, hero of Goshi, who had split Gore's head with his own club; and when he came to the village the chiefs themselves ran to salute him.

'Lord Henry, how good that you are come. What do you want? Only ask.' And the cook, smiling down upon them, gave his orders like a master, genial but knowing what was due. So many chickens for his mistress, who was coming that night, so many for himself, so many yams, so much sweet potatoes, cornflour and tobacco. Also he desired a girl for the next three nights, but let her be clean and fat. He would pay her well with beads and kerosene.

'Master,' they cried, 'all shall be done—and it is quite unnecessary to pay us anything. Only give us your favourable word with your noble lady that she may intercede for us with Bewsher.'

'Trust me,' said Henry laughing. 'You'll be all right as long as I'm all right,' and he strolled off with his new English hat over his left ear, his silver-mounted walking-stick twirling in his hand. He did not only act like a master but he looked like a master.

Henry, in fact, was acquiring steadiness and manner as he acquired cash. He had now fifteen pounds put away and felt like a man to whom fifteen pounds' worth of honour is due. He no longer got drunk every day and played the buffoon, for such conduct is unfitting to a man of distinction.

But as with civilized man everywhere in the world of cash values, his good nature, his sympathies had increased with prosperity and he was everybody's friend. As he made his way towards the river bank, the usual rendezvous of the ninth and seventh class, he was stopped every few yards by a shout of greeting from the little groups of men or the shrill laughing cries of women coming up from the waterside with pots for the rest-house. 'Welcome, Lord Henry, are you well?'

'How are you.'

'I'm well enough thank you, but my little Oni has a sore eye and I was just wanting you to come—just have a look.'

The path was close to the bank of the river which here ran through a glade or rather a canyon in the high forest, whose green cliffs were thirty or forty yards from the water's edge. The northern of these immense walls was in full sun glittering like a mountain of jade, a hundred and fifty feet high; the southern now at five o'clock was in shade; its blue oblique shadows reached the river bank and threw on the brown water dark shapes like those of fish which were in fact their uppermost leaves. Thus when a parrot or a monkey playing in the top of the forest a quarter of a mile away made the branches spring, the village children dancing in the shallows shouted, 'Fish, fish,' and darted after their moving shapes on the water.

The river bank was the children's playground as well as the young people's club. Here they played all day at hunting, fishing, marriages, wars, shops, built huts for themselves and planted farms of broken palm leaf bedded in mud; danced, sang, and rolled shrieking a hundred times an hour down the steep bank into the water. Nok children had no clothes to tear or make dirty and no restrictions of noise. They were the happiest children in the world in spite of fever, small-pox, dysentery and a dozen other diseases which killed half of them in the first five years. For dying was no trouble.

While the children played, their fathers and brothers sat gossiping and smoking at the edge of the bank. This was the time of year which did not count in Birri, the time before the rains when the ground was too hard for digging, and the big hunts were over. In another month or six weeks the first rain would fall and men would begin to reckon time again, dropping a stone in a calabash for each day until the due date for corn and yams to be ripe and lambs and children to be born. Meanwhile there was nothing to do but talk, hunt, fish, and perhaps make a war or a feast.

Henry was looking for the Fish among these groups, but his progress was slow. For each of them had something to say to him and he himself could not resist the laughter and cries of the children. He, too, shouted fish, and clapped his hands, looking at the Birri to see that they too were enjoying this game.

'It's the shadows,' he explained.

'That's it—from the trees.'

'That baby there—see, he really thinks it is a fish. Ha-ha—he's trying to pick it up from the bottom.'

Henry ran down the bank to help this baby, a very solemn baby of two or so, to pick up the fish of shadow from the mud on which it lay, in two inches of golden water, like the ghost of a dab. He picked up handfuls of mud in both hands and poured them into the baby's fat palms.

'Come and show us your fish,' cried the men above, and the baby, his brown body glistening with water, began to clamber up the bank, stopping now and then to look at his palms and to wonder at the melting of his fish. Henry was chasing the rest of the band through the water amidst a cloud of spray. Then when at last he was hailed by Fish from the top of the bank, he was sweating and breathless; his new green felt hat with the silk bow at the back, his clean white shirt and khaki trousers, the silver-mounted stick and sparkling

158

knife chain were covered with mud. But Henry himself was in the highest spirits as he scrambled on all fours up the rough clay, pursued by the yelling babies, and threw himself down among his friends.

Fish was surrounded by all the most eminent young warriors in Nok, for though he was not yet made chief on the council, he was already chief in influence and fact. That he was conscious of his rise in the world was made plain at once by his restless movements, his incessant broad smiles, the new confidence of his voice, and the manner in which he received Henry, with shouts followed by roars of laughter. The man seemed drunk, but he was drunk only with the excitement of his own glory.

'Henry—it's Henry. Hail, Henry. How are you doing, you Henry?' he shouted.

Henry, laughing also, was pushing with his foot at a little girl who was trying to catch at the flapping trousers which excited her curiosity and interest. 'Go away, you rascal you, I'm tired,' he cried out. But the child, though carried to and fro on the powerful leg like a fly on a piston rod, continued to hold on, gazing at the strange cloth until he pulled her away with his hands and rolled her shrieking with laughter down the bank into the water again.

'The rascal,' he said, coming back to his place. 'Who is it?'

'Why do you want to know? Do you want to steal her, you blackguard?' laughed Fish.

This was a joke and everybody laughed at it, politely; everybody except Obai who was sitting on Fish's left hand. Obai looked thin and sad. He had the look of calm despair common to black men and perhaps to animals in their time of disgrace or illness; his very attitude as he sat gazing across the stubble of the village farms at the walls of the forest expressed resignation. He was smoking a large brass pipe shaped like an elephant.

Henry, seeing Obai downcast, at once aimed his jokes and smiles towards him. 'How goes it, Obai—that's a good pipe of yours.'

'Yes, it's a good one.'

'Yes, a well-decorated pipe. Did you get it at Goshi?'

'No, it came from Benin.'

'Of course what you got at Goshi was a decorated belly.'

159

This raised a laugh.

Obai, without turning his head, asked, 'Are the whites taking all Nok?'

'Let 'em try,' cried Fish.

'Fish knows how to crack chicken's eggs,' said Henry.

Another roar of laughter greeted this joke. Fish when he had seen it at last, a minute or two after his first laugh, bawled, 'Yes, a white egg. What do you think of that, Obai?' Obai puffed his pipe and said, 'So it's true that Bewsher has sold us.'

'Who knows? White men are like other people. They do what suits them.'

The fat baby who had wrestled with Henry's foot came running among them closely pursued by a little round-faced girl of about six. The baby was still a solid oblong with soft thick legs and arms deeply creased and dimpled, but the little girl's legs and arms were already growing thin and long. She wore a single pigtail about two inches long on the back of her round head.

These two came flying among the men, then suddenly the baby took refuge between Henry's legs, revolved himself slowly round and sat down as if in a nest. He leant back against Henry's stomach with the expression of one who had escaped from the business of life into a refuge. The little girl, almost as abruptly, turned aside and threw herself down against Obai. Resting her elbow on his thigh and her chin in her hand she gazed at Henry's green hat with solemn curiosity.

But the men paid no attention to these visitors.

'And it suits them to take our country from us,' said Obai.

'Every man takes what he can get,' said Henry, who believed that he spoke the truth; and at once the young men grunted their approbation. For they thought that they recognized a truth.

'And who are you?' said Henry stooping forward to play with the little girl beside Obai.

The men looked at her and one of them answered, 'That's the one they call Bobbin.'

'Is she yours, Obai?'

Obai did not answer, but Fish answered for him that Obai had no house, neither wife nor children. His wife had been lost with the cough, that is, she had died of influenza.

'That's a pity,' said Henry, 'but I thought you were going to marry Osana. Now that's a fine girl. Strong, good-tempered, sensible and fertile—the best kind of a girl you could find.'

Again Obai was silent. Uli explained for him that Osana was married already to a Goshi man. This was her daughter who was now leaning on Obai.

'But Osana is not living with her Goshi man and everybody knows that he is an old fool and that she doesn't care for him. That's why she's always at home with her family.'

'She came to bear a child.'

'If I had a friend like Osana I wouldn't wait long before she belonged to me.'

Obai continued to puff at his pipe and gaze across the water at the trees. Fish smiled at Henry's foolish remarks, and began to explain that many Birri had friends among women whom they could not marry for one reason or another. Obai's friend Osana was betrothed already before they were friends, and his own friend Amo was not only betrothed but belonged to a different totem group. But Osana had promised her daughter to Obai and this was a common plan in such cases; a good plan also because in this way a man gained a wife with the spirit and after the likeness of his friend and had also a friend in his wife's mother. This was a great advantage.

'Why, yes,' said Henry, laughing. 'A great advantage. But what is a greater advantage is to enjoy a fine woman like Osana.'

Obai had laid the stem of his pipe across his knee so that the little girl could put down her lips and take a pull at it. As she did so she laid her fingers on the back of his hand to steady the pipe.

'Osana is married,' he said; 'how could I take her?'

'Aren't you a grown man? Did you fail at your initiation? How does a man marry a woman? Are the Birri made differently from other men?'

'There won't be any Birri when the white men come.'

'And my friend Amo is betrothed to a man in Paré,' said Fish. 'Besides neither of us is allowed to eat monkey so I could not marry her in any case.'

'What is preventing you?'

'Why, it would be——' Fish, astonished at the very notion, could not find a word to describe the impossibility of marrying a totem sister.

'Pooh!—and have you never played with her—don't tell me—I'm a Birri myself.'

'When we were children together we played at marriages. But that was before my initiation. Besides, any more than that would have been—well, it would have been—a very wicked thing.'

Henry spat on the ground. 'Wicked? Why wicked? Who made it wicked? Do the birds and the beasts make such rules. People in the great world laugh at such foolish rules.'

'You think they are foolish,' said Obai, playing absentmindedly with the child's pigtail. She having had her treat of tobacco was once more attending to the conversation with the air of a responsible person. As Obai's betrothed she felt her dignity and importance.

'They are not foolish for the jujumen that make them and punish people who don't keep them with fines and beating. If I was a jujuman I should make some more laws against eating and drinking beer and if anyone drank beer he would have to pay me a hoe or two English silli.'

'Yes, we Birri are ignorant and stupid. That's why old Umoké and his jujumen at Paré can sell us to the whites—and we do nothing but talk.' Bobbin gave a sharp cry. Obai had pulled her pigtail too hard and she could not prevent tears. Henry, Fish and the rest burst out laughing at this accident, and tried to comfort her by clicking their fingers and calling out, 'Hey-hey, Bobbin. See the little bird—see the monkey there was a long tail,' pointing out the silent wall of forest.

But the child clambered over Obai's leg as if to hide herself between his knees. She turned her back on the spectators of her shameful tears and clung to the man, who had not smiled nor even apologized, but lightly brushed her smooth head with his fingers as if to remove the pain. 'We are fools and they know we are fools,' he said in a voice trembling with rage. 'They are playing a game with us. First they take Goshi and now it is Lower Nok and next it will be Nok itself, and after that all our country. And what do we do? We talk about women and quarrel among ourselves. Yes, we are a worthless people and it will be a good thing when we are made slaves because that's all we are fit for.'

Henry was amused by this vehemence which annoyed everybody else. Obai had no longer the right to abuse the Birri. He was a small man weakened by his wound. Moreover, he was a nuisance because he was preventing a discussion which had taken an interesting turn towards the subject of women and marriage. Angry murmurs were

162

heard, and even Fish remarked that the Birri could not be expected to fight until the white men had given them cause. 'When they come to Nok, we shall see whether the Birri are a worthless people.'

'Yes, we shall see,' said Obai, getting up and walking away with Bobbin in his arms. She had fallen asleep.

'But how could I marry Amo—why it's—it's impossible,' said Fish, raising his eyebrows and stretching his enormous mouth in an astonished grin.

'For you perhaps,' answered Henry, tilting his hat over his eyes and gazing round him with a smile half of contempt for these savages, half sympathetic. 'But in the great world outside Birri men are not afraid to take what they want, and they would laugh at all these rules which tie you like sheep.'

'Have they no rules outside Birri?'

'Who cares for their laws. You can always go away from them. That country is not a little yam patch like Birri. It is the whole Sudan from sunrise to sunset, from Sokoto to Mecca.'

'What is this Sudan?'

Henry smiled patiently and began to explain what the Sudan was; it was all the land between the northern desert and the great forest, between the white man's sea (Atlantic) and the black man's sea (the Red Sea). It was nearly all the land in the world. And in this country, according to Henry, everybody did what he liked. Everybody was free and happy and able to acquire riches and to defy all rulers, chiefs, jujus and laws—everybody, that is, with any intelligence and pluck. And as Henry, who had spent most of his life outside Birri starving on one rubbish heap or another, or robbing wretches more miserable than himself, crawling about in the chain gang with a latrine bucket on his head, or sitting in the stocks with the skin torn off his back by the dogarai's whip, spoke of this happy land, enthusiasm gave him the words of a prophet, and his great voice, vibrating with the burden of his important message to these poor ignorant devils, his large gestures which moved his whole body, waked the baby slumbering against his thigh. It looked up with dreamy delight at the waving hands and began to sing a humming tune to itself in chorus with the varied notes which shook and rumbled inside the wall of carcase behind it.

Henry, like all his kind, had much eloquence and a great power of conviction. Now as he played upon his voice like an organ, jerked head, shoulders, arms, raised his hands against the sky and swung them about in a gesture including not only the whole glade of Nok which stood about them in the quiet evening as huge and still as a crater of the moon, but the whole world, he was a poet in full creation; and his creation seemed to him not only true but something more important than truth, splendid and desirable. He desired it himself and was convinced of its truth.

So also to the young men it seemed not only true but just what ought to be true. For they were assured already by their secret inclination, by the desire of their bodies, that the world was made for joy; they were surrounded by promises of delight in food, game, beer, women, war; and yet up to now they had not had any enjoyment at all comparable with their expectation. Their women were not amusing after a single half hour, food lost its attraction after every meal, game was scarce, beer gave a headache, war was largely a matter of dull marches and long vigils. Something was obviously wrong with things in Birri and it was quite time they were changed.

It was therefore Henry quite as much as Bewsher and Obai who produced the final unexpected triumph of Bewsher's policy when, in the next dry season, actually within a fortnight of the Bewshers' departure on leave (their steamer ticket had to be transferred to the next boat) all the villages agreed to a truce and a general assembly at Paré. For though Bewsher himself had broken the old narrow tribalism of the Birri, it was Henry who made them eager for experiment. As for Obai, he went round the villages like a madman preaching war against Bewsher and the whites. Let the truce last for ever, let the Birri join together in a great nation like the Fulani and the Yorubas. Then they would be among the greatest nations in the world and all would fear them. The whites would fly before them.

This also was an attractive notion to the warriors. Besides, it was quite certain by now that Bewsher had sold their country, lied to them, betrayed them, so that to Bewsher's delight and astonishment every village in Birri accepted his invitation. In the first days of November the whole fighting population of the country set out for Paré, not only the young warriors but all those chiefs who understood politics and saw that it would be wise for them to agree with the warriors in arms. But what was extraordinary was that these bands from twenty different villages, which had been at war with each other for as long as men could remember, now met with cries of delight and greeting. For the first time all had the same object, to drive out the Yorubas and the white men, to break the juju, to kill Bewsher. At night they camped together, drank and sang together, and perceived for the first time that the Birri were brothers. New relations are always delightful, they are full of love towards each other because they have not yet had time to know each other well. Thus the people from Goshi found that they preferred the men of Nok to each other and, if two men were seen walking hand in hand, it was safe to guess that they came from different villages and that, three weeks before, meeting thus in full war dress, they would instantly have attacked each other. The fashionable words across every fire were now 'The Birri are brothers. The All-Birri are great and noble. They will drive out their enemies. The All-Birri do not need foreigners in their country.'

Within three days more than twelve thousand tribesmen were gathered round Paré, feasting and playing together. Umoké welcomed them all and told them that they had come to hear an important announcement by Bewsher.

'We don't want the rascal here—we can rule ourselves,' they said, 'we are going to kill Bewsher and divide his flesh among every village. Then we shall not be responsible and we need not be afraid of his spirit or the soldiers either.'

Umoké smiled and said, 'That's not my business. I sent for you because Bewsher required you.' On the fourth morning Bewsher arrived, in his usual manner, with extreme suddenness. In fact, a party of young Nok chiefs under Fish who were living in the resthouse were taken completely by surprise when Sam walked in and addressing them as a pack of dirty apes, told them to get out quick. They retired quickly to the forest. From here among a force now amounting to at least fifteen thousand they watched Sam lay the breakfast table and pour water into the bath.

Most of them had seen Bewsher in camp. It was one of the sights of the country, popular with all the village lads. Now as usual he took his bath in the sun, sponging himself with furious energy and talking all the time to his boys and to Umoké, whose duty it was to visit his master at the earliest hour. Then having dismissed Umoké he ate an immense breakfast. It could be seen even from the bush how much he enjoyed his breakfast. Afterwards he lay down in his chair, lit his pipe and opened a book while the boy Sam took off his slippers and massaged his feet and legs.

The young drafts were asking already, 'Why don't we kill Bewsher now when good luck has put him into our hands,' and the chiefs were of the same mind. But when they came together in council it was discovered that the killing could not be carried out so easily as they supposed. The fact was that there were already half a dozen energetic and ambitious claimants to the overlordship of Birri, and their common enemy was Umoké and therefore the Paré juju. But if Bewsher was killed in Paré his body would belong to the juju which claimed a right to all persons killed in Birri. It seemed to the chiefs therefore that if the body of a man and especially a man like Bewsher were surrendered to the juju they would be acknowledging rights they wanted to abolish. On the other hand all recoiled from breaking the old law.

'If we do not give his body to the juju for division what shall we do with it,' asked one. 'We cannot divide it ourselves because we haven't got the proper knife.'

The debate went on for all that day and it was not decided when a message came to say that Bewsher had learnt of their assembly and desired to see all the chiefs at the rest-house. This occasioned another debate, which lasted all night and most of the next day. It was brought to an end only by the sudden appearance of Bewsher himself and old Umoké in the midst of the council. Bewsher's Sam had brought his chair and Umoké's boy his mat. Chair and mat were placed among the chiefs who, astonished as they were, sat motionless with the dignified expressions of frogs when the stranger passes and they cease to croak. Bewsher having saluted most of them by name and cracked several of his usual rude jokes, sat down in his chair and told them that he was very glad to see them. 'For twelve years,' he said, 'I have wished for this day, and sometimes I feared that I would never see it. It is indeed a very happy day for me (and staring at Bewsher they could see that he was indeed happy, smiling and jerking his head in quick movements like a bridegroom. Why was this? But it didn't matter). It is the very happiest day I have

166

known to be here with all the chiefs in Birri and know that they are friends together and will never fight with each other again.

'Some of you have been angry because white men have come to Nok. I understand your anger. The white men mean no harm to you, and if you are careful not to learn bad ways from their labourers you will gain benefit from them. You are angry with them and I am sorry for your anger. But I say that even if the white traders were wicked and dangerous like the Fulani it would be good that they have come, because their coming has made you friends. Your anger with the whites at Nok has done what I could not do, it has made you stop fighting with each other.

'The Birri people are now brothers in peace and the All-Birri nation stands among the other great nations, the Hausas, the English, the Yorubas, the Beni, those nations that are themselves brethren in peace under the great Sultan of England, my master. See then that you do not fall into disgrace with the great King, your father, by making war upon your brethren.

'When you have chosen your chief of All-Birri, the King will send him his word of friendship and power, but not if you are turbulent and quarrelsome.'

He stopped then and looked round at them as if for approval. In fact it was the proper thing for Birri in council, whether they approved or not, to make now and then a kind of grunt, meaning, 'I'm listening, I follow you.' And when now they sat silent, he looked at them in surprise.

But Bewsher was an unaccountable person. It was impossible to know what he would do. Instead of noticing, like a Birri chief in the same circumstances, that his remarks were not wanted, he smiled at them and made several grunts himself. Then he called out to his boy to bring him a drink and lifted it to them. 'This is health to the All-Birri.'

No one spoke. But the man was not at all disconcerted. He drank, banged down his glass on Sam's tray, lit his big pipe and at once began to talk again, giving them the most impertinent advice about their own affairs, the affairs of the All-Birri.

They were to elect a single chief over all Birri, and Umoké was the best man for the part. They were to have councillors from each tribe, re-elected every two harvests, to advise with Umoké. They were to write down the juju law; and then the council and Bewsher would consider if it needed alteration, and so on. He continued until Sam called him away to a meal.

After that the council took care not to let Bewsher know where he could find them. Their business was too important for interruption; who was to be chief, what was to be done with Bewsher's body?

Meanwhile the guards complained that he gave them no rest. During that day and the next he was turned back from every path leading out of Paré and even from the shore of the sacred lake which has no bottom. Two jujumen caught him there taking a photograph of the sacred crocodiles. But when they put their spears against his breast he laughed at them and said in Birri, 'A good joke is a meal.'

Finally it was agreed that an old man from Kifi, feeble and harmless, should be chief for five harvests and that Umoké should keep his rights as juju head, that is to say, he should dispose of Bewsher's body.

This settlement was received with great rejoicing throughout the camp and especially by the young warriors who foresaw that when Bewsher was killed there would be a war. On that night the drums beat from sunset to sunrise and not a man in the whole army except the guards was sober. Such a feast had never been seen for even before the beer went round the intoxication of new friendship and national glory had made everybody drunk with joy.

# XVI

ULI WAS SICK. This was his explanation of the fact that he could not work, that he was always getting drunk and fighting; this was his excuse for quarrelling with Atua. It was an explanation which enraged Miss Dans and irritated even Mr. Dobson; but Uli meant it for truth. When he had been sick in Birri he had felt the same self-disgust, the same emptiness within and without, the same lack of interest in things. In sickness a man did not care what he did or what people said of him; and so in the mission he did not care what he did or what others did or what they thought of him. Why should he? All these strangers, these Jamesus and Fredericks and Ojos and Musas had nothing to do with him; and they knew nothing about him, neither his family relations nor his own personal history. They were nothing to him and he was nothing to them. And life was emptiness, sickness.

One day Enuké came to the mission and told him that the Birri were going to make war on Bewsher; let him come now and enjoy a good war and win glory for himself.

'And what about the juju?'

Enuké made a disgusted face. 'Why, you were mad that time. I didn't tell about that or the women would have killed you. And I agreed for you, Uli.'

'You didn't agree for me, you little fool.'

'That's because you were mad—but now you will be wise.'

'What do you know about anything, you bush-girl?' said Uli with a rude laugh.

Enuké looked at him gravely. It seemed to her that there was nothing she did not know, for she had been well brought up and now she had borne a baby. 'You're sick, Uli,' she said. 'This is a bad place. Does your woman here make beer as good as mine?'

'You little fool, are you trying to catch me?' with another contemptuous laugh and toss of the arms.

Dobson, seeing the man capering round the visitors like a lost dog that has found its owners, at once invited Enuké to stay at the mission, and when the wild thing, frightened at this sinister proposal, bolted the same night back to her home, suggested that Uli should follow her. 'You had much better go back, Uli, than stay here. For you're doing no good in the mission, and at home I see you have a very nice and good wife. If you can teach her to be a Christian, so much the better, but if not, you can at least make her and your friends in Birri understand that we are not their enemies.'

But Uli answered with disgust that Enuké was a fool girl with no more sense than clothes, and since she would not live at the mission he would have nothing to do with her. Then immediately he got very drunk and gave Atua such a beating that only her personal appeal saved him from expulsion. It was obvious, in fact, that Enuké's visit, far from doing the wretched boy any good, had simply added another complication to his tangled miseries.

But the thought of being turned out frightened him very much and for a long time after that he avoided fighting. After each quarrel when he could not bear the mission he used to go away into the forest or the fields to sulk and plan the revenges which he was too prudent to carry out. For to beat Atua again might cause the loss of all his comforts, his rich food, his idle life.

One day when Uli was sulking in the edge of the bush he saw two white men from Nok come out from a by-path and go towards the Mission. The first was Jukes, the little pale man whom people called Baldhead. He was dressed in a black coat, short white drawers torn in the seat and shooting boots. The second, Redhead, wore silk pyjamas in purple and white, one brown shoe, and one native sandal tied to his feet with creeper. He had no hat but he carried a kind of umbrella made out of cloth and leaves tied to a stick.

Baldhead was limping on both feet and seemed very tired but Redhead was walking at ease, swinging his arms and talking. Once finding himself in front of his superior, he walked backwards for several paces in order to go on talking.

Uli knew that kind of man among his own people and was amused by his antics and by the dejected shuffle of Baldhead. He laughed heartily at the calabash hat and the odd shoes. But when he went back to the mission and heard that Bewsher was surrounded in Paré and that the Nok miner's camp had been burnt over their heads, he did not trouble even to understand the news. He was too bored, too disgruntled within himself to enjoy it. And when an excited messenger came to him from Dobson, saying that the judge had written for him, that he was going to the war, he was not at all pleased to be congratulated. On the contrary, the prospect of leaving the comforts and safety of the mission seemed to him still more unpleasant than his life there.

The letter was from Gore asking if Dobson could provide a bush-Birri to carry a message to the Birri chiefs.

'This is a fine chance for you to distinguish yourself,' Dobson told the boy.

'I cannot help war. War is wicked,' said Uli.

This was a quotation from Dobson himself, and Uli was therefore contemptuous when Mrs. Bewsher said to him, 'You're just too fat and lazy, Uli. I never saw anyone so spoilt. If you don't do what you're told I'll have Mr. Gore put you in prison.'

'War is wicked,' Uli repeated, not at all disturbed.

'No one asks you to fight. It is to stop fighting that Mr. Gore wants you. But of course he'll go.' She turned to Dobson, 'He must go. I'll make him.'

'But there is war,' said Uli. 'They are going to fight. They have wanted to kill Bewsher for a long time and now they've done it.'

He looked at Marie as he spoke. It was his revenge and a successful one. The woman shrank up like a dead corn leaf. She turned so white and ill-looking that even he felt a little alarm in case she should retaliate. But instead she screwed up her face like a wounded monkey and said in an angry voice, 'Don't talk such nonsense—no one in Birri would want to hurt Mr. Bewsher. They know perfectly well that he is the best friend they have.' Then she went quickly out on the stoop and Mrs. Dobson followed her.

This triumph was the more pleasing to Uli that it was accomplished merely by words and not by force; and that it involved no trouble or danger to himself.

But to his surprise Mr. Dobson was extremely angry, and said emphatically that Uli had no right to repeat such wild rumours to Mrs. Bewsher. 'And this work that you are asked to do is a good

171

and Christian work. If you still refuse to do it, I cannot allow you to stay in the mission.'

Uli was astonished and furious. He glared for a moment and then sprang off the stoop like an angry cat, turning round with hunched shoulders and vindictive eyes as if he would fly at him. Uli's temper, in fact, had deteriorated among his comforts. Ease had made him easily provoked. He was fat and venomous.

'Off with you,' cried Miss Dans. 'We're not going to stand any more from you, Uli.'

Uli walked across the compound as slowly as he dared to annoy the whites and maintain his dignity. Then to annoy Atua and vindicate his injuries, he flounced into the hut like a whirlwind and shouted at her, 'Where's my bag? Hurry up. Put some flour in it. Get some sandals. What are you staring at, you fool?'

'But what—what? I don't understand.' Atua was completely taken aback and confused by this sudden attack, just as Uli had intended.

'My bag and my sandals,' he bawled at her. 'Are you drunk?'

'But are you going away?'

'What do you think I'm doing? Hold your tongue and be quick. Can't you see I've no time to waste?'

'But, Uli, where?'

'Here, get out of way. I suppose I must do it myself.' He pushed Atua violently, causing her to stumble over the water-pot.

'A good thing you are going, you big head,' she screamed at him as she fell against the wall. 'I'm tired of you.'

Uli struck at her and chased her round the hut. At the door she caught up the woman's weapon, a hard-wood pestle four foot long, and aimed a blow at him that would have broken any of his bones. But he was too quick for her clumsy swing. He ducked, butted her in the stomach, pulled away her legs, throwing her heavily on her back, and then trampled her like a bush-cow, stamping his powerful bony heels into her body and face until her screams brought a crowd running to the door. Then he dived through them and ran off towards Alo without either bag or sandals.

The messenger, Gore's orderly, was waiting for him at the opening to the path. He commanded him to walk in front and said often, 'No games now, you damned Birri, or I'll shoot a hole in your back.'

But Uli did not mind the policeman. He was in high spirits. His heart was full of elation and pride. He was thinking, 'I came off well there. It was very neat, the way I got her down. I taught her something that time. And then getting through the crowd. They didn't think I could dodge them like that. It was a real surprise for them.' He was delighted with himself. And also it seemed to him that he had done something clever in leaving the mission, that some happy change had taken place in his condition. The tree trunks flickering past him in the light of the constable's lamp, the profound stillness of the forest, the feel of the path under his tread, these gave him the sense of holiday, made his feet spring heel and toe, his muscles dance. He did not inquire why he felt this joy, why, in spite of his blowing lungs and a stitch in his side, he smiled to himself as he loped through the forest in front of the trotting orderly. But all at once the word flew from his lips, 'And this war, do we go at once?'

'At once.'

'Are they going to fight?'

'Why, of course. What are they going for? But to shoot some of you damned Birri.'

'But if I go with them, they'll have to give me a gun.'

'You, you ape? What would you do with a gun?'

Uli jumped round upon him and crouched forward, stretching out his hands like claws, so that the policeman, taken by surprise, started back and almost dropped his lantern. 'Call me ape,' said Uli, 'you son of a hole, and I'll tear out your tripe.' He smiled and his eyes glittered in the lamplight green and gold like a leopard's. Like a leopard he was not angry but rejoicing in the chance of a fight.

'Go on with you,' said the orderly. 'You know I didn't mean anything.' And Marie, with her boy, catching them up, said impatiently, 'What is it now? Go on, go on.'

Uli laughed. He had frightened the orderly, he had shown him that he was not going to be insulted. He threw up his hand with the gesture of a warrior recovering his spear, twirled round and marched forward.

The news of the Birri rising had the same effect at Alo as a declaration of war in a more civilized country. Everybody found life more interesting. Mr. Ogbomasha Montmorency, a young clerk from the coast, homesick and running to seed in the bush, full of scorn and melancholy, became suddenly energetic and prompt. He followed Gore about like a dog, flew to do everybody's work as well as his own. The telegraph clerk, a seedy youth called Jones who usually crept about the station like a spy or criminal glaring angrily at black and white alike, came to the office with quite a new face, full of sympathetic devotion, to declare that he would keep the office open day and night and sleep on the floor. Moreover, such was the self-respect engendered in him by this loyal offer that he put on a clean shirt and washed himself for the first time in many months. Even old Dollar, dragging his heavy legs from the hospital to the barracks, seemed to move with unusual speed and liveliness, as he went to confer with Stoker about the medical staff for the expedition.

Only Gore failed to rise to the occasion. From five in the morning, dressed in a white canvas shirt and blue bow-tie with white spots, pale fawn trousers and bright brown shoes he sat at his table in the middle of about four hundred people, writing notes in his usual slow manner, and bargaining with traders.

When he had written each note or telegram he carefully read it through and added the file number. It seemed that he could not trust Mr. Montmorency, even at this critical hour, to disentangle carrier transport from medical labourers or a court case about a soldier from the new file of the Birri patrol.

He looked if possible more bored and cadaverous than usual, and he was dressed very much better. Nobody had seen the blue bow-tie before. It was a full tie almost Bohemian in shape and size. It said plainly, 'Please observe that I am not a military man. My job is quite different.'

Naturally it annoyed Stoker. But everyone, even Cottee, was indignant with the A.D.O. for his callous and shortsighted behaviour in the crisis. It was agreed that he showed up very badly. Cottee had hurried to Alo in order to make sufficiently plain the extreme gravity of the situation, which demanded the strongest measures.

He greeted his friend with the most impressive warmth, squeezing his hand and assuming for a moment the solemn fixed eyes of a long lost brother. This was not insincere. Cottee was a friendly soul and at the moment his natural affection for Gore was intensified by the feeling of a common purpose. They were all brothers against the Birri.

'What's the latest with you?' he asked.

'You're the best news at present,' said Gore, trying to get his fragile bones out of Cottee's paw.

'It was a near squeak. I got out of bed just as the pillow burst into flame. Jukes was actually on fire when we were running for bush. I had to smack his back to put him out and he thought he was speared.'

'You were lucky.'

'The men weren't. Five killed at least, if not seven.'

Gore, still with a sympathetic expression, looked down at his desk and read on it a form just brought in by the messenger.

Priority 192.71. your 19.24. A company left two hours ago Birri co-operate Stoker. Advance on two fronts essence plan operations. Resident.

Gore pencilled on a blank form 20.24 your 192.71. Please delay all movements troops your side till further information received. Gore.

'A bad business,' said Cottee in a tone agreeable with Gore's expression. Gore shook his head sadly and gave the wire to the messenger.

'I was wondering if I could be of any use to Stoker,' said Cottee.

'I'm sure you could, but first go over to my place and give yourself a large drink. Then you can see Stoker yourself.'

'Thanks, old man, but I don't feel like a drink till I know how things are going. I don't want to be left out of this.' Then suddenly finding his voice and look too cheerful, he exclaimed in a tone of the most mournful and passionate intensity, 'My God, when you think of poor old Monkey in the hands of these devils—by the way, is there any more news?'

Gore sadly shook his head and ejaculated with unexpected sharpness, in Hausa, 'Not a farthing more than threepence, so you can go outside and think it over.'

An excited rat-faced youth clad in a very dirty Hausa gown, who had silently pushed up behind Cottee, now burst into a tearful wail. May God curse him if he could sell sandals at threepence. A long bundle of the sandals, made of raw cow-skin with the hair outside

175

and strung like kippers on a rope, suddenly flew out between the white men. 'A shilling, May God curse me if anybody could sell for less.'

The sandals touched the tablecloth. Two messengers and an orderly, transported with horror at the sacrilege, fell upon the huckster and kicked him out of the door.

'I was surprised to see Stoker hadn't got his company away yet. I should have thought he'd have been smarter than that,' said Cottee, confidentially lowering his voice. But he did not want to decry Stoker so much as to exploit the bond of sympathy with Gore.

It was then that Gore revealed, quite calmly, the fact that Stoker had been ready for some time, but he, Gore, had not yet decided whether to let him go or not. Cottee was amazed, shocked. 'But, good God—but surely, every minute's precious—at a time like this.' Gore played with his pencil, and answered politely, 'That's true,' and then becoming very hearty again cried, 'But you must be worn out—just slip over to my house.'

'Really. Gore—not exactly my business—but dammit, there's a good many lives lost already—and poor old Monkey's at stake.'

'Quite so,' said Gore, for the first time turning his pale, heavy-lidded eyes on the man, 'That's the trouble. Excuse me for a moment. He turned to reach for another bundle of wires from the messenger. This time there were three. He read, 'Clear the line. D.O. Alo. 193.71 your 19.24. Reported here Bewsher surrounded somewhere near Parre or possibly Bary or between Barry and Nock Stop Suggest encircling movement from both sides put Stoker in immediate communication with O.C. here arrange details Stop Commandant suggests advance on two fronts most favourable movement providing synchronized Stop Wire condition Elema fords and probable availability food supplies Birri in line drawn Pari-Kunama. Resident.

'Clear the line. 194.71 your 19.24. Is Parre or Pari identical Barri marked on War Office map 1910 Stop Lambert's sketch map 1923 shows Pari Stop Notice also Berri twelve miles west Parri Stop Should this be Paré Stop Reply at once for Commandant and O.C. Troops Kunama Resident.'

'I think you're making a terrible mistake,' said Cottee.

Gore, murmuring some apology, with a perfectly inexpressive countenance, sat down and drew towards him a block of wire-forms.

Cottee felt himself dismissed. But he went away, as he said afterwards three or four times to Dollar and to Stoker, absolutely flabbergasted by the way this business was being messed up.

'Of course I like poor old Gore, but he was never exactly brilliant and now he's the complete mandarin; he won't take advice, and he can't take responsibility.'

There was a little pique in this but no temper. After four o'clock when the marching orders finally arrived Cottee was in the highest spirits. For he was accepted as S. and T. officer to the expedition and Stoker had fitted him out with bush kit from the company store. His last grave anxiety that he would have to go to war in a grey flannel steamer suit and buckskin shoes was happily removed; there was no danger that he would look like a fool.

He was going to enjoy this show, and it might easily make him a rich man. All Birri would be opened up, including Paré. Also it would be in highly favourable state for development; the people submissive and ruined; the government ready to welcome anyone bringing money and work.

Marie arrived at eight o'clock and delivered Uli at the office whence he was dispatched at once to Stoker at the fort. The company was making its last preparations and the zero hour was ten.

The effect of this news on Marie was unexpected even to herself. For two hours she had been walking through the forest with the orderly's head travelling smoothly in front of her and the lantern throwing its pattern deep among the tree trunks. In this rhythm of motion and light it was easy for her to move like a machine and she was aware of nothing between stages until, close to Goshi, a kind of tension or pressure which had gradually invaded her brain and muscles attracted her notice. She saw then at once what was wrong with her, that she was praying, or rather her body was praying, without any kind of volition on her part.

For a few minutes she observed this phenomenon with cold surprise and disapproval. Even in her preoccupation she found it queer as well as painful, even frightening. It alarmed her and she resolved to stop at once.

But she could not stop because the condition was outside her will. Tension, the sense of imploring, as if (she put it to herself) her whole body was stretched out to God, remained in spite of reasoning. She

177

ached with that petition which could not be put into words, which had no object.

She remembered somebody saying to her in a kind voice, when as a little girl she had been going for her first trip on a fishing-boat, 'Eat plenty, darling'; and she thought, 'When Mama used to teach me my prayer and my hymn, perhaps it was because she knew what life was like. It was because she loved me and not because she loved God.'

But as she told Gore at a later time, that feeling was one of the worst she had known. And it made her a little crazy, 'As you all noticed that night.'

Gore, of course, assured her that nobody had noticed anything, but this was not quite true. Everybody had noticed something.

The first was Cottee, who met her on his way from the rest-house. The news that the troops were actually to march had sent her flying after Gore who was said to be in the town sorting carriers. But she had missed him there and now she was hurrying to the fort. She said that the soldiers must be stopped; it was as good as killing Monkey to let them inside Birri.

When Cottee, full of tact and sympathy, began to question this, and reminded her that at Nok she had wanted to use the troops, she made the unexpected answer that the only thing that could save Monkey was just that he was Monkey.

Cottee might have said that this was the reason why the man was in danger, but he answered politely.

'Yes, of course, you can't beat him for bushcraft. He always has a dodge.'

'Like the man who had a fire extinguisher put into his coffin. Why, Frank, there's ten thousand Birri round Monkey and even bushcraft can't turn him into a balloon.'

'Then you don't think that a quick move from this end——'

'But don't you see that his only chance is the way they feel about him,' and she explained, still more oddly, that the Birri would find it difficult to kill Monkey. Because he had gone to them as a friend and no one liked to kill an unarmed man who had come in friendship. It was really quite difficult to do so. She had seen that herself at Nok when a chief had tried to stab him.

'I see.' He gazed at her.

'It's not the Dobsons' notion,' she said angrily. 'It's just plain sense.'

'Ah yes, of course,' he hastened to soothe her, 'and he's all right—we know that.'

This conversation took place on the road opposite, and nearly midway between the fort and the civil buildings. In front of them the station could be seen lit up like a fair; a long fair struggling over half a mile among trees and cottages with its chief attractions clustered at the ends. One was the civil station with its houses, offices, dispensary and hospital, the other was the fort and the officers' houses. Lanterns bobbed between, three or four at a time. The carriers massed round Gore's office had lit a fire which illuminated a kind of Walpurgis night of ragamuffins, soldiers, doxies from the town, traders and grave turbaned officials of the Emir's court. A white horse with a scarlet saddle-cloth, tied to the office verandah, was conspicuous from a great distance.

Two other fires flared on the parade ground, making the long wall of the fort behind stand out against the black sky like a sharp gold frame to the scene, and showing on the parade ground a regular array of small pyramidal heaps, like stooks in a field of bright yellow stubble. The stooks, however, had a brownish look, as if they had stood too long and grown a trifle rotten. Colour-Sergeant Maggs could be recognized even at this distance bustling up and down between these lines in full marching kit. The fire glittered on his steel and brass. Stoker and Dollar appeared only from a nearer range. They were standing by themselves about twenty yards behind the left-hand fire. At this range also the stooks were seen to be soldiers in their fatigue jerseys, each sitting behind his kit laid out for inspection.

And this sight caused such alarm in Marie who apparently had not expected the troops to be so forward in preparation, that Cottee barely prevented her from running among the men. He averted a grave breach of military etiquette only by persuading her that her mission would have a much better chance of success if he made the first approaches.

Marie, always respectful of official ceremony, agreed then to stay by the fire. Cottee went up to Stoker and explained the situation. His sympathy with Marie and his natural interest in a point of view, caused him to add, 'Of course, there is something in it.'

179

Stoker and Dollar, who were discussing the sick list, did not see this. They looked at him in silence. Then Stoker said, 'What, that we ought to trust to luck?'

Cottee wished now that he had not bothered about points of view. He turned red and damned himself. Why couldn't he remember what blockheads these people were. It was no good trying to reason with them. They only thought you a fool for your pains, and what was more, they made you feel like a fool.

'Of course,' he said, 'that's just Mrs. Bewsher's idea. That shooting might be riskier than letting it alone.'

'These wives,' Stoker murmured.

'We've got to remember she's da chikki (pregnant); two months gone,' said Dollar.

'Of course,' cried Cottee, in full retreat—'of course—that explains a lot.'

'I don't see what we can do,' said Stoker. 'She may upset your friend Gore again, but so much the worse for him. So you can't do anything about these two, Dollar,' with a glance at the hospital sheet.

'They can't march.'

'Won't march.'

'Just as you like,' said Dollar, whose heavy, slack body and sagging cheeks had acquired from the emergency, from belt and uniform and medal ribbons, an air of dignity and resolution. 'Can't or won't. They don't know themselves which it is by now. But if you hurt their feelings they'll lie down and die on you.'

'I wonder.' Stoker turned towards the colour-sergeant and a storeman who was opening ammunition boxes. They poured out a stream of cartridges on a blanket and all three stooped to count, dividing the heap into little fans of ten.

'She's waiting,' said Cottee, and after a moment's hesitation he added, 'Sir.'

Stoker, without looking up from his task or ceasing to count, answered, 'Yes, you must tell her something—but take her away.'

Cottee turned round, but Marie had approached already to within a few paces and now, eager to interpret any movement as a sign, darted forward. Her eyes, her expression, the cock of her chin alarmed even Dollar, who muttered, 'God save us.' Cottee was quick to intercept her. His gesture was again that of the devoted staff officer officious to rescue his general from impertinence and interruption. 'It's all right,' he said. 'They're not going yet.'

But Marie had already burst out, 'Captain Stoker, you're surely not going to start shooting when Mr. Bewsher is in the middle of the Birri.'

Stoker, who had jumped up, and old Dollar, gazed at her with polite blank faces as if at a respectable gate crasher. Cottee tried to catch Stoker's eye with a look of sympathy for his embarrassment.

'You know it's entirely his own policy,' said Marie.

Stoker answered in a sympathetic voice, 'You can be sure we'll do our best, Mrs. Bewsher.'

'But you can't do anything good at all—I'm sorry if you think I'm butting in, but I have a kind of special interest in the thing.'

'It's very difficult, of course,' said Stoker, but Marie, to everyone's relief, suddenly turned round and walked away towards the civil station. The three men stared after her.

'She'll get at Gore now,' said Cottee.

Stoker, leaning once more over the cartridges, said that it wouldn't surprise him, and so much the worse for Gore. 'Six—eight—ten——' he counted. 'Deal that lot out, Sergeant—you can understand poor Mrs. B. being a bit deficient in nerve—it's Gore that's beyond me. Where do these politicals get their pacifism from. Is it Oxford, or where?'

'Just a fashion,' said Dollar. 'It came in about the time that the top-hat went out. I believe Lugard started it out here. At any rate these lads all copy it as soon as they arrive. It's just like school over again. The little boys look to see what the big boys do and if a first-class Resident went about in a dog collar, they'd all be hooking themselves up behind.'

Stoker got up, dusted his knees and gave orders for the ammunition to be doled out. 'Zero hour is ten, and we parade here, but of course you needn't appear. As for you, Cottee——'

'Yes, sir,' said Cottee, coming to attention.

The sergeant-major's voice from behind made them all start, and spoilt Cottee's gesture of loyalty. 'Judgie ya zo'.' He saluted like a wooden toy on a string. Behind him, in the bright yellow light of the wood fire Gore was seen moving towards them at his usual long paces.

The A.D.O. still wore the foppish blue tie which had irritated

Stoker that morning; also he seemed even more unmilitaristic in pose, his long back more rounded, his chest hollower.

Although it was now half-past nine o'clock he was wearing a hat, but on the extreme back of his head; and this again was not usual with Gore. It was simply another reminder, conscious or unconscious, of his difference from the soldiers.

He came right up to the group before he said in his polite rather high-pitched voice, 'I'm afraid we'll have to put you off again, Stoker. I've just had a letter from old Umoké—he's the head chief in Birri—to say that he's collected all the chiefs at Paré for a Durbar. We'd never heard anything about this before and it's just possible it may explain why all the Birri are at Paré and why we can't get messengers through. The letter's four days old—it was sent to Bewsher at Kifi—but it does give us just a hope that things aren't as bad as they look.'

The three men listened in silence, staring at Gore; Stoker with contempt, Dollar with cynical amusement, Cottee with a feeling of wonderment that any man could dare to make such a fool of himself.

At the end of the speech Dollar tossed up his big head and gave a short laugh which was echoed by Colour-Sergeant Maggs from the background. Stoker said, 'I must say you've got a nerve.'

'What about my men at Nok?' cried Cottee. 'Don't they count for anything? Seven men cut to pieces.'

Gore began to explain that it would be time to hunt for the murderers at Nok when the Birri had dispersed. But Stoker caught him up at once. How could he do so? How would he catch any of the Nok without using force?

'It's been done pretty often in the last ten years.'

'Yes, by bluff, and now the Birri have called a show-down.'

'That's the question,' said Gore. 'Have they?'

'That's the very word for it, sir,' said Cottee, warmly approving his captain. 'Bluff—and if you've only got a busted flush or a ten-high, you're for it.'

'A busted flush—that's not very polite to Mr. Gore,' said Dollar.

But this was too subtle for the moment. Stoker was too angry for such quips. 'All I've got to say is that if you haven't got the guts to make up your mind one way or another, you'd better clear out of your job. Because all you Cuthberts are fit for is to dodge responsibility at the cost of other people's lives. It's going to be Bewsher's now. In France it was millions, and to-morrow or the next day when we really get started on the show and the Birri have got everything nicely ready for our reception, it will be some of my men.'

'But they are only soldiers,' said Dollar.

'Come, old chap, make up your mind,' the good-natured Cottee pleaded with his friend.

'Yes—well'—Gore's manner was apologetic. 'I'm sorry about it. But that's how things are just now. Of course, I'll let you know at once if I get any more news. I'm expecting a messenger any minute. I suppose I can get you at the fort any time to-night.'

Stoker did not answer, but turned round and gave the order to dismiss. Colour-Sergeant Maggs was heard addressing the air, since he had no confidant of equal rank, to the effect that this was just about over the edge.

Gore walked away towards the office. He was not surprised by the insults of Stoker and Dollar, much less disturbed in his intentions.

He offered to their anger and contempt the immense nonchalance of a professional spirit, the real *esprit de corps* which gives to every member of an organized body, a church, a regiment, a service, the strength and detachment of an impersonal force.

These people were amateurs. They didn't understand his job and they couldn't be expected to because they had never been inside it; they had never experienced it; they didn't know it in its essence, in its details. It was the scrupulous respect for detail fixed in Gore's mind by education and perhaps a bent that way, which possibly caused him to spend more time over shaving and tying his tie, to be more particular about the neatness of his office table and the set of his orderly's fez, at a time when every moment was valuable, than when he had all day to be finicky.

As soon as he turned away from Stoker and Dollar he forgot them and closed again with the important questions, was he not putting too much trust in his agent? how long should he wait for his return (the man might have been killed)? had Umoké anything to gain by selling his master? what would the Resident say to this last change of plan, and how could he be made to see its advantages.

But he was extremely tired and although, as he walked slowly towards his office, his brain was already engaged with the necessary wire to the Resident, he found that it did not give him the phrases he needed. He felt something like dismay when he saw Marie running towards him, with a gait and expression eloquent of nervous excitement. 'Oh, Harry,' she began to call out to him from ten yards away, 'have you been to them—Mr. Montmorency told me—what a blessing, and just in time. But I just knew there was some explanations.'

'Yes, this letter of Umoké's.'

'Thank God you stopped the soldiers.'

'It seemed the obvious thing.' He gazed at her out of his red-rimmed eyes, sore after a sleepless night and thirty hours' work, much of it in a badly-lit office. He swayed slightly like a sapling in a breeze and his mind suggested, 'Letter received from Umoké, head chief of Birri, inviting Bewsher—what a relief to see Marie taking it like this. She certainly has guts.'

'I'm afraid this is a rough time for you,' he said.

'What about you? Your eyes have gone right in. A couple of aspirins and a long sleep.' She took his arm and turned him towards his house.

Gore liked her arm in his. The contact by itself communicated something that he needed. It was easy to forget in Alo the unique sensation of possessing a friend, and the effects of a friendly touch upon the arm, the uncritical, undemanding presence of someone like Marie who knew how to give.

She gave and then you wanted to give. You didn't give because you hadn't the time and because she had a husband, but the desire to give was itself a happiness so keen and unexpected that all at once you found life extremely interesting and even admirable.

'Why do you never come to stay in Alo?' he asked. 'Couldn't the Dobsons spare you sometimes?'

'Do you think I've gone Christian too?'

'What? I beg your pardon.'

'Frank thinks that I've gone foursquare and that's why I wanted to stop the war. You don't think that, Harry?'

'Of course not,' said Gore with indignation, though he did not know in the least what she was talking about.

She sighed and her fingers tightened on his arm. 'I'm glad you don't think so badly of me.'

'Good Heavens!' warmly repudiating the very notion.

'Though I guess lion-tamers' wives are apt to be virtuous Christian women.'

'You know, Marie, you're absolutely worn out. It's you that ought to be in bed.'

She stopped and looked at him. She appeared to be amused by something. Gore, disturbed more by the tone than the matter of her conversation, gently urged her towards the Residency. But she resisted and said, 'You needn't be afraid. I'm all right.'

'Of course you are—that's to say you're just about all in. And if you crock up now you'll go into hospital and Dollar won't let you travel.'

This was at once effective. The Bewshers were supposed to be going home by the next boat. The haggard, exhausted woman said firmly that she had never been better in her life, but she agreed that was she tired. She would go to bed if Harry promised to bring her any news. And as her loads had not come could he lend her pyjamas and a clean towel and some aspirin.

'Are you sure that's all you want?' he asked her as they stood outside the Residency.

'You do think it's all right, Harry?' For a moment a look of terror appeared in her round eyes, her half-open lips.

'Certain sure. Not the least need to worry. I should take three aspirins if I were you.'

'That letter really explains the whole thing.'

'I can't see any other interpretation.'

She looked at him thoughtfully and sighed. 'Well, I can depend on you, Harry.' But with a sudden change of note decidedly cynical, 'for comfort anyhow.'

So that he was left as he once more turned towards the office wondering how far, after all, she had managed to deceive herself.

The messenger dozing in the porch jumped up, Mr. Jones shambled towards him with a handful of wire forms, a dim figure squatting in the shadow of the back wall got up and staggered into the light. It was the Birri agent, but with one eye knocked out and his body, face and legs streaked with blood from half a dozen gashed wounds. 'Zaki,' he fell down partly in salute, partly in exhaustion.

'Who did that to you?'

185

'The Paré people, lord. It is war.'

'And the big judge?'

'They mean to give him to the juju.'

Gore sat down to write another note to Stoker, giving him authority to march. The Birri agent, grasping twenty florins in his two hands, the reward of his fidelity, but possessing also the more valuable reward of immense self-satisfaction in his exploit, his wounds, the exclamation of the messengers, the praise of Gore and the effect of his news, was grinning and groaning at once on the way to the hospital.

It was not discovered till then that he had been sitting at the office for three-quarters of an hour. But the reason was quite simple. Knowing the sensational value of his news, he had resolved to give it to nobody but the little judge in person.

# XVII

But the oddest and most uncomfortable incident of the night occurred at two o'clock when the soldiers were drinking a parting glass on Gore's stoop.

They were to march at four and it was agreed that nobody wanted to go to bed. They wanted, it appeared, to talk about wars, patrols. Nobody admitted to any enjoyment of war; it was not the fashion to do so at that time. But everybody had an exact recollection of his war adventures and told them with unusual gusto.

Stoker, who had been on the Duchi patrol, described the arts of cave fighting. The Duchi patrol had taken eight months; what they had really needed was gas.

'How long do you think this one will take, sir?' Cottee asked.

'Impossible to tell.' Stoker already pondered his words like a commander-in-chief.

'If we could only get a few gas shells, what?'

Stoker shook his head. 'Every show is different,' and Maggs, sitting bolt upright in his chair, with his big nose elevated and the points of his moustache newly waxed, with his tumbler grasped like a rifle at the present and his heels together, turned eyes right to his commanding officer and barked, 'And that's a fact, sir.'

It was at this moment that Gore caught a glimpse of somebody moving in the shadow behind Dollar's chair. But before he could recognize Marie she was in the middle of the party saying something about a trick.

It was obvious, of course, that somehow she had heard about the patrol and that this was another effort to stop it; but the woman was in such a state of excitement and the men were so much astonished by this apparition of the D.O.'s wife in blue pyjamas six times too large for her that nobody understood exactly what she did say. They all heard the words murder and something about the name of Jesus—at this point the pyjama trousers already turned up eight

187

inches seemed to grow shorter and sink towards the floor. She clasped her hands.

Gore and Cottee leapt out of their chairs together. But Cottee, as usual the more adroit in a social crisis, was the first on the spot. He bent down, said something in his most cheerful and polite voice and the next moment he was leading her across the compound towards the Residency.

In less than five minutes he was back again in his chair. But for some time conversation was difficult, and again it was Cottee who had to come to the host's rescue with an amusing story about the Gallipoli landing.

Suddenly a dirty small boy with a lantern clambered on to the stoop and said in an impudent voice,'Sarkin Dunia ya zo' (King of the world, he comes).

For a moment there was astonished silence, and then Bewsher's own voice was heard from the direction of the Residency calling for Sam, and Cottee jumped up with a laugh. 'By Jove, here he is.'

Dollar without getting up also laughed, but his laugh seemed to mean, 'Sold again.'

Bewsher could now be seen at the edge of his own stoop talking to Marie. They appeared very calm. No doubt the lantern boy who stood between them was a check upon any romantic gestures. There was, however, something expressive of a lively emotion in the skip with which Marie finally disappeared into the house as Bewsher turned away, and in his own lively gait as he came hopping down the road towards Gore's, twirling his stick and grinning. The grin of his white teeth in the middle of three days' dark red beard could be seen twenty yards away. His hat cocked over one eye defied the world to put him down, much less any number of pagans.

As the party came down from the stoop, already preparing their looks of welcome and congratulation, he stopped, swung round to bawl some more orders at Sam in the darkness, then turned and looked at them with his head on one side and that characteristic expression, at once delighted and sly, of the horse-coper who has brought off a good stroke. 'Hullo?' he said, 'I hope you haven't waited dinner.'

It was obvious that the man was bursting with joy, that he was ready to burst out laughing in their faces. But he played the rôle, much less embarrassing to them, more easily fitted into the social complex, of the lazy conjurer, who brings off his greatest feat with the most nonchalant indifference; and everybody gratefully took the tone from him.

'It seems you've kept the Birri waiting for *their* dinner,' said Cottee.

'Yes, I suppose it was rather inhospitable of me to reserve all the best cuts for myself.'

'We were just off to look for your remains, sir,' said Stoker, a remark which caused Maggs to laugh with great loudness. A very small joke by his C.O. tickled him far more than the best civilian efforts.

'Yes, so I heard. I'm sorry you've missed a show. Who got the wind up? Gore or headquarters?'

'I waited as long as I dared,' Gore began.

'It was you, was it? Well, I'm surprised, that's all I can say.' Bewsher looked at him with the mournful expression of a father deceived in his favourite son.

'If I'd had my way, we'd have gone off this morning. So you mustn't blame Gore,' said Stoker. 'We heard you were eaten.'

'Sur-prised,' said Bewsher sadly, still looking at Gore. 'I didn't think you'd go rushing for a gun at the first market yarn; and I hear you've been babbling to the whole country.'

Gore smiled and then looked extremely bored. It was no good defending himself, too long and too complicated.

'You'd better go and tell the Resident that the Empire is not in any immediate danger.'

'Yes, sir.' The dejected figure was once more seen nodding its way towards the offices; a spectacle which amused several of the party. Gore certainly had no luck.

At last, Gore reflected, the damn thing was nearly finished. But it took him another hour to make the Resident understand that the Birri patrol must be deferred at least till Bewsher went on leave, that Bewsher (this required the most tactful and subtle wording) would probably not go on leave at all if it were not deferred.

'And now for bed.'

But he was not for bed that night. When he returned to his house he found it occupied still by the whole strength of the station.

189

Bewsher, fed, shaved, bathed, dressed in full white mess kit and the old green cummerbund of the Northern Provinces, his most festive get-up, with a powerful grog in his hand, was sitting at the gramophone. His air was that of the man who makes the music. Marie, in a green silk frock, cut very low, was dancing a full-time waltz with Cottee. Both of them looked a little insane. Stoker and Jukes were the other couple. The solemn parade ground expression of the young soldier and the resigned face of Jukes, who acted lady, as he turned slowly and painfully round in the one-two-three of the pre-war dancing academy, touched Gore's peculiar sense of humour. But he had not time to smile before he was seized in Bewsher's powerful arms and whisked across the floor in a series of breath-taking jerks. Bewsher, however, smiled at him in a most genial manner, and said, 'We're enjoying your party so much—it's really very thoughtful of you—the dance was an inspiration—such a good idea to provide whisky as well as fizz.'

Gore, who had very little whisky and no champagne, resigned himself to teetotalism for the rest of the tour; but he found that the whisky had actually been sent over from the Residency. Cottee had brought a dozen of champagne from what he called his bribery and corruption stores and Dollar six bottles of medical comforts. So that even Gore had the illusion, between four and five, of a permanent kind of happiness, in a polka with Sergeant Maggs, a species of wrestling match with Jukes, whose smiles were very near to tears, a perfect dance with Stoker who insisted upon his dancing extremely well, and a reckless gallop with Marie, who made love to him.

But she, as well as he, confessed themselves glad when at five o'clock or thereabouts the gramophone stopped. The spring, broken some time before and secured with wire, had slipped from its anchorage.

Thus while Bewsher and Stoker, with the delighted anticipation of schoolboys (no one had ever seen Stoker look so happy), were taking the thing to pieces, the others, the more contemplative and intellectual members of the company, gathered in a corner.

Gore for the first time heard the story of the escape. Apparently Bewsher had walked out through the bottomless lake of Paré. It had not proved deeper, in the deepest place, than his waist, and the sacred crocodiles had had the fright of their lives. The lake, fatal to all intruders, had not been guarded, and the chief difficulty had been to persuade the servants and the carriers that it was preferable to risk the crocodiles who might not bite to the Birri who would certainly do so.

'I wonder how he did persuade them,' said Gore, looking across the dimly lighted room to the square figure and round sandy head bent over the gramophone. They heard him say in an excited voice, 'There you are now—pull—pull—gently, oh damn, it's out again. You know, what we really want—to make a proper job of it, is——'

'History didn't relate,' said Cottee, 'but I fancy there were some very sore behinds among the staff.'

'A very fortunate escape.'

'And now he can e'en start all over again.'

'He's luckier than we are, what Jukes?'

'I beg your pardon.'

'You ought to be in bed, old man, with that pain of yours. When are you going to cut him up, Doctor?'

'It can't be done here.'

'You think it should be done?'

'Ay—and soon, or——' He lifted his thick hand and let it fall on his knee.

'Then send up the price of tin.'

They were sitting in a kind of alcove at the corner between the wall of the bedroom and the back wall of the stoop. Gore's house consisted of two small rooms, one at each end of the great clay platform on which they had been dancing. Even by lantern light the dusty, uneven earth, the rough mud walls and crooked window holes, the sagging thatch of the roof covered with the tunnels of white ants, had a squalid and desolate appearance.

The little group in their dinner jackets and mess coats (Dollar was wearing a white jacket with black trousers, Gore was still in his holland-coloured office suit) huddled together as if for comfort. It was an hour of disillusionment.

'My God, what a night,' said Cottee. 'On the top of everything else, I suppose it isn't etiquette to go to bed before our esteemed resident has finished with his new toy.'

'I think he deserves a party.'

'But I think you won't be sorry to exchange the chilly tropics for reliable central heating in the real noo Jerusalem.'

'I don't know, Frank. I'll hate to leave Birri.'

'For Noo York?'

'We're going to Lady Bewsher in Somersetshire.'

'I can't help that, Doctor. I've got two boys at school—if this place closes down I must get a job on the plateau.'

'You know what's best for yourself, but how will the boys be educated if you——' He stopped, noticing that he was overheard, and said in a different tone, louder and rougher, 'I've told you what you can expect.'

Marie shrugged up her thin shoulders and twisted in her chair.

'You're cold.'

'No, Harry.'

'But it must be Noo York. What about that lecture tour on the Golden Age of Birri Compared with Fifth Century Athens.'

'Don't laff at me or I'll cry.'

'Is it true, Mr. Gore, that the government will refuse compensation for our losses in Lower Nok?'

'I'm afraid I can't say.' Gore was on his feet. 'The matter will have to be looked into.' He went into his bedroom.

'I don't know what looking into means,' Jukes murmured.

Dollar said something in his strongest accent about some other affair that wanted looking into, and at once, as usual when Dollar made the smallest joke (this apparently referred to Jukes' inside), all the men laughed. Gore was heard laughing on the other side of the wall and even Jukes himself laughed, though not with a very humorous sound. He said thoughtfully, 'I hear Mr. Bewsher has written to Umoké. I suppose they'll try to shut up the whole district if there's no patrol.'

'We'll fight that.'

'When could he write?' Marie asked, incredulous.

'I beg your pardon.' The lady had been forgotten in the interest of the discussion. 'I understood him to say—when he went to shave——'

'The lion-faced Umoké must be feeling a little jumpy.'

'Ah! your politics—you've driven Gore away.'

'Well, Doctor, they will go on, you know, in spite of everybody.'

'Mr. Bewsher will do anything to stop a patrol, that's quite certain,' said Jukes.

'What do you say, Gore?'

'Things are rather mixed at present, I'm afraid.'

'Were they ever anything else?'

'Except whisky in Scotland.'

'Yes, indeed, since the war,' said Jukes.

'Since Adam and Eve and Kick me—but you modern anthropologists don't agree with that, Mah-rie.'

She moved her lips as if smiling and held up her arms for the coat which Gore had brought for her. But she did not listen to Cottee or notice Gore's skilful handling while he wrapped her up.

The grimace was for the enthusiastic young woman of eighteen months before who had written to America about 'a civilization of athletes and poets, Greek in the beauty of its golden age, but more secure—savages truly noble, bound in the strong web of natural loves and duties as eternal as nature's own laws.'

Of course, Cottee had been right to laugh at her. All these men who accepted so easily the insecurity of things, who simply did not imagine any other state of affairs, were right. Only fanatics and fools, communists and sentimentalists like herself could believe in a natural order of things, fixed and eternal, divinely appointed. The lion-faced Birri—no wonder they laughed. The golden age of Birri, like that of Greece——

She gazed across the uneven floor, in waves of light and shadow which trembled in the flicker of the yellow lamp flames, and saw Obai and Uli walking hand in hand across the residency compound at Kunama, two of the most beautiful men she had ever seen, of the noblest carriage, the frankest look. They had been her Greeks of the fifth century, moving in friendship over the bright worn pavements of the Agora and discussing Plato's last discourse. But Obai and Uli had been talking about Bewsher (the first time she had heard his name) and probably they had been talking nonsense, like their Greek prototypes.

Her smile became more derisive. But she felt in her breast an intolerable longing—she wanted to cry—for the silly young woman who had seen in a little community of naked savages the pattern of an earthly paradise. The same silly young woman who at college had adored the Greeks and wished that she had been born two thousand four hundred years earlier.

The golden age of Greece. Galleys full of agonized rowers bleeding under the whip—chained to battered leaking ships—kept from sinking

193

altogether only by the endless patching and plugging of the anxious carpenters creeping about with their tools in the stinking bilges.

The lamps flickered in the draught and the waves flowed towards her, she, too, was on a bench listening to the dismal laughter of slaves and there was Gore with a weary dejection nailing up a plank and Bewsher strutting on the captain's plank, shaking his whip at them while they screamed curses.

But the voyage was over. They would soon reach harbour. No, of course, there weren't any harbours for the spirit, no rest. The slaves were chained, the captains, prisoners of the ship. And some day Bewsher would crack his whip for the last time. They would throw his old carcase into the sea, Gore would lie drowned among the rats, and she, if she did not die before, would toil on across the black waves—to nowhere—the ship itself, the ship of the whole earth, was rotting under their feet, at last it would open up in space like a burst basket.

There was silence in the corner. Outside beyond the mud pillars of the verandah the false dawn was melting into the clear night air, making it thick and white. The bare level of the compound beyond the two stooping figures at the gramophone table and the bare sky emptied of stars, seemed like two parallel surfaces of the same neutral blue-grey, not much wider apart than the height of the house. A cold breeze blowing between them like a north wind coming under a door made Cottee shiver in his thin shirt and dinner jacket. He looked at the group of merry makers, Dollar in a long chair, sprawling like a burst sack, Jukes, crouched on a box with a look of calm dejection, and Gore, sitting in his favourite attitude with his elbows on his knees, his arms stretched out in front of him and his long hands drooped, staring straight in front of him towards the cold oblong of dawn with a look that contemplated nothing; the picture of resignation, of enduring patience.

Marie, grey rather than white, with pinched cheeks and heavy dark lips, sat perched on the front bar of her chair, clasping her fur coat tightly round her with bluish transparent fingers like a pigeon's claws, and gazing at Bewsher with enormous round eyes full of wonder and pain.

'So you'll be sorry to leave Birri,' said Cottee, grinning at her.

She answered without moving, 'I don't know.'

194

'You'd be quite clear about it if you had to stay—like me.'

Marie said nothing to this. But Cottee persisted in bringing her down to earth. 'I didn't know you'd enjoyed Birri so much.'

Maggs appeared striding across the compound like a vigorous and martial ghost. For Maggs there were no moments of depression, no melancholy scenes; in fact, no scenery at all. He waved something and called, 'Here you are, sir.'

'Good man—that's capital.' This was Stoker in great satisfaction. 'Now we shan't be long.'

The sound of a file was heard and Bewsher's voice saying with a thoughtful and enquiring tone, 'The real question is whether the spring isn't the harder——'

'It's not that I've *enjoyed* it,' said Marie dreamily, as if the enjoyment of life were after all a minor point.

'But it's been a noo experience,' said Cottee, thinking to show his penetration of the American mind. Marie turned her head slowly and looked at him as if at a new phenomenon, then at the others, and said vaguely, 'Experience—yes.'

'Fever alone is quite illuminating.'

Suddenly she woke up and said, 'You folks think I'm frightened to go on.'

Cottee and Gore, recollecting the unfortunate episode at the council, assured her forcibly that they had never dreamt of such a thing. Even Jukes roused himself from his private desperation to smile and touch his beard and murmur that Mrs. Bewsher had been an inspiration to the whole district.

'Yes, I'm a coward.' Her voice trembled.

'Oh no, Mrs. Bewsher. You're tired.'

Everybody was greatly alarmed, for it seemed that she was about to say something tragic or cry.

'Let me get you a drink, Mah-rie.'

'He ought to stay, but it seemed such waste.' There were now certainly tears in her voice. Her face began to crumple.

'That's done it,' said Bewsher in a voice of rising triumph. 'By Gad, that's done it—that *has* done it.'

Marie put her hand into Gore's, who, taken by surprise, turned to her with a quick movement of solicitude that made Jukes look the other way and Cottee cock his head sideways with humorous intention.

195

'It's our dance, isn't it?' she said. Gore jumped up.

The gramophone made a noise like a motor car struggling up hill on bottom gear and then broke into a yelling foxtrot. Bewsher came dancing down the floor by himself holding an imaginary partner and singing, 'On the Bam Bam Bammy shore.'

He stopped in front of Marie's chair. 'Where's the lady?' he asked in surprise and indignation.

'She just went off with Harry—I thought they were dancing.'

But they had danced only as far as the drink table where Marie was swallowing a neat whisky and grinning in mockery at Gore while he assured her that she was the bravest little woman in the world. Drink made Gore sentimental as it excited Cottee to waggishness. When she saw Bewsher she threw herself into his arms with a whoop and they executed together the most surprising variations on the foxtrot that have ever been seen in Alo. To Jukes and to Sam equally they appeared so scandalous that for the moment the white forgot his misery and the black his aching fatigue.

About six o'clock in the morning, when the office messengers came yawning on duty, they were startled to hear raucous voices bellowing a song from the little judge's house and one other voice, a high woman's voice, taking the treble.

'What is this song, clerk?' they asked Mr. Ogbomasha Montmorency, and he answered with a contemptuous face, 'The song says that if you have any misfortunes you ought to put them in your bag and continue to laugh.'

'Al hum dill allahi,' said the head messenger, as the thin voice soared up far above the others on the last word, 'what pagans.'

'True,' said the clerk, mournfully, 'but these white people, you understand, are not fair specimens of our Christian religion. They are a lot of unbelievers—damn heretics as you might say.'

Mr. Montmorency was also feeling the flatness of peace and the renewed melancholy of his lot at Alo.

# XVIII

Uli in the guardroom was shut up with another guide and a couple of Hausa murderers, about equally suspect. For Uli was reported a skrimshanker and he was certainly a renegade.

But Uli himself was in very good form. 'It's a good thing for you people that your captain is taking my advice,' he told them. 'I know the ways of these bush Birri. They'll drop on you from the trees and make pit-traps in the path. I can tell you we Birri are up to all the tricks. We know how to fight.'

'I suppose you'll play a trick on us.'

'Me—no. Why, I'm going with you——'

Nobody in the guardroom thought the worse of Uli for fighting against his own people. To the soldiers as well as himself war was like a trade or a game. They despised Uli, not because he was a traitor but because he was a bushman.

'I was the best warrior in Birri,' he bragged.

'We'll have to make you captain.'

'Why no, how could that be? Captains are white.'

They laughed at him, and for a moment he was confused. He sat and looked at them with his lips pushed out in uncertainty and suspicion. For a moment his elation, his holiday feeling, was checked. Downtown the carriers standing by for the column were making a feast. The drums had been beating for two hours.

Suddenly Uli, who was seated just within the guardroom door (he was not permitted outside), heard in the middle of the Alo drum tunes a broken rhythm saying something in Birri.

These notes, though not loud, were clearly perceptible to his ear as words spoken in one's own tongue in the middle of some foreign babel, and they had the same kind of effect. They filled Uli with curiosity and excitement. They made him feel like an exile.

He was so astonished that he uttered an exclamation and jumped up. The sentry, at the door, alarmed, lowered his bayonet and ejaculated, 'None of that.'

Uli had not been thinking of escape but only of hearing that drum again and interpreting it. He looked round. The guardroom was a hollow cube of mud about eight foot in each dimension, lighted from the guard lantern hung in the middle of the low door. Its two window-holes high up under the palm-beams of the roof, were less than a foot square.

Uli darted at a window, caught the brittle lower edge with his hands and pulled himself up to the opening.

The drum was in the middle of a long speech. It seemed to talk from the forest over behind Alo, and it sounded like a Paré drum. What was a Paré drum doing in the Alo bush?

Then suddenly a Nok drum interrupted from the opposite point of the compass, from the east. It said clearly: Where are you? Answer: This is Nok, answer.

Uli dropped from the window and flew across the floor to the other hole. What were these people talking about? What was going on in Birri? He had not thought of Birri for a whole year. He never thought of the past. His mind, like most people's, was entirely concerned with his own affairs in the present. But now at the sound of these Birri voices he felt deprived, as if he had lost a year, as if his time at the mission had been an interruption of his real life. He pressed himself to the window, like a bird in a cage that hears the notes of its own kind from the trees outside.

Paré was speaking in a phrase which he could easily interpret. 'Paré comes, Paré is on the road.' And at the same moment Nok answered by declaring its name, and Goshi from behind Paré, in a faint sharp sound like the taps of a woodpecker repeated 'Goshi, Goshi. Where are you, Nok?'

Uli, caught half-way between the windows, stood muttering, rolling his eyes. The soldiers peeping through the door under the lantern, were laughing at him; the prisoners stared at him from their dark corner with disgust and hatred. They appealed to the sergeant, 'Stop him, how can we get any rest?'

A soldier remarked, 'He's up to some trick.' Another called out, 'What's up, Birri bastard?'

Uli, noticing for the first time that he was being laughed at, stared foolishly, panting. Then gradually intelligence appeared in his countenance; all could see its progress from the first perception of their interest and curiosity to a final inspiration of cunning. He looked at them with an air of surprise and at the same time with so sly and altogether Birri a face that the soldiers smiled and nudged each other. It was quite easy to distinguish the genuine surprise in his expression from the false in his voice when he asked leave to go behind the house.

'Sergy,' the sentry called, 'prisoner wants to go to the latrine.'

The sergeant of the guard in his brown fatigue jersey and his red cordon was sitting on a box at the corner of the shelter. He was a tall Shua Arab, black as a stove, with the sharp, arrogant manner of his race.

'You want to go to the latrine?' he asked, fixing Uli with his suspicious cat's eyes.

Uli pressed his hands on his stomach and crouched backwards moaning; he closed his mouth and visibly held his breath. Half a dozen voices bawled at once, 'Hi, stop him!' The sentry and a soldier with one spring leapt upon him, caught his arms and ran him into the open.

'Take him along,' said the sergeant, 'but no tricks or you'll get a bullet into you,' and he sent two men to look after him, with orders to shoot on the least provocation.

Uli still wore the agitated expression of one in extremity; and amid his moans and gestures of urgency he protested continually against the unkind suspicions of the sergeant.

'We know you Birri,' they told him. 'You'd better not try anything.'

One man stood on guard at the only door of the latrine; the other entered with Uli, rifle in one hand and Uli's wrist in the other.

This precaution was necessary on account of the pitch darkness within. Suddenly Uli's head struck him in the stomach with a force which laid him winded and helpless on the floor and the next instant, the soldier at the door, in the very act of stooping forward and saying, 'Hi! what's that?' received a blow on the forehead from a rifle butt, end on, which silenced him more effectually than a bullet. Before the few men strolling about in the neighbourhood and the women scattered along the lines preparing their men's food, with that diligence and care which wives do not show except when husbands are about to leave them, had even guessed that anything out of the common had happened, Uli was prancing over the Fort wall; and before the sentry at that corner of the Fort could make up his mind whether he had to do with a runaway prisoner or one of the soldiers' boys escaping from some amorous difficulty with an irritable husband, he was a hundred yards across the clearing. 'Shoot!' bawled the sergeant, and the man fired; but he did not see whom he fired at.

When Uli reached the forest it was silent and apparently empty even of the beasts, a sign to him that it was not empty of men. He slipped out of his mission clothes and into the hollow between the buttresses of a cotton tree, where he remained crouching till the moon rose. Not till the moon was high did he begin to look about him, fixing his glance for several minutes at a time on the same point. One of these glances, intent and piercing as a rat's, distinguished gradually in the course of thirty seconds a smooth surface, a polished branch in the network of wrinkled bark. He moved towards it at a pace no quicker or more sudden than those of the shadows moving beside him as the world turned and the moon passed overhead. At five paces the polished branch attached itself to a shoulder, a side barred with ribs, a spear leaning across a neck. These had not moved at all in half an hour. Uli's motion became circular. He passed behind a tree into deep shadow. Shading then his forehead so that the moonlight might not be reflected in his eyes he slowly raised his head to see the man's face. It was that of a Paré man with five cuts on the cheek and three on the forehead. The man was awake; his eyes were open and gazed past Uli with the stare of an idol. Uli slowly lowered his head and retreated backwards towards the shelter of a tree trunk. It was not safe for him to be caught by a Paré. He was also confused at finding Paré men where he had heard the Nok drum. Could he have made a mistake in the direction? That had never happened to him before. For the moment he was confused and when suddenly hands grasped his ankles he gave a sharp cry. Instantly he was surrounded by warriors; the forest hissed with their passage like alarmed snakes. Dark shrubs grew up on legs, branches turned into arms and saplings into spears, the living creatures of the forest again sorted themselves into the fixed and mobile. Black human bodies with muscles silvered by the moon passed between the black and silver bodies of the trees like moonlit waves flowing past the piles and shadows of a pier. Men and trees continually melted together and parted. It was only possible to distinguish the blackness which was wood and the shadow of it from the blackness and shadow of the rippling sea of flesh by the recurrence of the same forms and stripes in the same places, the same repeated patterns.

Uli stood trembling with terror and delight. These Paré might be going to kill him but they were Birri. All about him were bodies made of his own kind of flesh. He could not help smiling and touching the arm of the man who held him, caressing Birri skin even while he felt in his stomach fear of death. A chief appeared before him. 'You are from Nok,' he murmured in a voice less penetrating than a whisper.

'I escaped from the soldiers,' Uli whispered, smiling anxiously at the chief, and licking his lips.

'Are you not Uli of Nok?'

Uli shook his head, but half a dozen voices in the group about him murmured, 'Yes, he is Uli.'

'Hold him here,' said the chief.

For another hour Uli sat side by side with the Paré men. Once more the forest was silent and nothing could be seen but the black and white, and nothing moved but the moon. Then a rustle was heard as if a breath of wind had moved the leaves a yard or two away. It grew, took form and became in Uli's ear these words, 'Obai sends for Uli, but do not make a noise. Come,' said Uli's guard, standing up. They moved quickly away through the trees, crossed the Goshi road, and came suddenly upon the men of Nok. Obai, and four other chiefs, two of them from Paré and two elders from Goshi, were sitting round the bottom of a little steep dell smoking and murmuring together in council.

Uli was received coldly and was asked why he had come, as a spy or a friend.

'As a friend. I heard your war drums and I came to help.'

'Can you show us the best way to approach Alo?'

'Are you going to fight the soldiers?'

'Yes, we are going to destroy all these whites and their soldiers.'

This was from Obai who seemed to preside over the others from a higher seat on the bank.

But the other chiefs protested. They were already too far from Birri. What if the soldiers attacked Birri from the other side while they were away? Besides, it was a bad plan to attack soldiers across the open ground. The young men did not know how far rifles could shoot. It was Bewsher who was the enemy, who had given away their lands to his friends. Let them go home now that they had failed to catch Bewsher and wait for another better chance.

Obai jumped up in a fury, 'Ah! you cowards, are you afraid of a few whites and Hausas with guns?'

Uli saw at once that he could commend himself to his leaders. He exclaimed that it would be easy to kill Bewsher without attacking Alo.

'How so?' Everybody gave him attention, and already he felt like an important person.

'Bewsher is going to Goshi. We have all been awaiting him there for a week. His wife was waiting for him there and three times they had new bread made ready for his coming. You have only to stay here until he passes on his way.'

'He may take the other road.'

'Then go to Goshi.'

All but Obai were very pleased with this news, and congratulated Uli.

'Moreover,' said Uli, 'if you kill Bewsher in Goshi and go away quickly into Birri you will be safe from the soldiers.'

'Why?'

'The judges will not let the soldiers fight in Birri. I have been hearing about it this very day. The soldiers say that if it was not for Stork they would be at Paré by now. But the judges fear war.'

'How is that? Fear to make war? Why should they fear when they themselves do not go to war.'

'It is a religious matter among the whites at Goshi, I too was taught that war is wicked.'

This provoked another long and excited discussion. Obai again demanded an attack on Alo, on the grounds that the soldiers would not be prepared and that the judges were already in a panic. But the elders, especially the Goshi men, were against him.

Uli saw that he had secured his position and took care to avoid quarrels whose bitterness alarmed him. That old good nature which had made him popular in Nok had returned to him with his comrades, and he felt confused and stupid when Obai waved his arms and spat abuse and the Goshi chiefs perspired with irritation. He

202

had not come to Birri for quarrelling but for friendship and glory. He withdrew quietly and went to find himself a spear, throwing stick, and shield among the Nok contingent.

At dawn nothing had been decided, and it was too late to fight that day. Fires were lit in holes and hollow trees and the warriors heated their food and warmed their stiff limbs. Uli sat among the picked men of the headquarters guard with his back against a tree trunk; it was indifferent to him whether Alo or Goshi was attacked so long as he was at war again among the Nok. And now, having eaten, he drowsed in the morning sun, delicious warmth after the cold night. What keener happiness than this, to be in peace and idleness during war. It was complete idleness, for one was not allowed to do anything, and yet an honourable idleness, because it was a soldier's.

The next man chatted lazily with him. 'You're coming back to Nok?'

'Yes, I'm tired of foreign places.'

'They said you had a wife there.'

'No, only a woman to pass the time. Enuké is my wife—from Lower Nok. Do you know her?'

'Why yes, I know her. I thought you'd left her.'

'No, she had a baby so she was no good to me for a time. But now a year has past, and I thought I'd go back again.'

'One gets tired being away.'

'Yes, it's not suitable.'

And then for two or three hours he sat looking at his own toes without any thought whatever and smiling all the time with the most profound satisfaction.

In the evening when the fires were put out, he lay sandwiched in a row of his comrades, his cheek on the next man's shoulder, his arm locked across his side. He did not fall asleep at once like the others because what was commonplace to them was a novel delight to him. How much more pleasant to lie like this in the forest with other soldiers all at war together, than in a mission bed. How much sweeter than to lie with Atua, that soft, stinking creature in her stuffy hut. He fell asleep slowly and waked more slowly than the others. He was not yet awake while, spear and parrying stick in hand, he rushed towards the Goshi road. There was an alarum.

At the edge of the road, the darting figures became rigid; Uli stood like a tree and did not move his eyes for half a minute. He found himself close to the road, where it curved away at both sides; when at last he turned his head, fifty yards or more was in view. He could now hear a rustle of bare feet, and even the creaking of a hammock. Then Bewsher's voice echoing for a great distance among the trees could be heard talking and laughing. A dogarai in a ragged red gown appeared carrying a lantern whose light was drowned in the moonlight, then two soldiers, and a small boy with a stick and a thermos flask balanced on his head.

A whisper came down the line, let them pass, and Uli understood the reason of it when the hammock appeared, for it was followed closely by ten or twelve more soldiers. It was true that these soldiers could not have beaten off an attack. They were marching at ease, as careless as the two men of the point who had lounged behind the dogarai with the lantern. They no more expected to find a Birri ambush on the Goshi high road, twenty miles outside the Birri border, than Bewsher himself. But no doubt their presence had been enough to decide the prudent majority of the council that it would be better to kill Bewsher a little further away from Alo and a little nearer to their own forest refuge.

But that was not Uli's business. He was enjoying himself. All his senses were awake in a harmony of living. He stared at the visitors whom he was not to kill just yet with sharp interest, straining his eyes to notice every detail, his ears to hear each word. Uli loved all spectacles, all ritual; even to sit in the street and watch ordinary people in their daily movements was a pleasure. This procession in the moonlight fascinated him like a child at the theatre. The glimmering spot of yellow flame moving through the silver moonlight, the scarlet rags of the dogarai, the important-looking small boy (what a joke that he would get his throat cut to-morrow) the chair hammock shuffling along on its eight legs all out of step, like some clumsy beast; the white woman in the hammock with her small white face, dark eyes, her laughing mouth while she said something to Bewsher, strolling beside her with his pipe in his mouth and his usual one-sided grin. As Obai said, Bewsher was not a serious person. He always seemed to be playing.

Even the sweating carriers, grunting and muttering, the dignified

Henry with his grave, important look and his silver-mounted walking-stick, who brought up the rear with four more soldiers, afforded keen pleasure to Uli. He remembered Henry on the Kunama road, a miserable, starved wretch ready to lick your feet for a cigarette or a bowl of broth; now he was a man of power and wealth. Look at him. Look at his fat legs, his fat chin, his great soft belly. What a clever rascal he was. It was wonderful. It was good to look at Henry.

Henry's back disappeared at last round the bend in the road and almost at once a finger touched Uli's arm and a voice whispered, 'Bush.'

He went back and was ordered to cut wood and block the road behind the soldiers. Already a hundred men were weaving thorns and scrub among the trees to make a broad entanglement. Obai ran about admonishing, instructing. It appeared that he was quite reconciled to the attack on Goshi now that he had seen Bewsher walking into the trap. 'Now we are sure of him,' he said. 'Only don't waste time. For the other soldiers may come.'

An hour later every path was filled with warriors draining towards Goshi. Uli moved after the man in front of him with eyes cast down to see the foot or two of path between their feet. He moved like one joint in a centipede; but to himself he seemed released, free; released from futility, free of boredom; once more Uli of Nok, a somebody in the world, his own world.

# XIX

Bewsher had two objects in dashing off to Goshi in the middle of the Birri crisis. He hoped to end it, and he wanted to get away from the wire which made him dependent on the Resident and from the troops which frightened away the Birri. He had already written to Umoké appointing Goshi as a meeting-place where the chiefs could meet him in safety. The escort would not be in the way for its orders were to proceed to Kifi as a guard to the stores belonging to the Marine Department.

Bewsher had not liked this arrangement, which seemed to him suspiciously like the beginning of a patrol. He acquiesced in it only to get rid of the escort.

But the Resident had reached him. A wire, sent by hand from Alo, arrived at the Mission at eleven o'clock to tell him that the patrol could not be delayed beyond another three days and that in any case the Alo company would be sent forward to Goshi in order to cover the Mission.

Bewsher answered at once 'Birri situation extremely favourable peaceful settlement provided no provocative movements troops.'

But he did not sleep. From twelve to three he had been walking about the room and the compound, smoking cigarettes and gazing now at the wall, now at the roof or the sky with an expression of mild and pensive surprise which in Bewsher revealed a high degree of melancholy. Now and then approaching Marie's bed and gazing at it with amazement as if he had never seen anything like it before, he would at last perceive that she too was awake. Then he would say in an indignant voice, 'You ought to be asleep.'

'What about you, Monkey? Are you worrying about those wretched pagans? If I were you I'd never want to see any of them again after the way they've treated you—or the government either. When you go perhaps they'll begin to find out what you've done for them.'

'What I can't understand is why I haven't heard from that damned old rascal Umoké.'

'You've given them fifteen years of your life and all they've done is to try and cut your throat for you. It makes me so mad at the meanness and injustice of the whole thing that I'll just be glad if they do get themselves shot up. It'll serve them right and it'll serve the government right if the Birri make them fight a real war and cost them a hundred thousand pounds. That will spoil their estimates for them, and I hope it happens.'

Bewsher smiled derisively at this outburst, and murmured, 'They've been good years.' He wandered away again. In a few minutes Marie heard his voice stating in a tone of gentle regret, 'It was a mistake to clear out of Paré like that. It never pays with pagans to get cold feet.'

Marie had never seen him so dejected. Apparently it was beginning to penetrate even into his obstinate brain that he was beaten, that the control of affairs in Birri had already passed out of his hands. Marie was glad because it was time that he should realize that. He was due for a medical board in a week and she had Dollar's promise that he would be sent home. Probably Alabaster and the soldiers were counting on that too, and that was why the patrol had been dated for next week.

It was a good thing that Bewsher should begin to see the plain truth that everyone else had seen for weeks, before it had to be revealed to him by a violent shock. She dreaded that moment when the doctors finally told him to go and the soldiers marched into Birri.

'It's bad luck that Alabaster doesn't understand pagans—never did and never will. A regular desk-wallah.' He was back at the side of the bed, his head slightly on one side, the cigarette smoke curling between his fingers. His forehead was deeply wrinkled and his pale eyes were full of a kind of naïf astonishment at the amount of his bad luck. His voice was a sigh. There was nothing exaggerated about his depression. He might have been regretting the loss of a golf match. But it was extreme for Bewsher and also comical. His whole figure clad in crumpled pyjamas and an old Burberry made Marie want to laugh at him, to jump out of bed and embrace him, to tuck him up and say, 'Don't cry any more, but go to sleep like a good boy and to-morrow you'll be quite happy.'

For she was happy. She was so happy in the thought of escaping from Birri at last and taking her husband away with her that she,

207

too, could not sleep. She did not want to sleep. Long after Bewsher himself, having consented at last to creep into bed and protesting to the last that he was not sleepy, was snoring and tossing in a heavy restless doze, she lay awake. Relief, and gratitude for the Paré mercy, the thought of a happiness without daily anxiety, a secure enjoyment of the life which was so full of delights for her, excited her nerves to such a pitch that she could hardly bear to lie still, even for Bewsher's sake.

'I shouldn't be a bit surprised to see old Umoké walk in this morning,' said Bewsher. He was lying on his back smoking his first cigarette of the day. The very voice in which he spoke, a lazy, meditative voice, told Marie that the man was restored. For a moment only she was faintly surprised by this sudden recovery. She was accustomed to Bewsher's sudden rebounds of optimism.

'I'm glad you went to sleep at last,' she murmured.

'I believe I did get a horse's wink in the small hours.'

'That's Goshi.'

'And Sunday.' He yawned, and even the yawn was contented and luxurious.

There was a pause. The Yoruba watchman passed slowly, tapping with his stick and humming through his teeth a hymn tune. Bewsher hummed with him the last three or four notes.

'That's the German one,' he said then, 'what is it? Luther's?'

Marie was falling asleep. The sleepy and contented mood of Bewsher acted as soporific. Her eyelids began to fall together.

'There he is again,' said Bewsher. 'No, it's a mosquito. But when you come down to Mamma, in Somerset, that's what you'll hear on Sunday morning in the summer. It comes in with the sun. The church is in the garden and the Sunday school in the old coach house. You can hear the little blighters wake up and do a really big sniff when teacher gets on to Elisha and the three bears.'

'Darling, does it say how many bears?'

But Bewsher, like an old-established husband, ignored the interruption and pursued his own thoughts. 'It's a funny thing—I used to grumble at being fetched home for a Sunday. But now it seems to me the best kind of day I ever spent at home.'

'I always said you were the religious one,' said Marie.

'H'm,' said Bewsher. He was not listening to her. He let his head

208

sink back on the pillow and gazed at the roof where a nest of small birds were already cheeping for food. Swallows nested in his own gable at home. He had heard that cheeping a thousand times.

'That's really why you like coming here,' said Marie, as if talking to herself, 'and why it does you so much good.'

Umph! A sigh of pleasure through his nose. It was not only the cheeping. There were a dozen other sounds when you listened for them, country sounds. The grind of cart wheels on a stony road, the clap-to of a shaking gate, the heavy chopping of hooves, the rustle of leaves, the whirr of a reaper, larks and then a church clock striking in the distance. The cart wheels and the hooves were far off, perhaps a drum tapping and rattling in the bush, the jingle was something on the watchman's belt, the clock was a bird calling twenty times from the direction of Alo. A lizard jumping from the top of the wall and dragging his tail over the hard earth was the gate and the reaping machine. There he was again, slap went the gate and bounced twice in its socket.

'And why you and John are such good friends,' said Marie, as if she asked a question.

The jingle grew louder. A stick dragged on the ground exactly like a braked wheel. The Yoruba passed slowly, moaning another tune; his intonation was the very note of a sleepy choir on a summer morning. Flies buzzed in that nasal drone and there was also the authentic yowl of a farmer with his mind bent upon dinner. 'Roast beef and horse radish,' Bewsher muttered, 'followed by two hours in a hammock with the top button of the trousers undone. And please God no damn women will call.'

'What darling'—in a startled voice—'what did you say?'

Bewsher did not answer. He was waiting for the Yoruba to pass the side door and now he picked up the tune, first humming, then suddenly, delighted at his good memory, striking into the words, 'I—heard—the—voice—of Jesus—say. Come unto me—and—rest.'

'But, Sweetheart, don't you think that is most beautiful?'

'One of my favourites—we always had it at Millcombe.'

Marie, now quite awake, had risen on her elbow. Bewsher could see her eyes and nose close to the net. The brightness of the eyes and the note of the voice told him that she was in a highly emotional state, and her emotion was at once communicated to him, not in a specific form, but as a stimulant to his own feelings.

Unexpectedly she said, 'I wish I could be like Minnie and Dawl Dans, living in all that beauty—it's like a different world.'

'I think you do.'

'Oh no, Monkey, I've no real religion.'

'Why don't you get one then?'

'Would you like me to?' Again he could see her bright excited eyes and parted lips close to the net and felt a keen movement of pleasure.

'Certainly I would. It's a very good idea.'

'But, Monkey, you can't just choose a religion like a lipstick—you've got to feel a conviction.'

'It's a great pity you weren't brought up to it. If we have a girl we'll put her on the right lines from the beginning.'

'What if it's a boy?'

'Oh! all children.'

'But not men,' said Marie with a faint note of mockery, of disappointment. There was another long pause. Then suddenly she appealed to him. 'But, Monkey, you do feel that the *idea* of it is beautiful, to make Jesus an example, to teach people to love each other, to make them kind and good, to give them peace. Don't you feel that it's the most beautiful *idea* for a religion?'

'Of course I do, it's a first-class religion.' He spoke with force and meant what he said. He was charmed by the idea and also by Marie because she thought it beautiful, because she was the kind of woman who melted at the thought of Jesus, of his love and pity. This was the kind of woman a man wanted for a wife, one whose goodness would earn his respect. What a stroke of luck that he had obtained her in Marie whom he had married for quite other attractions. But he had always been the luckiest of men.

'Why then is it different for men?' Marie asked, looking at him gravely. Bewsher was looking at her also with a grave and resolute expression. There was a short silence. Then he pulled up his net and said, 'Shall I come and talk to you, my dear?'

This was a euphemism which meant usually everything but conversation. Marie was taken aback. She blushed. Then she began to laugh at him. He quickly slipped out of his bed and under her net.

It was Marie's habit everywhere she went to take an early morning

210

walk while Bewsher tackled his letters. Especially she looked forward to her walks in Goshi which was the biggest clearing in the division. The path between the Mission and Goshi village was more than a mile from the forest on either hand, towards Kifi and towards Alo. Marie had learnt to hate the forest, not only because she saw in every mile of it an ambush waiting for Bewsher, but because its terrors made it impossible for her to be at peace within herself. When she was in the bush she was always preoccupied with mean fears of which she was ashamed. It was degrading to tremble at every sound, and hate the very sight of the Birri, especially as she could not confess these sensations to Bewsher. But on the Goshi road there was no cover for enemies and the wild Birri were never seen.

It was still cool. Marie was glad of her short, padded coat and walked briskly. Now and then she looked at the sky which was turning pale green, the rough broad plain, and the distant black walls of the forest. The plain, usually untidy and harsh with its refuse of the fields was now partly covered by long streaks of greenish mist, the fields were in every shade of blue, grey and purple, and when the mist threw a breath across them, watergreen. Each time Marie looked about her she said in devout tones, 'How beautiful.' But she was not observing the beauties with great attention. Her ejaculation was a kind of prayer, and sometimes she said, 'How beautiful,' when she was looking at the dusty road with the smile of a dreamer mixed with a little cynicism which was her usual expression, when she was happy. As usual she seemed to mock her own romantic frame of mind, but in fact she was in such a condition of gratitude and relief that it was difficult for her to think at all, much less to laugh at herself.

Next to the evening when she liked to talk to her friends, Marie loved the early mornings when she could be alone and feel in the silence and calm clear light that the whole world was in sympathy with her mood, that there was in space a mind which loved beauty and which had sympathy and tenderness for all creatures.

Possibly this was an illusion, like other intimations of immortality, but this was no more hindrance to Marie's keen delighting in it than the make-believe of a theatre to a sympathetic audience. She found in the brightness and immensity of the spectacle in front of her something large enough to house part of the majesty, beauty and eternal being of the god she desired, and therefore she placed him there and rested in the midst of him.

Bewsher had his Sunday morning feeling and she had her early morning walk. For Marie, Sunday in Goshi, on the Goshi road, was a true experience of God. She did not believe in him any more than she believed that little babies came from heaven trailing clouds of glory, but every nerve in her body exulted in the thought of him, and when, looking into the empty air, she smiled and said 'How beautiful,' she was communicating with the spirit of love itself. Love made the poem and love filled the sky with a material god in whose lap she had always wanted to rest, safe and glorious and happy among a world full of safe, glorious and happy lovers, without the indignity of laws and the folly and wickedness of conflict, none greater than another, none less. Her smile was like that of a grown up taking part in a game with children but her spirit was in Paradise.

The message from Umoké arrived by a Goshi boy at half-past six. It had been sent the night before. The boy admitted that he had been afraid to bring it to the mission until the morning. But it was entirely satisfactory to Bewsher. Umoké asked forgiveness for the bad conduct of the young warriors at Paré and promised that they should be punished. The Nok murderers were already tied up at their own village and the chiefs waited only for Bewsher to come and try them. 'All trouble finish now,' he wrote, 'the Nok fear too much.' He urged that Bewsher should meet him in Nok that evening.

But as Bewsher, who was having breakfast on the stoop, pointed out to the Dobsons, there was no great need for hurry. 'I'm not going to trek in the heat of the day and deprive myself of your company just because these rascals at Nok have got the wind up about a patrol. It won't do them any harm to wait a little longer now that their tails are well down between their legs. On the other hand, Nok is a better place than Goshi because it's further from the telegraph office. I don't want the Resident making difficulties.'

Miss Dans was disgusted at the very notion. 'But Mr. Alabaster couldn't possibly send the troops after that letter? It would be just murder.'

'You never know,' said Bewsher, who appeared, as usual in the morning, cool and businesslike. But as he sat at the table between the two admiring ladies he could not prevent himself from smiling at their enthusiasm.

Bewsher was always sure of sympathy at the Dobsons'. They never, like Marie, accused him of selfishness or pigheadedness. They understood perfectly his feelings about the pagans because they had the same kind of feelings about their own work. So that now he found himself in very congenial company, and the party, while they were planning the details of this new important peace mission, which road to take, how many carriers, when to start, was like a family of brothers and sisters. Even Doll Dans had in her voice, together with the briskness of the competent, the affectionate tone of a sister at a crisis of separation and danger.

Minnie Dobson, though she had retired, as usual after every meal, into her long chair, took with her a pile of underclothes and socks. Mrs. Dobson and Miss Dans had now for many months supplemented Marie's very inefficient mending. At every visit they were shocked by the condition of Bewsher's clothes, which were certainly in a ruinous condition at the end of a nineteen-month's tour. Miss Dans sorted out from loads filled with half empty jam jars, mouldy bottles of chutney, old newspapers, broken plates, enough sound tins of vegetables and fruit to last a fortnight. It appeared that Marie at least had not counted on eating any more meals in the Nigerian bush.

Thus when Marie walked in, she found herself on the edge of a scene of domestic bustle in which Bewsher himself, smiling with the embarrassed air of a hero among the overwhelming attentions of his family, formed the centre.

'What is it?' she asked in astonishment.

Bewsher was startled. His smile became guilty. For the moment he could not answer. He experienced that most irritating self-consciousness of the husband who knows he is doing the right thing but dare not confess it to his wife. But it was precisely at such a moment that he could rely on the Dobsons.

'He's going to Nok,' said Doll Dans, without even looking up from her tins and bottles. 'Umoké sent a message. Minnie, do you think this tin is gassy or is that just the shape they made it? I must say I never saw such stores in my life.'

'What nonsense,' said Marie. 'Nobody could go to Nok. Nobody could go into Birri at all. They'd just kill you as soon as you put your nose into the bush.'

Bewsher, still with the same nervous smile, began to explain that in fact Birri was now perfectly safe, the tribes had capitulated. Nok was in a state of panic.

It was a good speech, reasonable, well put, cheerful and matter of fact in tone. It would have convinced anybody except Marie, who did not listen to it. She interrupted twice with irrelevancies. She still refused to believe that he was serious. But she was growing more agitated. She looked once or twice at the stores spread out on the floor, at Minnie sewing the spine pad to a bush shirt.

'But, Monkey, it's simply absurd,' she exclaimed. 'It's suicide.'

Bewsher once more pointed out that the pagans were suing for peace, that it was to their interest to secure it as soon as possible before they were attacked, that they knew this to be their last chance.

Marie began to argue, contradicted him and all at once it appeared that there was going to be an unpleasant scene. The woman lost control of herself and began to scream in a shrill voice that no one had ever heard before. She accused him of selfishness, obstinacy, of thinking of nobody but himself, all in the furious senseless tone of some hag abusing her drunken husband in a slum. She even looked like one. She had become all at once haggard, exhausted.

Now again Bewsher had reason to be grateful for his friends, whose moral courage was equal to anything, and who besides were accustomed to deal with such cases. While, looking extremely foolish, he was still murmuring something to the effect that he was very sorry about this—he had no idea—but he hoped—etc., etc. Minnie Dobson, whose languor had quite disappeared, got up and led Marie into the inner room. She was heard to say that she knoo just how she felt. She'd felt the same herself, as if she could scream right out. In a few minutes she came back and shaking her head at Bewsher, who was getting up from his chair with the promptitude and desperate face of a man summoned to a forlorn hope, beckoned her husband. Dobson, though he could scarcely have expected the summons at once, went in and for a long time the party on the stoop, still busy with darning and sorting, could hear his voice beyond the curtain murmuring consolation. The result was that when Bewsher finally was allowed access to his wife, at half-past seven, just before service, he found her more contrite, more tearful and apologetic than if they had fought a full-dress battle throughout a whole day and night. So far from having to invent a new defence, he was obliged to defend Marie from herself. 'John tells me I'm a noosance to you and everybody and a disgrace to my country as well as yours, and I guess he's right. For if I cannot trust God to look after you when you're doing God's own work at least I ought to be ashamed, says John, to work on the other side. I am ashamed, Monkey; I'm so ashamed I'd like to die. Go along now and get eaten soon as you like, and I won't drop a single tear on the pot.'

Bewsher was delighted, charmed. He was equally relieved to escape all the last stages of a violent quarrel and shocked to see the effects of passion on Marie. She was so worn down and broken by the rapid succession of panic, hysteria, rage, shame and the expert handling of Dobson, who had, no doubt, as she once put it herself, gone straight to her most sensitive nerves and played the banjo on them, that she seemed to have no strength even to lift her hands. Only the voice had life in it, and that was a false, galvanic kind of life, like that of a muscle which plays tricks after the owner is dead.

Bewsher was full of pity and love. He put his hand behind her head and explained again how little danger there was in this last journey, and how much depended on it. This was the turning-point for Birri.

He was slightly disconcerted even after his experience of marriage and Marie to find that she had not even listened to his arguments and apparently took no interest in his political hopes. At the first pause in his eloquence, she asked pensively, 'Do you believe it yourself?'

'Believe what, darling?'

'That God has been looking after you.'

'I've certainly had uncommon luck.'

'John says it was God. You don't believe that, Monkey, do you?'

'That walk out at Paré was rather providential.'

'He says it's a scientific fact.'

'My luck?'

'No, that love is stronger than guns.'

'I daresay there's something in it,' said Bewsher cheerfully. 'And now I suppose I'd better put my coat on for chapel. You're sure you're all right, my dear?'

She held tightly to his hand and answered, 'I guess I don't want to lose a husband—I'll never get another.'

'No such luck to lose him this time.'

215

'A scientific fact—now wouldn't that be nice. But it's just non-sense—when little children die of cancer and the whole world is just one big dog-fight.'

'I'm sorry to go, darling, but there's the bell.'

'Don't go, you can hear it all from here.'

'But don't you think it will look rather rude if neither of us go. Besides, I told Dobson——'

'Go along then and play.'

The service on this Sunday was held not as usual in the chapel but the central room in the mission house. The real reason of this alteration was to let Marie hear it, for the Dobsons felt that it would do her good. But the reason given was that the congregation was a small one. No one had come from Goshi, and the convert Birri, who had quarters about the mission, had mysteriously vanished. Even some of the servants, including Henry, could not be found. Bewsher's explanation was that the Birri were suffering from a bad conscience, that his own presence combined with the passage of the Kifi detachment had frightened them all into the bush. The mission Birri in fact, as well as the absent servants who were all Birri, had probably been playing a double game. He would certainly not be surprised to find out that Henry was a traitor and spy.

This consideration was added to the other numerous reasons for the satisfaction with which Bewsher came to the service. The highest was derived from the occasion. For he thoroughly enjoyed any kind of religious service in which he could take part, that is to say, sing and understand, and especially these at Goshi, where he could rely upon his favourite hymns and a good sermon. He took a front seat between the two ladies and waited with a little smile of anticipation. He was at peace with the world and especially with his wife.

The first hymn was,

> Rejoice to-day with one accord,
> Sing out with exultation.

Good, this was the stuff for the troops. He opened his mouth and rejoiced.

> Now every voice shall say,
> Oh praise our God alway,
> Let all his saints adore him.

On the last line Bewsher's voice came in with a triumphant bellow and then finding itself alone in the middle of a soft passage was suddenly deflated to a noise resembling the baa of a sick lamb. But he didn't care a damn. He even smiled at Doll Dans to see if she had enjoyed the incident. She, however, was looking straight in front of her with a very severe expression. She was probably still thinking about the condition of Bewsher's mincing machine which had been her indignant theme for the last half hour. It seemed to her a disgrace to her whole sex and the stars and stripes as well that Marie should allow her mincing machine to be in such a state.

Dobson, in a long prayer, was thanking God for his mercy shown to a dear friend and commending him to the same sure keeping in all his enterprises. It was not till this point that Bewsher perceived that he was the dear friend, and that the service was a thanksgiving for his escape. Then he was touched as well as amused. He looked forward to the sermon with a keener interest. What would Dobson make of the combination of luck and bush-craft that had got him out of Paré.

But you could always rely on Dobson to put up a first-class show, good plausible argument on reasonable premises. He never played tricks with texts or hit below the belt with sentiment. He was as honest a preacher as he was a man. You could trust him to play the game as well as a layman.

The subject proved to be faith, and the preacher began in his own and Bewsher's favourite style with an argument designed in this case to show that the simplest operations of reason were impossible without faith. For instance, that a man must take upon trust such things as the principle of causation upon which all science was constructed. And then he went on to show that as without these *a priori* principles of reasoning the world of knowledge would be a chaos equally senseless and dangerous, so without faith in God's providence the world itself, the real world of man's spirit, appeared as a cruel and pointless accident, something quite inexplicable upon any grounds at all.

'The world without a provident and loving God has been compared with a lunatic asylum, but this is quite inadequate to describe the horror of the conception. Can we really imagine a world without justice, mercy, or indeed any object at all, a ceaseless warfare of race against race, in which it is equally possible for good men and bad

217

to perish without the smallest advantage, in which we may say the good are more open to destruction than the bad just as in a country without government the best elements are quickly destroyed by the most violent and ruthless. In this war, moreover, not merely a whole race but its culture, the noblest accomplishment of a nation, could disappear like a stone into the sea without leaving a trace or even a recollection. Consider friends, what this means. That all the famous and noble deeds of their heroes, the anxious labours of their wise, the inspired masterworks of their artists, the loving self-sacrifice of their teachers and their saints be made as nothing, things that need never have been and will never be known again.'

Bewsher coughed slightly and moved in his chair; the cough and movement expressed approval. That last bit had been well done, very good indeed. Of course the argument was not new, but there was no harm in an old argument if it was a good one and well expressed. Yes, here was the next step. 'But fortunately it is not necessary—it is not even possible to imagine a world without justice, mercy or love. They are facts of experience.'

That was a very familiar passage. Had he read it somewhere or was it from the old vicar at Millcombe? But the vicar usually stuck to a text, stuck to it like a fly in treacle. My God, what sermons! It was like a knock over the head to remember them. Why was it that these Nonconformist fellows produced so much better stuff? Probably for the same reason that a gunman is quicker on the draw than a traffic policeman.

Would it be a good plan to hang the Nok murderers from their own roof trees as soon as he reached the place or bring them through Birri in chains? He would have to see how the land lay. But now that he had them in his hand it might be a good thing to put the fear of death into them.

Bewsher caught himself looking out of the window with his nose gripped between his fingers in a reflective but not very decorous attitude. He hastily turned his eyes towards the preacher, crossed his arms, straightened his back. Dobson was leaning forward over his little schoolroom desk with a look of excitement and earnestness which betokened the rapid culmination of his argument. His round well-shaven face was slightly flushed, his eyes, usually so mild in expression, gazed indignantly through the gold-rimmed spectacles.

They challenged contradiction. They defied the world. 'And angels are stronger than tanks. That is not romance—it is a fact—a fact that explains why slaves are now free and why little children are no longer sent into factories at five years old. Did the slaves and children have any guns? Their own parents and masters swore that they should never be free, that their services were economically necessary. But they are free because of God's love, and that is stronger than all the guns and whips and economic considerations in the world.'

First class, said Bewsher to himself, smiling with friendly congratulation. That change of voice when he put the question, and the pause afterwards—a K.C. couldn't have done it better. A damn good man if ever there was one.

Dobson, now flushed and perspiring, not from physical exertion, for he used very little gesture, but the force of his nervous excitement, spoke more slowly and in a lower voice. This more intimate and domestic tone conveyed even more strongly the sense of the man's profound feeling. Bewsher perceived this at once and admired the art of it while he appreciated the sincerity of the emotions. He was indeed very much touched by the last part of this sermon.

'The veriest savage hesitates to kill the man who comes unarmed and in the name of friendship. Even the name will serve. It has served scoundrels before this, slave traders, spies. It has served missionaries, doctors, teachers, magistrates in every part of the world. I need not say how clear and fresh is a recollection which must be in all our minds to-day, where one who went in the cause of peace and amity among thousands of armed enemies vowed to seek his death, yet passed through them for days untouched, and finally escaped by what we must humbly call a miracle. May we not ask ourselves what would have been that man's fate if he had followed what are called the dictates of common sense? If he had sought to rule these pagans by force instead of love and trust, if he had gone among them armed and threatened them with vengeance for his death. It is as certain as I stand here that he would be dead now. It is certain as the sunrise that he owes his life to the fact that I have stated, the strong repugnance of any man, however fierce, ignorant and deceived, to kill an unarmed man who comes to him in friendship. And that fact, a scientific fact of experience, is proof alone that there is a god in the world, a god whose spirit is attested by the fact not only of our inner experience, but as clear in operation to our eyes and to our critical judgment as these rays of light which fall upon this desk from the open sky. God is love and love is strong. He that fights in love's name shall be saved and his work shall endure for ever.'

This excellent address was followed by the hymn, 'Now thank we all our God.' No better choice had been possible. It was not only a prime favourite of Bewsher's, but it expressed exactly his feeling of the moment. He was in luck, lucky in his wife, in his friends, and above all, most unexpectedly, lucky in Birri. The game was in his hands now, and he knew how to play it. Federation, native courts, a code of law; in a year Birri would have a body as well as a soul. The tribe would be saved as a people.

And with federation accomplished he could afford to let the traders in. In fact, he would want them, for he would need money to build the courthouses and markets and to make the roads, and that would make his peace with the government. The missions were another pair of shoes. They got at the women, at the very foundations of the domestic system. Think of the Dobsons at Nok and Paré, thoroughly sincere, active, intelligent people with their whole minds on the job of winning souls, and all the knowledge and experience of civilization behind them. No Birri would have a chance against them. They'd play the devil in no time. That would be putting the pike into the pond and no mistake.

He would bar the missions altogether. It would take five years at least, perhaps ten or twenty, to form a thoroughly useful native creed and ritual out of the juju, and pump in the right kind of ethics. Play the game. What would that be in Birri? Probably have to be turned right round. Must ask Marie. Last verse. He took a deep breath:

> *All praise and thanks to God*
> *The father now be given;*
> *The son and him who reigns.*

Bewsher went straight from service to Marie. He wanted to ask her to knock him up a speech for the Nok Birri. Her Birri was very much better than his. He found her lying on her back with her eyes wide open and an expression which meant that she was preoccupied.

'How goes it, my dear?'

She gazed at him for half a minute before she answered, 'Did you like the address?'

'Very much—absolutely first class.'

'After all, you can't get round facts, can you, Monkey?' She was like a child asking for a lump of sugar.

'Facts are facts, no doubt about it,' he declared with emphasis.

Minnie Dobson came in apologizing and put a thermometer in the patient's mouth. Marie had accepted the thermometer before she knew what Minnie was doing to her. She was neither amused nor surprised. Her mind was too busy, or rather her whole being was too much involved, with the discovery which, like those rewarding the chemist or the physicist after years of research, had seemed to her at first only another step in a commonplace routine of explanation and now began to reveal itself as something enormous, revolutionary; that transformed her whole conception of life.

'It's true,' she said to herself. 'There's no way out. Only a coward could run away from it. Or is it all nonsense?'

She shivered with excitement. Her body turned cool and light. She seemed to be floating on her bed on golden waves. And even though she perceived that the waves were the sunlight reflected from the undulations of the mud floor, she had the same feeling of elation, of lightness, of confidence and delight. What peace to float like this, cool and tranquil in the security of God's love, God's justice. Or perhaps it was only that she had a temperature.

Minnie took out the thermometer, looked at it and showed it to Bewsher. Both of them smiled and Minnie said something to her about the heat.

Marie did not hear her because she was not listening. She knew already that she was not suffering from fever, or no more than she had at any time in the last twelve months. But Minnie was a molly coddler, in Bewsher's phrase, and liked to take temperatures.

Now she went away, and at once Bewsher, losing his nonchalant social air, knelt down by her bed, and kissed her and murmured, 'Poor old girl, it's a damn shame.'

'Darling, when are you going to Nok?'

He hesitated. 'Well, of course—there's no great hurry.'

'But I want you to go, it's such a great chance.'

'You do see that?' He was delighted. Then suddenly he took her face between his hands and kissed with such energy that she was startled.

'But why, Monkey——'

'By Gad, you don't know what a difference it's made to me—to have you backing me up.'

'Oh but, Monkey, you don't understand.' She pulled at his shirt to draw him near while she explained to him her great discovery. But she could not find words sufficiently convincing, that would not sound absurd.

'What don't I understand?' he said putting his lips to her fingers. Monkey, for all his clumsy shape, was deft and easy in his gallantries. 'Oh, damn the woman.' This referred to Minnie Dobson who came in at this moment with a cool drink and a fan, an ingenious machine worked like a clock by weights and gear wheels. She put a tablet in Marie's mouth and gave her a drink. And then said something to Bewsher, who, smiling over his shoulder as if to say, One must submit to these good women, went away with her.

The tablet was soft and bitter, probably aspirin. Marie swallowed it automatically and lay gazing at the silent twinkling fan which sent a hot stream of air upon her face.

She fell into a doze and when she waked the sun was over the zenith. She judged that it was lunch-time and began to get up, in a panic at her lateness, before she remembered that she was supposed to be an invalid. But how absurd that was. She had never felt so well, so light in body and mind. She put on her slippers and walked into the stoop. There was no one except Doll Dans sound asleep in a big chair. Even in her sleep the woman wore a determined air. She lay flat on her back with her feet together and her hands at her sides like a soldier on parade. Her spectacles, however, were crooked, and one lock of hair had detached itself from the smooth cap of brown to wave about in the slight eddies of the hot wind.

Loud snores came from the verandah where Bewsher could be seen on his own bed, stripped of its poles. Apparently it had been removed from the room while she had been asleep. Bewsher asleep had the patient, careworn expression of an old soldier.

He appeared suddenly unlike himself, not the nonchalant and cheerful Monkey whose very enthusiasms were a kind of game, but the man of the world armed and hardened by experience, trusting in nobody and nothing but himself. Marie, looking at the wrinkled brows and compressed lips, thought with pity, 'And he could rest in peace if he only knew—if he could only see——'

She stooped to kiss him, as if the kiss itself would convey to him some of that comforting repose which filled her own spirit, but Bewsher's frown suddenly deepened, he threw up his arms and muttered. Marie darted away on tiptoe. She did not want to break his siesta. Afterwards she could tell him, prove to him what was so obvious.

She moved across the compound towards the Goshi road. She had forgotten the sun, still high enough to be dangerous, but when she felt it striking through her hair, she thought dreamily, 'But it can't hurt me now, it's God's sun.'

This, of course, was half in joke. Nevertheless she felt a temptation to risk the experiment to see if the sun would hurt her now, and she did not hurry to put herself in the shade of the chapel. But she perceived that in this she was playing a kind of game unworthy of the moment. She was a little ashamed of her frivolity, which had the air still of a doubt.

Everybody was asleep. Even the kitchen dog, yapping at her, seemed to yawn between barks and ask itself, 'Why did God make me such a martyr to duty?' Snores came from all the boys' houses. In the shade of the kitchen two of Bewsher's Alo carriers, powerful Hausas with the flattened, cynical countenances of old professional vagabonds, were lying with their hands locked together. A third was resting his head upon one of their stomachs. A thousand times she had seen such a spectacle, carriers hand in hand, friends heaped together in their sleep like a litter of kittens. No one came to hospital without at least one anxious comrade and often with half a dozen and his family as well.

With what courage one naked savage from the forest would venture among his enemies in Goshi merely to accompany another to the mission hospital and with what patience he would sit outside for a whole day, two days, in order to be within call of the sufferer.

Marie, looking at the snoring carriers, felt again that wave of triumphant conviction and joy which had carried her into another world. She had called the Christian faith another world and that was true. She was in that world now, the world of faith in God, in love;

her whole being said to her, 'It is true.' She did not need to argue with herself. Her mind, her heart assured her of the fact immediately, as she knew that the sun was shining all about her. As the sun filled the air with its transparent flame so God poured his love through all creation invisible only because it was everywhere.

The dog was now almost hysterical. Marie, not to annoy it further, turned towards the hospital. At the same time, the hospital orderly, a boy called Garuba, came out in his clean white jumper and stood looking towards Goshi, shading his eyes with his hand.

Suddenly he gave a shout and ran back into the hospital. A commotion was heard, excited cries. Half a dozen figures appeared on the stoop, looking towards Goshi. The shout had brought out several of the boys and some of the women from their compound behind the hospital. A small boy ran towards the kitchen shouting something—about Goshi, and the carriers sitting up with bewildered looks of awakened sleepers asked, 'What—what?'

The small boy ran past without answering. But now the whole mission was awake. Half-naked women shrieking at the tops of their voices scuttled towards the mission house carrying in their hands clothes and babies. The hospital patients streamed out limping, staggering, or actually crawling on all fours, in the same direction.

Marie had been seen. An excited crowd pressed round her, shouting that the pagans had come. The boy, Sam, excited for the first time in her recollection of him, was trying to induce her to go to the mission house. He spluttered, 'Run—run—quick, quick, quick.' His small hands, with their yellow palms, circled about her arms desiring to catch her and push her into safety, only too polite and well trained to touch their mistress.

Marie was astonished, and kept on saying, 'But what is it—what is happening?'

'Look, look.' A dozen fingers pointed not only towards Goshi, but in every direction, across the plain which seemed to Marie to wear its usual empty and sun-dried appearance. At this time, about three o'clock, it was speckled all over with the short dark shadows of old yam heaps, piles of rubbish, corn stacks and shrubs and clumps of weeds such as cover all African farm lands. This was what the plain always looked like during the middle hours of the day.

But as Marie watched, still smiling, as much amused as surprised by this sudden fuss about nothing, she saw that some of those dots

224

of shadow were in motion. She narrowed her eyes to stare. There was no doubt about it—one of the yam fields had thrown out an arm across the road.

The movement, which excited her interest, produced a panic among the rest. They bolted; only Sam remained, imploring, his hands reaching to lay hold of this stupid white woman. But he did not look at her. He was looking over his shoulder.

'Very well, Sam—run along. I'm coming.'

But the boy would not consent to run. It was obvious that his self-respect would not permit him to run while his master's wife was in danger. 'It is true,' thought Marie, looking affectionately at Sam. 'He simply can't put himself first. It's just so common a thing you don't notice it.'

Dobson and Miss Dans were already standing at the edge of the stoop looking overhead towards the plain. As she approached, she smiled up at them, expecting some comment upon her escape from her bed and her reckless exposure to the sun. But no one even looked at her. She climbed up beside them.

Bewsher came lounging from the back stoop, red from sleep, his hair sticking out in tufts like a cornfield after a storm. He, too, did not notice her affectionate mocking smile. He was already staring at the plain.

The movements among the shadows had become more noticeable. As Marie once more turned her eyes that way, a whole flight of arrowy black shapes was seen to rise from one yam field and swoop across into the next. A thicket of scrub suddenly gave birth to a number of small scattered shrubs which sailed across two cornfields and the Goshi road like bundles of grass carried on a strong wind, and finally dived into a hollow about a hundred yards from the station. The effect was startling, and for the first time Marie gave her mind to these strange phenomena.

'What is it, darling?' she asked, smiling at his bemused, half-awakened look, and then at once noticing that this was a silly question, 'What do they want?'

'That's what I'm wondering. Where are my field-glasses?'

'In the bath basket, I expect. Shall I look?'

'If you would, and you might bring my gun at the same time.'

Marie, already going towards the bedroom answered that Sam

had the gun for cleaning. It was probably in the back stoop. Then the Dobsons said something and there seemed to be discussion.

She could not find the glasses, and while she was looking for them in a uniform case, Doll Dans came in and said, 'It's not his shot-gun but the automatic.'

'He's not going to shoot at them,' said Marie, startled, beginning to wake up.

'That's what we're afraid of—he seems kind of excited.'

'But he never has before—he doesn't believe in it.'

'He thinks they've come for him this time, and he wants the gun for his pocket.'

The pistol in its brown holster was in full view of both of them. It lay among a heap of boots, books, tobacco tins, newspapers and sandwich cases in the wicker-bath lining, which served on tour for all such small hard objects.

Marie picked it up and slipped it out of its case. It was familiar to her hand for she had cleaned it and charged it for Bewsher a hundred times. Now, with an accustomed gesture, she pulled out the magazine to see that it was filled.

But she was not thinking about the pistol. Her whole mind was engaged with this problem so casually presented to her. Doll's last remark made her understand even more clearly its nature. She turned very white and said, 'You wouldn't shoot.'

'No, but then—it's not the same for him.'

The woman spoke in the most matter of fact voice; nothing showed her nervous tension except a slight colour on her cheekbones and a certain deliberation of speech.

Marie knew that this quiet moment when not a sound could be heard anywhere was critical for Bewsher's life and her own happiness. She trembled and looked at Doll as if for advice. She wanted to ask her, 'Are you sure that this God of yours can be trusted even by those who trust him? Are you sure about these facts?'

But she knew, even as she looked, that it was no good asking such a question. Doll Dans' religion at least had nothing to do with facts. It was her passion, her life, and she did not ask whether God was to be trusted. She gave without condition or bargain. Probably she would like to die for Him, whatever He was, as people died for kings they had never seen and creeds they could not understand.

'At least it's about the only chance,' Marie said.

The other slightly compressed her lips as if to forbid them to speak. She was determined not to play the partisan.

Marie accepted her responsibility, and now her mind was not confused any longer. Her judgment was as active and concentrated as an animal's at bay. She weighed the chances.

'Have you got it?' Bewsher's voice shouted from the stoop.

She opened a uniform case and pushed pistol and holster down among her clean linen as far as they would go.

'I think you're right,' said Doll gravely. 'He doesn't want to do anything mean at a time like this.'

Marie was running towards the door. Bewsher and the Dobsons were at the edge of the stoop sharply black against the glittering sunlight of the fields. But about midway up this background appeared a new dark band of shadow, a dusty brown hedge. Marie, coming breathless to her husband's side, saw that this hedge was the Birri, standing twenty or thirty deep and thousands strong round the edge of the mission clearing. They feared to put their feet on the magic ground of the white man's juju house. Only their spearheads, twinkling and flashing, seemed alive.

But not all of them were afraid. A party of ten or fifteen had just been noticed advancing under cover of Stoker's fort. It was upon this manœuvre that the mission party were intent when Marie came up. Bewsher, without looking at her, held out his hand.

'But I haven't got it,' she panted.

'Then get it, my dear, quick as you can.'

'But, Monkey, isn't it all against your own policy to——'

He turned sharply round and looked first at her, then at Doll Dans who had now modestly rejoined her, then at her again with an expression which she knew very well. He had looked like that when she had first produced her theory that the Birri civilization was the natural pattern of society, and again at her suggestion that faith had cured him of poison. It was an expression which meant, 'What's bitten her now?'

'But there are thousands of them,' she said, making a frightened grimace.

His glance had shifted over her head towards the chapel compound. At the same time the refugees in the middle room began to scream something about the chapel. The party turned simultaneously and saw a mass of pagans standing in the shadow of the chapel not

227

twenty yards from them. Others were streaming from the other side of the building.

Bewsher snatched up Mrs. Dobson's steel-covered scissor-case from the table, and then looked round as if for something more offensive. The screams of the servants were answered by a battle cry from the warriors who rushed towards the mission house.

Mrs. Dobson and Doll Dans, as if by an agreed plan, ranged themselves side by side and fell on their knees. Dobson stepped in front of them and spread out his arms. Bewsher put the scissor-case in his pocket, and ran out into the chapel compound, holding up his left hand like a policeman stopping the traffic, and shouting angrily, 'Stop, stop, what are you doing—you fools, you good for nothing.'

He ran crookedly away from the mission house, edging towards the chapel, so that the Birri turning towards him left the mission on their right hand. When suddenly he stopped, they also stopped, and those in front, who had been darting at him with raised spears, sheered away on each side. Some who could not escape to the sides even turned back, as if his furious gestures and curses had been physical blows beating them back from him. So for a moment he was seen in the midst of the pagans who eddied round him like the divided waters of a river, with in front a clear space like the hollow in front of a post or rock which holds up the rush of the water. They still did not like to face Bewsher.

But one who did not give way was Obai. He stood right in front of Bewsher so that perhaps for fifteen seconds, a long time in a fight, the two were alone in the open ground. The boy was crazy with excitement. The sweat poured down his cheeks, his eyes were bulging from his head, his whole body was quivering like an over-engined frail boat. 'Kill the whites,' he screamed. 'Death to the white scum. Birri for the Birri.'

Bewsher, with his eyes on the youth, knew his danger. He smiled and said, 'Is it you, my friend? What's all this?'

Obai, ducking as if to avoid a blow, ran a step or two forward and raised his spear for a stab. His eyes were half closed and his hoarse cries became inarticulate. He was in the extreme of terror and courage. Bewsher whisked out the case, and aimed it at the boy shouting, 'Go back, or I shoot.'

228

Obai did actually go back. As the sun flashed on the steel he recoiled a yard back in automatic terror of the expected bang, crouching and bending his head.

But at once he recovered his purpose. He stood up, opened his chest as if to say, 'Shoot,' and then repeating clearly and proudly his national cry, made a single leap forward and stabbed Bewsher in the chest. At once a score of others closed in with spears and clubs.

Bewsher fell on his back with a look of ludicrous amazement and indignation. He was heard shouting something again about 'bloody rascals,' in a voice expressive quite as much of surprise as indignation. In fact, Bewsher's own feelings as he lay on the ground with two or three spears in his body, though, of course, full of official indignation, was not empty of a kind of amusement as if some part of his mind were remarking to him, 'Well, old chap, the joke is on you. You're not going to get away with it this time.'

# XX

He had, however, very little time for any reflections indignant or sardonic because from the moment when Obai first struck him to the time when he was most certainly dead with ten or fifteen spears in him and his skull smashed was not much more than fifteen seconds. Almost before the Mission party had understood what was happening his body had vanished round the corner, dragged by the heels at full speed by Uli and half a dozen more of the tribe from Nok.

What saved the mission was the fact that most of the pagan leaders ran after Bewsher's body in order to keep their eyes on this great piece of booty and that their followers were looking in the same direction. Dobson and Marie who jumped off the stoop and ran a few paces towards the corner were not noticed until Marie, realizing that she could not get to Bewsher in time, opened fire with the pistol.

At the same time Sam let off Bewsher's shot-gun charged with No. 4. The effect of this double fusilade in the rear, the loud explosion of the gun and the cries from every direction of those who had been pickled, startled the mixed forces of the enemy so much that they trotted after their leaders.

Dobson was carried off his feet, but in a moment after the second barrel of the gun went off found himself sitting in the middle of an empty yard in which nothing appeared abnormal but a couple of dropped spears and a small patch of blood near the chapel.

It did not seem that either Sam or Marie had succeeded in killing anybody though many had certainly been hit.

Marie herself had disappeared. She had run round the corner after the Birri calling out threats and reproaches to all whose names occurred to her and telling them what would happen to them if they injured Monkey. But fortunately for her (as no doubt she would have gone as far as the bush) an exasperated pagan, just beyond the corner of the chapel, stood for long enough to throw his club at her, which struck her in the throat and chest, and brought her down.

But she recovered very quickly and half an hour later when the soldiers arrived (the blocked road, reported by the first morning traveller out of Alo, had brought them hot-foot) she was so cool and so self-possessed, so helpful with advice about the probable route of the Birri that it was difficult to remember her situation.

Fortunately she was convinced, or pretended to be convinced, that Bewsher was a prisoner. She gave the most elaborate directions about securing his release, whom to approach in Birri and how. So that Dollar, who was in most unusual spirits, could be excused a little professional jocularity while he assured her that she was as good as new.

But Dollar used his most breezy and official tone to all these people because he really had not time or mind to devise a special one for them. He was now the soldiers' doctor and war had begun.

The soldiers, in fact, possessed the whole mission. While Mrs. Dobson could be seen through the door of the inner room lying exhausted with horror and grief, and while little Miss Dans and Dobson equally pale and, as it were, shrunk out of importance or consideration, stood with the cheerful doctor beside Marie's bed, Stoker in a Sam Browne and Gore with a huge Webley strapped to his belt were interrogating Sam and Henry about the direction taken by the Birri in their flight, and just at the door Colour-Sergeant Maggs gesticulating with both hands, his stick and his moustache, was bellowing a continuous stream of abuse and instruction at the troops in the compound.

But it was not the bustle, the uniforms, the professional language of war which seemed to the Dobsons blasphemous in the mission room; it was something not professional, something like enjoyment.

'They're all just delighted to think that they can go and kill,' said Doll Dans. But even Mrs. Dobson knew that this wasn't the truth. Dollar did not want to kill. Even Stoker and Maggs were not thinking of it. Their heads were full of maps, dispositions, supplies, strategy, a thousand complicated and interesting matters. They were artists handling a new subject, with as much disinterested enthusiasm as any missionary planning a campaign for souls. That was what distressed the honest and sensitive Dobson.

231

It was, in fact, only Gore who showed any real animosity against the Birri. After a little private interview with Marie from which both were noticed to emerge with an unusual colour, he was heard to say that it was time those b——rs had a lesson and they were going to to get it bloody quick. Language which shocked both Stoker and Dobson, who unfortunately overheard it, in about equal degrees.

Gore was wrong in supposing that the Birri would regret anything. They are not a people who regret their mistakes or even remember them; and in this they are like all other peoples. A people has as little regret as gratitude and for the same reason; that it consists of individuals, and each individual feels in himself so little responsibility for producing misfortune that he goes carefree of good or bad feelings in the matter.

Besides, they had no time to worry about the past. The patrol lasted three months, during which about thirty Birri were killed and three soldiers; many hundred goats and a fine leopard. Three villages were burnt. The Birri fought well, but Stoker out-marched and out-manœuvred them at all points.

The casualties were light and the damage easily repaired where housebuilding costs nothing. But the Birri war had the unexpected result of breaking up the Birri. The old patriarchal government disappeared and the people became a mob. Large numbers of the young men drifted away, even during the campaign, to join the flotsam of wandering labourers and petty thieves in the neighbouring provinces.

When Mander took over a year later he found the division in such a state of social and political disintegration that he was extremely glad of the help of the new Paré company, floated by Cottee after Jukes' death, which provided the nucleus for the remnants of the Paré tribe; and the Nok mission under the Dobsons which gave the river people a centre.

But it proved impossible to make the septs work together and the latest suggestion is to split up Birri between Alo and Kunama. In that case Uli, or rather Enuké, at present chief of a small hamlet in the Nok bush, would probably be a district head. For Mander says that Enuké is one of the few people he can depend on. She may be a trifle conservative in her principles but they are principles and not chatter.

Henry, who was headman of carriers throughout the war, and made the usual large profits out of his rake-off and the wages of the dead, sick and wounded, has opened a store in the Paré minefield and is doing a splendid trade in condemned tinned meats slightly-blown, second-hand caps and trousers, aphrodisiacs and smuggled gin. Abortions sixpence.

The patrol was also a technical success. Obai was betrayed by Paré and hanged. Stoker even succeeded in recovering Bewsher's body, that is, at the earnest request of the Dobsons and Marie, he sent back to Goshi a chop box said to contain the body. He would have used another kind of box and a larger one if he could have got it. But Marie and the Dobsons did not need any apology from Stoker whose delicacy, typical of a gentleman and a soldier, caused him to scrape off the lettering on the box and stain it a dark brown colour appropriate to its purpose.

Stoker's orders were that the box should not be opened. He said that the sight of the relics, much injured as they were, would be too painful. The story of course went round that they were fragments of pagan. This was a slander. The coffin did contain Bewsher's smashed and mummified head, a horrible object whose bare-tooth grin made even Stoker feel uncomfortable, and a bagful of his finger joints. The other bones were probably Birri and one femur was certainly goat.

The funeral at Alo was most impressive. There was a firing party from the new company. The bugler played the Last Post. Gore, who was mourner for the Government, put on a brand new uniform and even his medal ribbons.

Marie was there with the Dobsons. She had waited to see something of her Bewsher again in spite of the doctors who had been trying to get her home for the last four months. She was seven months gone and getting big. Cottee, who attended with the other Europeans, took one look at her, frightfully thin and misshapen, the face of a spectre with huge eyes like the holes in a skull, set upon the swollen body in its dingy black cloak, borrowed from Mrs. Dobson; and looked away again. He hoped he would be able to dodge an interview. That would be too much for him altogether. Even at the moment he was feeling pretty low. Yet how unnecessary it was to produce and indulge all these mournful ideas. Monkey

Bewsher had lived a good life and died the best kind of death, quick, unexpected, and in the midst of his prime. Marie no doubt was to be pitied. She had lost her Bewsher. But on the other hand she had inherited a pretty good income; she would be a well-off young widow instead of a wandering journalist of doubtful reputation and more doubtful future. She was placed in life on a sound financial basis. No doubt she could not value that in her present mood, but she would do so in another year or two. It seemed to him, sentiment apart, that she had made a success of her African adventure.

He called afterwards at the Residency where she was still living, but Mrs. Dobson, on guard, told him that she had been sent to bed. They were leaving next day by river to catch the boat for England, and it would be necessary to start early.

The young man was more relieved than disappointed. Yet he was disappointed too. It was a comfort to escape from the labours of condolation and the certainty of painful emotion, but also it was dull.

He had tea at the fort with the new C.O. and Gore, who was more gloomy and pessimistic than ever. For Gore the world was going to the devil. A new dark age of persecution, superstition, tyranny and general wretchedness impended. Glory and loveliness stood on their last legs.

Cottee as a successful man could smile at Gore's romanticism as he had been annoyed by Bewsher's. For Bewsher's attempt to keep the Birri out of the general flux had sprung from the same source; as Jukes used to say all these officials were playboys moved by some impractical notion or other. For even if civilization meant for the Birri a meaner, shallower kind of life, how could any man hope to fight against it when it came with the whole drive of the world behind it, bringing every kind of gaudy toy and easy satisfaction?

The fact was, of course, that people like Gore couldn't suit themselves to a world in transition. They were inelastic, too much attached to the old standards. Gore's very eyebrows seemed fixed in the melancholy question, 'Why should everything go to pot at once, the sound and splendid as well as the bad? Why not keep the good and reform the rest? That wouldn't be hard. You've only got to be a little reasonable. Wait a bit, good people. These things you are destroying can't be replaced in a hurry and they may be necessary to you. Loyalty, truth, tolerance, kindness, even modesty will be wanted again—and you will enjoy the graces of life as soon as you know what they are. Only wait till things are better—till you are better off—till you have leisure—till you have time to think—to know what life really is about. A pathetic, a ridiculous sight. Like the old lady in the Russian story whose house was raided by drunken soldiers and who went down alone to face them in the hall. "Friends, here is all the money, and the food is in the larder, but please be careful of the furniture and the pictures. These cabinets hold only the china you see—nothing is hidden in them and they are beautiful —unique. The china is irreplaceable." So of course they said, if this old woman has risked her life for these cabinets and teapots they must be full of money and they smashed everything to pieces, and when they could not find any money they put the old lady on the fire to make her confess—What did she expect?

And it wouldn't have been any good to tell that old lady that beauty would not perish with her Sévres—that the roots of beauty were as indestructible and as fertile as life itself—that though cruelty and lies might carry all before them for a time, they had never yet succeeded in abolishing the things of the spirit. It wouldn't be any good because she was herself a period piece—her tastes and virtues had the forms of her time and she couldn't learn to appreciate or even understand any other. She was part of her period and it was made of sentiments and attachments and associations which by their very nature could not be transferred. The greater a period, the stronger the allegiance and interdependence of its human parts,— the more difficult its liquidation, the more painful for these fragments. People like Gore and Bewsher couldn't help themselves. Feudal anachronisms, servants of the king. He knew Gore's family; his own had been like it; parsons, soldiers, doctors, civil servants, magistrates, none of them rich; their whole inheritance a few old swords, bibles, medals and stories; strong in that ungreedy pride which says to kings and dukes and millionaires, 'You have your part to play and I have mine.'

How could they bear to see everything they valued, and rightly valued, suddenly overwhelmed and trampled into rubbish by movements as wild and unpredictable and stupid as a stampede of bullocks.

What comfort to them to know that the time of liquidation could not last and that when it crystallized out into the new civilization it might take forms more austere and rigid than anything known to them—a new feudalism of service, bleak, cruel, heroic, magnificent and highly intolerant of quacks, demagogues and Pecksniffs. They would not like it any better even if they could live to see it.

They were to be pitied. For man only had one life and if he wanted to enjoy it he had better suit his taste to his times and not try to change the times to suit his taste. Moreover, a period like this just because of its quackery, its confusion, its lack of standards, its cynicism and cowardice, offered to a man intelligent and detached enough to seize them extraordinary chances of amusement. There was scarcely any limit to what he could do, given effrontery, money and the proper jargon; and if the new Paré flotation came off, Cottee would be rich.

Even now he could afford to do himself extremely well. In three weeks at the shortest he would be hearing the corks pop; and catching sight of the long, quixotic profile in the next chair he could not refuse the thought, 'Poor old Gore, when he's rotting on a twopenny pension in some third-rate suburb I'll be a rich man; and we started together. Of course, one mustn't say so, but mine is the better fate—there's no comparison. Moreover, I shan't give up enjoying the opera—it's all nonsense about good living blunting the sensibilities. A dash of hoggery now and then may even improve and refine the artistic reactions.'

Afterwards he walked with Gore back to the political station. He was still in very good spirits, reflecting, with a cigar in his mouth, upon his successful tour, when suddenly upon turning a dunia tree at the corner of the native market, they came plump upon Marie.

She was dressed as at the funeral, in the same dingy black cloak, much too long for her, and a white sun hat; so that with her short, bulky form she resembled from behind, an African monk.

It was impossible to avoid her. She turned at once and greeted them eagerly. Then she held up her hand to take an arm and after a moment's hesitation hooked it into Cottee's. Probably because she liked him least. They walked on together. Cottee, who with a deep regret had already sacrificed his cigar, produced suitable words and condolence.

'Why yes,' she answered, 'it's been pretty bad for me. I suppose you heard about the gun.'

'I heard the boy fired a gun and saved your lives.'

'Why no, I mean Monkey's gun, the pistol.'

'All I heard was that it couldn't be found.'

'I found it but I wouldn't let him have it because I had a hunch it was safer for him to trust in God. And if he'd shot Obai he'd be here now.'

Cottee did not know what to say to this. He glanced sideways over the woman's head at Gore, but Gore's nose was directed forward, his eyes as usual gazing downwards.

'Doesn't it make you laff the way I fell for it. And it wasn't John Dobson's god—it was just the oldest kind of juju. But I guess religion is like real estate—the Get-rich-quick always picks upon the worst lot because it looks so cheap—he doesn't wait to be stung—he just stings himself.'

'Bewsher was bound to get killed in the end,' said Gore.

'Why, Harry, you can't make out that I didn't kill Monkey; I killed him with that hunch just as much as if I'd shot him myself.'

Neither of the men said anything. Cottee made as if to do so, thought better of it and cleared his throat instead.

'I always wanted things too badly,' said Marie. 'It was just the same when I was little. I made myself sick at all my parties and when I got big enough to grow my hair and lose my complexion I said that the finest man in the world would be too good for me. But still I went out and looked for him. And when I found him I wanted to keep him for ever. I just started right away trying to find a safe place for him, even if I ruined his life and broke his heart. And when I couldn't get Monkey safe out of Birri I just had to have Birri safe for Monkey. But I didn't see that if Birri was safe, Monkey wouldn't be Monkey, and if the world was meant to be a safe place there wouldn't be any men like Monkey, and if no one was to die or suffer there wouldn't be any love, and if no one was to get killed there wouldn't be any life worth living.'

Marie's voice had lost some of its quality. It was hoarse and rough, perhaps from crying; and even while she spoke, they knew that she was crying though they did not care to look at her. But it had still that power to move, common enough among those who speak with conviction, but always surprising in the force and suddenness of its effects; the power that fills a penitents' bench, that makes an audience of city men stuffed with dinner rise from their seats and shout. It made Cottee's heart beat and his eyes fill. It transported him once more into another state of being, where men and women were born to heroic destinies, and life was the magnificent stage of their glories and their suffering; and it seemed to him, moreover, that the men and women who lived in this other romantic world, call them sentimentalists if you like, were the only ones who knew how to live at all. The rest were the cowards, like himself, who were afraid to love, who were afraid of being laughed at; who mutilated and tamed within themselves every wild creature of the spirit in order to be in safe and comfortable possession of their own farm-yard and on good terms with the neighbours.

He found himself at the grave, a few steps from the path, or perhaps Gore had allowed himself to be guided thither. Startled as he was, he had the presence of mind to take off his hat; Marie stooped forward as if to touch the mound still covered with strange looking bush flowers. Cottee could now look at her. She had slipped her wrist out of his arm. He half turned towards her, gazed sharply and curiously at the small white face, the big sensitive lips made relatively bigger by the thinness of the cheeks. But no, the fancy dissolved like a transformation scene. This ugly little woman a tragic queen, Monkey Bewsher a hero, it was absurd.

In fact, Cottee recovered from this fit of poetical fervour even quicker than the last. He was older and not so impressionable. Even while he stood watching the girl he felt his pulse run slower, his excited feelings returning to the ground where they passed a comfortable existence under his own control.

It now appeared that Marie wanted to kneel down. She put out her hand for assistance and Gore stooped forward to take it. Cottee, half alarmed, half amused by this new development, so characteristic of Marie, looked at the tall A.D.O. with an expression which, though perfectly decorous meant, 'Here's a nice game. What will she do next—and what exactly ought we to do?'

That was the annoying thing. He would not mind kneeling himself if that was the proper procedure, but was it? Gore met his eye in passing but without any change of his own features, which appeared even more melancholy, more hollow-eyed and hollow-cheeked than usual. Holding Marie's hand he bent towards her with that grand air which she herself had described when she said

238

that Mr. Gore always made her think of King Arthur at the court of Mark Twain.

Cottee, disappointed of sympathy in this quarter, reflected again that the man was a damned official and probably enjoyed ceremonies like this. There was a good deal of hokum about him too.

Marie was painfully settling herself upon her knees. She looked up and apologized to them. 'I'm not praying, but where Monkey is, the ground feels kind of different.'

Prefatory Essay by Joyce Cary
written especially for the Carfax Edition of
**AN AMERICAN VISITOR**

THE original American visitor was a young wife with three young children, who told me once that in America 'we believe that children should get their own ideas of right and wrong.'

She was a very pretty, charming, gay young woman with a strong sense of duty towards the children and society. And I did not take her seriously. I accepted her remark as a fraction of the polite small talk that people bring out at a party, noticeable only because it was new to me, like a piece of foreign currency among the equally worn coins of Great Britain.

I still remember my stupefaction when I found that she meant just that; that it was her practice to leave children of five and six to decide all moral issues for themselves, without guidance.

I pointed out then that young children (I had four of my own) *asked* for guidance, but she considered this moral laziness on their part and a temptation to parents which they ought to resist.

She was, in short, an anarchist of the most extreme kind, but the name did not disturb her. She thought of herself as a good American who gave her opinion as an ordinary American opinion.

I did not quite believe her and afterwards when I visited America I found, as I might have expected, there are as many different opinions about education there as in Europe. But at

243

that time I was impressed by her conviction; and I knew something of her countrymen in Africa which seemed to support
her statement.

Once, for instance, when I was in the bush visiting some
flooded villages, I had a message from the Emir to say that a
'preacher white man' had arrived and was talking to the people
about Isa (Jesus) and about 'wars': what should he do with this
stranger?

This was in Borgu, primitive and remote, where there had
lately been 'big trouble'; that is to say war between followers
of a certain chief and a large body of tribesmen. And the
country was therefore closed to strangers (traders, prospectors,
missionaries) unless they had a permit of entry.

The object was not so much to protect the strangers who,
after all, knew they were taking a chance, as the natives. For
if they murdered a white man there would be a patrol and
more 'big trouble' among people who had not yet settled down
after the last.

But the preacher was quite safe at the capital. Moreover I
wanted him. One of my jobs was to carry out the first nominal
census (that is, a real census in place of a calculated one;
statistics, instead of guess work) and I wanted clerks who
could write in the Latin alphabet.

I had found that such scribes who wrote only in arabic
often could not read their own writing.

Up to that moment I had had to conduct my own writing
class—of a dozen members, most of them old gentlemen with
long grey beards, repeating the A,B,C, and painfully copying
from a home-made blackboard. I was delighted at the prospect
of a mission school to do this work.

So I wrote to the Emir and said 'The preacher is friendly.
Give him quarters and wood and chickens and tell him that I
am returning at once to salute him.'

But as soon as the preacher had received this message, he
ran off out of Borgu as fast as he could go. According to the

Emir, he did not like 'judges' and especially myself who was the 'big' judge. In fact, I was a very small judge, but the Emir regarded me as 'big' because I was the only one in Borgu and his opposite number in the state of Kaiama.

I do not know whether this story was true. I sent out enquiries but I could not trace the missionary. If he is still alive, I should like to hear from him.

But the statement that he hated judges sounded familiar. I knew a good many preachers, especially from America and Scandinavia, who had a horror, amounting to hatred, of the government official.

A friend of mine, a man of fifty, all by himself in an isolated station, a hospitable man, well-read, well-travelled, had the greatest difficulty in persuading two missionaries, the nearest white men within fifty miles, even to speak to him. For them, he was the equivalent of anti-Christ.

His crimes were that he left native religion alone, that he drank two whiskies and sodas every evening, above all that he represented the British Empire and administered the law.

Rightly or wrongly, too, I thought that this antagonism threw light on the American refusal to join the League of Nations, a refusal which even then threatened to smash it.

I was a strong league of nations man—I was in a country full of social and tribal conflict where it was hard to devise even the elements of security and a reasonable life, especially for the masses. I knew something at first hand about lawlessness as well as despotism. The everlasting conflict between authority and freedom was not an academic subject in Nigeria, it cropped up every day in a country where the traditional frame was in collapse and law had to be built while the queue waited.

I wrote an enormous book in the twenties which I was never able to finish, about a district officer who was, at once, a despot and an anarch; that is to say, a law to himself. Bits of this work came into Castle Corner, but in short form. The book itself was given up; it is still in being but no one, least of all myself, will ever get a clue to its massive ruins.

But the subject still pestered me and when I set out again to give the picture of a different kind of ruler, Bewsher, and his dilemma, I remembered that young anarchist mother— with a mind completely closed to any need of authority— which trusted *absolutely* to providence in the narrowest sense.

I had, as I say, never forgotten an experience which had been like the sudden opening of a secret door into a new world of the mind.

I thought, too, that having been brought into that world, I could understand better the antagonism of certain missionaries (not by any means all American) to Government.

What I did not realize then was how many of the Americans who were against the Empire, were also behind Wilson, that is, they *did* want an international law but detested 'imperialism.'

It might be said of them that they identified the League with 'democracy' and democracy with 'God's way to peace'; that they were still anarchists; that they believed that peace could come by a 'natural' development, without enforcement of law; that still they had not faced reality—that just as no state can exist without police, if only to regulate conflicting purposes, so the world needed some power, imperial or international, only to enforce law.

But the truth seems to lie deeper. It is that the faith which lies beneath anarchism is just as necessary to the world as the reason which creates systems of law.

If none had ever rebelled against the law in the name of freedom, we should still be living in the stone-age under the tyranny of some juju priest-king or tribal Politburo.

And the modern democratic state *has* developed by something like a natural course of events, and it *does* pursue, however erratically, the good life for its people; it *does* hate war.

The anarchist in short, has a good case. But so have those who say that without law, and authority to enforce law, we shall soon be back in an age still more barbarous and tyrannical than that of the primitive tribe.

And the modern democracy, as we know it, has a powerful system of law. It differs from the totalitarian state not so much in its law enforcement as in its ideas, its administration, its purpose, and its emphasis on the individual life rather than the collective achievement.

Democratic freedom, security, in the last resort, rest on a balance of power and an attitude of mind. Too much law, too much security, and you get a tyranny, a rigid machine; too much freedom and you get anarchy; too much nationalism and you rush into war, too much pacifism and you open the way to Hitler and Stalin, more and bigger wars.

And one extreme leads to another. Sooner or later, freedom corrupts or destroys the rigid state machine; and if it is only a machine, it falls apart like broken metal. The chaos in Germany after the fall of the Nazis was far more complete than the confusion which followed the Kaiser war. For the Kaiser's machine had not been so complete, so ruthless.

I was asked about the American visitor, So what? And this is all the answer one can give. There is no rule. The situation in family life as in politics is always unique; it has to be dealt with by the imagination, by a creative effort of the mind. And since only individuals possess imagination, there is always need of the individual ruler whatever he or she is called.

It is the essential job of political officers, whether they are mothers in their nurseries, or 'Pagan men' in the back bush or the first ministers of great states, to take responsibility for dodging their own laws or breaking their own rebels.

J. C.

# ABOUT THE AUTHOR

Joyce Cary, who died in 1957, was born in 1888 in Donegal, Ireland, of a Devonshire family long settled in that part. He was given for first name, according to a common Anglo-Irish practice, his mother's surname of Joyce. He was educated at Clifton and Trinity, Oxford, and also studied art in Edinburgh and Paris. Afterward he went to the Near East and joined a Montenegrin battalion for the war of 1912-13, and was attached to a British Red Cross party at the front.

Subsequently Cary studied Irish Co-operation under Sir Horace Plunkett, and in 1913 joined the Nigerian political service. He fought in the Nigerian regiment during World War I and was wounded at Mora Mountain. On returning to political duty, as magistrate and executive officer, he was sent to Borgu, then a very remote district, where he made close acquaintance with primitive native life. His health, however, had never recovered from war service and he was advised to retire from tropical Africa. He then began to write, and his first novel, *Aissa Saved,* was published in 1930.

In addition to many novels, Joyce Cary wrote books and pamphlets on political theory, and the film story of *Men of Two Worlds* with an African setting. Joyce Cary's last novel, *The Captive and the Free,* was published in 1959, his collected short stories, *Spring Song and other stories,* in 1960.